Out of His Mind
-- *Medical Revolutionary?*

The story of Dr Eddie Price.

By

Kirstine McKay

*DISCLAIMER: All quoted conversations are paraphrased from Dr Eddie Price's recollections and may not be a totally accurate account of what was, in fact, said at the time.
In a small number of cases the names of companies and their employees have been changed for confidentiality.

"I will go happily to 'an unmarked grave' in the knowledge that my writings will be recognised and appreciated by a future generation." (Dr Ernst Codman, advocate of hospital reform and founder of Outcomes Management in patient care)

Contents

Introduction

Edward Daniel Price is a deep thinker....in many respects he has thought beyond his time. From early in his youth he had the capacity to ignore the many distractions of his social and cultural environs that tend to consume and blind the majority. With great clarity he saw an energetic connection between a body's systems, between eastern and western medicine, and prophesied a future of a true health system, rather than what he called the current "disease system". Such was his beliefs that his published articles and subsequent books, as far back as 1973, detail concepts and theories that are only now, some 46 years later, being acknowledged and accepted on a broad scale. And yet more still await recognition.

Edward Price was a trained doctor who didn't like seeing people sick. Driven by this unease, his desire to contribute to the world and through his study of medical management, he made it his mission to work out how he could improve the health of more than just the patients lining up at his practice door. Dr Price claimed that the medical system's current perceived goal was the prevention of death. He felt that quantity of life was overrated, and led to a system trying to avoid the unavoidable whilst spending huge quantities of time, resources and money in this endeavour. The alternative, according to the doctor, was to redefine healthcare as a system to support patients to enjoy the highest quality of life and experience a sense of well-being. He established that medical treatment results and patient ailments and recoveries were not being measured. He questioned how the system could function to its best ability if there was no understanding of whether procedures and treatments were effective or not. More radically, Dr Price claimed that the most effective treatments, those that would actually prevent illness in the first place, were not being prescribed by doctors. He also highlighted the need for governments and health departments to employ multiple drivers and incentives for behavioural change in order for his ideas within the medical system to be embraced and achieved by practitioners. According to Dr Price, the humane side of medicine had also been neglected and the modern doctor needed to play a more caring role. He proposed that management skills would produce this humane system. He believed by implementing these concepts, not only would it radically improve the health of nations, but it would save governments and health insurers billions of dollars and increase the work satisfaction of millions of doctors and health providers worldwide.

Dr Price recognised that his ideas were revolutionary and that they would require an entire shift in the paradigm of the medical system. He was so passionate about his convictions, that his ideas would make such a positive impact on the health of the entire world, that he dedicated his entire professional life to championing them and striving to be heard.

In his first book Is Medicine Really Necessary? Dr Price advocated the use of measuring the outcomes of medical encounters through a series of highly structured questionnaires called PROMs. He discussed the idea that a functional health assessment was the catalyst for a more effective healthcare system and claimed that if behavioural change was implemented in preventative health, not only could this radically improve the health of nations, it would save governments and health insurers billions of dollars. He felt that his ideas could, should and would change the health systems of the world. Dr Price continued his research and championing of PROMs and published a further book, Supramedicine, which he thought would surely change the way medicine is taught throughout the western world. It supported a holistic approach to medicine, acknowledging the impact on health of a patient's environment, habits, activities and social situations....what he referred to as "supra-systems". Convinced his ideas were the future of medicine, he became an occupational medical practitioner and established his own company to promote the use of PROMs. Doctors, health providers, hospitals and insurers are provided a platform through "eHealthier" to enable patients and clients to complete electronic PROMs.

Dr Price relentlessly presented his ideas to the medical community and to every health minister to hold the portfolio. He rode a roller coaster with hope when a glimmer of interest was shown and then a plummet of disappointment when time after time his work was passed over. With a conviction that his concepts could change the quality of life around the world he refused to accept the defeat of his ideas due to them being seen as "subjective" and "not based on science". He turned to science. He claimed that the way western medicine is practised is out of date and that Eastern medicine is more accurately addressing not just the machine of the body, but its underlying energies. He believed that there was an underlying science – Complexity Science.

Inspired by his findings interlinking psychology, science and health, Dr Price wrote his third book So You think Medicine is Modern? In this he discussed the connection between complexity science and functional health and what he believed would be the way medicine would be practised in the future. This included the use of behavioural vaccines against heart attack and stroke - non-pharmaceutical pharmaceuticals. Instead of writing a script for drugs, a doctor would write a lifestyle script. Through science he also found solace and understanding as to why so many of his theories could not be "seen" by so many, likening them to the invisible concept of Wi-Fi.

Recently, PROMs have become widely accepted in the medical community as an effective, reliable and important tool in the management of patients, although to Dr Price's frustration they are still not used as a diagnostic tool nor used for caring or prevention. According to him, they are one of the biggest reforms to be seen within the modern health system.

Now in his early 70's, Dr Edward Daniel Price spends his days consulting in occupational health. He is also developing an app that enables efficient use of PROMs within the health system. He believes the future is in eHealth, using PROMs in an IT framework for on-going patient-led care and doctor-to-patient communication in conjunction with face-to-face consultations. Dr Edward Price is a champion of PROMs and has been their unsung hero in Australia for the last 46 years.

Chapter 1

Edward Daniel Price

A baby is delivered into his father's arms. It's how many of our stories begin. But....this baby wasn't just wrapped in a blanket and handed to a glowing father. This father, Dr Henry Price, delivered Edward (Eddie) Daniel Price in his own small hospital in the bustling city of Beirut Lebanon, on the 2nd of September 1946. Henry wrapped his son not just in blankets....but in layers of history, of cultural and religious anomalies, of expectation and unrelenting standards, and of love; always love. Of course Eddie's mother Ursula was there as well, but as in most of her life, her role seems somewhat diminished, or at least clouded by time, by THE times when women's lives and stories were seen as supporting roles to the main male events. Her own tortured family history is all but an echo collected through ghostly whispers and supposition rather than from her own lips....a father's suicide to claim insurance to support his family in post war financial distress, life as a Jew in Nazi Germany, a splintered family, a mother taken to Auschwitz....and never returned.

Eddie's father, originally Hans Manfred Preiss, was a proud German Jew and medical graduate, who fled Nazi Germany in 1933 and morphed his identity to become Henry Michael Price. In Lebanon, which was under French mandate, he found refuge in a flourishing society where he was able to establish himself as a respected doctor. He later met and married Ursula, who had also escaped Germany and was living in Israel. When war broke out between Germany and the English / French alliance, as a German in a country administered by the French, Henry was hauled into a concentration camp. His get-out-of-jail-card was, reluctantly for the pacifist doctor, joining the French Foreign Legion and heading back to Europe and into war. Following the fall of France, he became a Medical Officer fighting with the British Army in North Africa. When peace came in 1945, Henry resumed his life back in Lebanon and he and Ursula started a family. Their first child was a son called Michael, born on the 5th of May 1944 and then came Eddie. Eddie was born *"very young"* - as was the family's standard joke. He was named Edward Daniel Price after his grandfather – on whose birthday he was born. Henry greatly admired his father and the fact that Eddie was born on his father's birthday, unconsciously set up a special bond between father and son.

With a cloud of instability looming over the Middle East, the taste of violence still raw in his mouth and now with a young family to support, Dr Henry Price wanted out. As with many families at this time, they were stateless and the prospect of finding a safe and welcoming place to call home was greatly desired but extremely uncertain. Australia was seen as a good country with plenty of fresh air, sunshine and opportunity. Dr Price assumed that after serving the British army as a doctor and an officer in both Benghazi and Tobruk, he would have his medical qualifications recognised by the Commonwealth Government of Australia. Henry was convinced this country would be where his family would find refuge, happiness and ultimately a home. His wife Ursula was not so convinced. Australia was a long way from her longed-for Israel and beloved brother Herward who was her only surviving family member. Not only would it be hard to leave family, friends and the beautiful Mediterranean climate with its glorious blue summer skies far behind, but the logistics of the family's departure would present its own problems. Ocean liners were still the main form of transport but, in the post war world, they were all busy repatriating ex-prisoners of war and soldiers around the globe. The Price family's request for passage was not a priority and they featured a long way down the waiting list. Henry, determined to begin his family's new life in Australia as soon as possible, instead arranged flights to Cairo and then on to Australia on a standby basis. But again, they were low priority and standby turned out to be very protracted. In frustrated desperation, Henry persuaded a pilot of a cargo plane to make room for his family of four and they flew to Singapore on the 3rd of September 1947, the day following Eddie's first birthday. Soon after the hopes for the future of the Price family launched from Singapore Harbour, via Fremantle, Melbourne and Sydney and docked in Brisbane in October 1947. It was the start of a long journey with the dream to finding a new home far from the fear and prejudices that haunted their family in both Germany and the Middle East. Sailing into Sydney Harbour Henry was enchanted and proclaimed to his family, *"It's beautiful, yes? This will be a good home for us, I know. We will succeed and be happy here. You just wait and see!"*

For the next year and a half, the family's life was in limbo, waiting for Dr Henry Price to complete medical studies that the Australian government deemed necessary before this experienced doctor could start working in Australia. With little money and very little other support the family eked out a living in a small weatherboard cottage in New Farm and then later in a flat in Clayfield. Michael and Eddie attended preschools and, with their ever-attentive mother, made the most of the life they could afford in Brisbane. The frustrations of their father through, being forced to study final year medicine for the third time in a third language (first German, then French and now English), made for testing times in the Price household. He had already practiced medicine for many years and he had the further pressure of needing to be employed to support his family. The boys soon learned not to make noise when their father was studying and their mother was conscious of organising play out of Henry's hearing.

"Figas! Figas!" Michael excitedly pointed to his baby brother.

"More snails!" exclaimed Ursula.

"Why are they all over the baby and his pram?! Michael, did you give these to Eddie?"

"Yes!" replied three-year-old Michael.

"They're a present. Figas (snails). *Eddie likes figas as presents!"*

Michael's generous, but somewhat slimy, offering was a regular one and as such he became endearingly known as "Michael Figa".

In January 1949 Eddie, his mother and brother found they were alone and scraping by financially in Brisbane while Henry took up a position in the Broken Hill hospital. The posting only lasted three months. Henry soon realised the town not only depressed him, but offered little opportunity for his family. He took a gamble and purchased a practice in the NSW town of Wollongong. By May 1949 the Price family were together once more.

Wollongong became the backdrop of what, on paper, is a very "Australian" upbringing. They were happy and healthy, without a care in the world, except for the scores of the cricket games held in the dusty back streets of this industrial sea side town. Eddie flourished at school, excelled in sport and despite his father's own struggles due to prejudice and power in the Wollongong medical community, felt relatively unscathed by the fractured world that was reeling from war and what was emerging as cultural annihilation by the Nazis of Eddie's own tribe.

Henry was a proud, stern, authoritarian man with very high expectations of himself and of his sons. Life at home, although driven largely by Eddie's extremely capable mother, was dictated by the standards and discipline of his father. At 7:30 every morning his mother and the two boys would be sitting down at the table and only then would his father enter and breakfast could officially begin. Similarly, Saturday lunch was a sacred family affair for Henry and in later years would clash with Eddie's desire to participate in weekend sports. He may have been a difficult man to live with but Eddie admired and absorbed his father's moral code that one should contribute, make a difference to the world and leave it a better place. Henry's experiences in Germany certainly confirmed his beliefs that everyone is equal, is valuable and worthwhile, and that you treat people as you yourself would like to be treated. It was an expectation, but also something that emanated from Henry's own persona, in the way he conducted his life. Along with this noble trait, Eddie also inherited his father's short and sharp temper, evident from an early age. One evening a game of canasta was organised in the dining room behind the surgery. Michael partnered his father and Eddie partnered his mother. The first games were won handsomely by Michael and Henry and Eddie was extremely annoyed and angry. It was time for the third game. Ursula and Eddie won, and Eddie cheered and cried

5

out with joy.

Suddenly Henry stood up, *"I cannot play a game with this child! He is miserable when he loses and then runs around and cries and screams with happiness when he wins. This is no way to play."* Eddie ran to the bedroom in tears. He piled all the furniture up against the door as high as he could, and then cried and cried loudly for hours. His mother eventually handed him his dinner through the bedroom window. It was late that night when Michael was allowed into the room.

Ursula was the centre of Eddie and Michael's world. She was firm, predictable, extremely loving, a safe anchorage, a haven of security and an ever-willing bowler to the cricket fanatic that was young Eddie. For Ursula, family was of utmost importance, yet her own childhood was all but a shadow of memories reluctantly exposed in brief and scant moments throughout her life. She had recollections of a loving and generous family with a home always open to foster children, but then with a tragic disintegration. During Germany's economic catastrophe in the 1930's, Ursula's father, Paul Rosenberg, was a director of an insurance company, and faced ruin. In order for his family to be financially saved through his life insurance, he committed suicide in 1931. Paul not only left money to support his family, but also a close friend whom he had fought with in the First World War, George Grunewald. George became Ursula's mother's confidante and lover, but not her saviour. Ursula's mother joined the Jewish underground delivering messages to thwart the Nazi atrocities. In 1943 she was betrayed, taken to Auschwitz and murdered. "Uncle" George was criticised by some for not doing enough to save her but he was still loved by Ursula and her brother Herward. Following her brother, Ursula, by then a 25-year-old medical student, fled to Holland and then onto Israel and to safe haven from the Nazis. It was, in fact, Herward who introduced Ursula to Dr Henry Price who was then residing in Lebanon. The family move to Australia was the final blow to Ursula's family breakdown.

Aching from the distance between herself and her brother in Israel, Ursula worked hard at fostering a loving relationship between her two sons. Michael was two years and four months Eddie's senior and the two were firm allies and partners in many adventures. Michael was Eddie's hero. Eddie thought his older brother was fantastic at everything and was all-knowing. The boys often dressed as twins as whatever Michael wore, Eddie had to don the same. As their father's surgery was often taking over part of their family home, Michael and Eddie shared a bedroom, if not a bed, for most of their childhood. Separate beds were always available but Eddie enjoyed having someone to go to sleep near, and talk to, before falling asleep. He would often creep across to Michael's bed, cloaked in his beloved snoopy blanket, where they would start telling jokes, playing games, tickling or wrestling.

"You're on my side of the bed. Move over to your side of the bed," cried Michael.

"You've taken my blanket. I need more blanket," implored Eddie.

Michael sighed, *"Well stay on your side of the bed."*

"I am on my side of the bed," insisted Eddie.

The boys built a firm bond that would last a lifetime. By day the boys were outside playing sport or exploring their world. Many afternoons were shared with the Bell family. Betty Bell and Ursula would be chatting in the kitchen, shelling peas, whilst the four Bell children, Michael and

Eddie had wonderful adventures and became firm friends. They rode bikes, ran races around the block, explored the fairy creek, went on outings, and built cubby houses out of blankets, and canoes out of corrugated iron. They played never ending games of Cops and Robbers – tied each other up and spent hours and hours picking delicious blackberries together. Their spoils after a scratchy afternoon in the brambles were blackberry pies, patty cakes, scones and jam. The Prices also had a big sand pit in the backyard which became a pool after lots of rain. On one occasion Eddie, the youngest at four, was volunteered as test pilot for a box the children had successfully floated. Even with his modest weight it was enough to have the box sink and Eddie shrieked for help.

"The water is up to my ankle. The water is starting to go up my leg. Do something!"

"Grab this rope," instructed Michael.

"Missed!" shrieked Eddie. *"Missed again!"*

"Grab it this time," begged Michael.

Finally, Eddie grabbed the rope, was pulled to safety with great cheers from his brother and the Bell children. Despite the dramas, their shenanigans continued.

"Hey Eddie! Hold onto this apple so I can pretend to shoot it with the air-rifle. We'll be like William Tell!" explained Michael one day as they played together on a friend's property.

"Don't shoot me!" instructed a worried Eddie.

"Don't worry. I'm aiming to miss!" promised Michael.

Michael underestimated his aim, grazed Eddie's arm and promptly demanded his silence, *"Don't tell Mum and Dad!"*

Animals were gathered by the Price household. They owned cats, two dogs, guinea pigs and Eddie had rabbits.

One day, whilst cleaning the rabbits' cages and giving the animals free reign of the lawn, one of their Alsatians Josephine, a very timid dog, was attacked by one of the rabbits. It chased her around and around the yard. Eddie stepped into the melee to rescue Josephine and the rabbit turned and bit him instead. It latched onto his hand and was swung about the yard by an ever-increasingly panicked Eddie.

However, he redeemed his animal husbandry status one morning whilst the family were having breakfast with milk acquired from a local farmer.

Henry and Ursula both commented, *"This milk tastes different."*

Eddie agreed and added, *"I wonder if the cow is pregnant?"*

Henry enquired with the farmer and indeed it was. Dr Price was ecstatic; surely Eddie's ability to diagnose a cow was a sign that he was destined to follow the family tradition into the medical world. He'd realised that Michael, who spent all his time with mechanical objects, in designing vertical take-off planes that could be folded so they fitted into a person's knapsack, and drawing pictures of planes and reading books on planes, probably wasn't that way inclined. He was delighted to think Eddie might follow, not just in his footsteps, but in those of his grandfather, father, aunt, cousins and sister's husband. Eddie was just six years old. The layers of expectations from his father were ever present. His father's theory was further confirmed with one of the family's cats – Alli. The brothers were watching the cat give birth on the verandah and Eddie proved a most enthusiastic birthing partner crying, *"Push, push hard Alli!"*

Out of the litter of six, two kittens were born in the same sack. Three weeks after the birth Eddie noticed that one of the kittens was struggling and wondered of his father, *"Could this be because it's one of the twins?"*

Dr Henry Price was proud, calling out to his wife, *"Ursula noch mal.... Again, again! I told you he's born to be a doctor! It's in the genes."*

Another expectation that the Prices placed upon their children was that they were to be raised as part of the proud global Jewish community. The family were not particularly religious, but from an historical and cultural perspective, they wanted their children to understand and love their heritage. The Jewish community in Wollongong was not very large and Eddie was not particularly close to any of the other children as they were from very different age groups. At Sunday school where they were introduced to Hebrew, he spent more time climbing out of windows and causing as much distraction as possible rather than in absorbing any of the teachings. At school there were no scripture classes for the only Jewish boy so he was left to roam the playground on his own. It was up to his parents to instil a sense of pride and protectiveness of Judaism.

Jewish culture was not the only education he'd get from his father. Eddie was seven years old when one day his father amassed a pile of medical books and grabbed the brothers and sat them down to explain "the facts of life".

"Boys, children do not come from the birds and the bees. A stork does not deliver them," said Henry and then he proceeded to show his sons the clinical pictures, in very thick medical books, of different parts of the male and female anatomy and how they come together to make children. If only Henry had been privy to the fact he'd been usurped! It was Michael who'd been the first to explain to Eddie that, *"Humans do that too,"* when the boys were witness to their

two Alsatian dogs, Gaston and Josephine, having sex in the backyard.

Eddie was confused, *"Out here, in the backyard?"*

Michael rolled his eyes, *"No, stupid. In bed."*

Henry would be slightly less disheartened to know that he had at least confirmed what Eddie had found to be rather dubious.

Despite their father's, at times fierce temperament, and despite not once attending any of Eddie's beloved cricket or football matches, he was always a loving and doting dad. He was there imparting his knowledge and ensuring his sons were well educated on the human reproductive cycle. He was the only parent to turn up in the middle of the night to one of Eddie's scout camps on Mount Keira to check the boys were all right after being flooded out of their tents. Henry was also conscious of the lack of culture the boys were exposed to in working class Wollongong. The closest the boys were to experiencing a cultural performance was the circus on its yearly cycle of sideshow sensationalism. This rather base cultural event (in the eyes of Henry) showed its true calibre when on one occasion Michael was suddenly curled in an elephant trunk and lifted off the ground. The family was horrified. The circus was nonplussed. Henry was determined that his sons should experience a rather more refined and cultured upbringing. Their yearly vacations to the Chateau Napier Hotel in the Blue Mountains harped back to the youth Henry had himself experienced, with lots of horse riding, picnicking and swimming at Blackheath. Henry had experienced lots of horse-riding in the British Army and had enjoyed it immensely. He encouraged all the family to take horse-riding lessons and go riding with him in the forests around Katoomba and Blackheath and particularly the track along the Megalong Valley.

At home the sound track to their lives was an ensemble of classical music - Bach, Mendelssohn, Tchaikovsky and Danny Kaye and to pander to their youthful sensibilities, the Peter and the Wolf records. Their father delighted in passing down old German legends and the stories of Wagner's or Mozart's operas. *"He held him up by the ankle and dipped him in the dragon's blood, which would protect him from arrows, but he had to hold him by his heel. So you know what became of him? Well, he wasn't protected on his heel and that became known as his Achilles Heel."*

And then there were the concerts, operas and musical comedies by Gilbert and Sullivan up in Sydney. Every second weekend the family would travel to the Canberra Oriental Hotel in Kings Cross and spend the evening being entertained by shows such as H.M.S. Pinafore, The Pirates of Penzance, Gondoliers and The Mikado. They were outings the entire family looked forward to and enjoyed immensely, save for the afternoon naps at the hotel enforced by their father, *"You will sleep in the afternoon. I hate it when you yawn during the show. It spoils the show for me."*

Whilst Australia and Australians basked in the freedom and prosperity of the 50's, the backdrop to the Price family's drama was the impact of the Suez crisis on family members in Israel. Ursula would often comment, *"I just hope Herward is okay. We need to ring. We need to ring"*.

The on-going tensions of the Middle East were forever playing on their minds. These events also played an important role in expanding the international awareness of their sons and fostered an engaged social conscience that they would carry with them for life.

In 1950, aged three, Eddie was enrolled in St Michael's

Kindergarten in Church St. Wollongong. The building was directly opposite Michael's Infants school. The close proximity to his sibling did little to quell the distress of having to leave his beloved mother. Eddie cried non-stop for four hours on his first day. Once he did settle in, he found kindergarten fun and looked forward to it every day. He loved the playground and playing outside on the wooden monkey bars, exploring out the back of an old broken down barn, playing in the sand pit, sand jumping and playing King of the Castle. He loved singing and playing barbers - with one girl being quite enthusiastic about wanting to really cut his hair. One incident, with his friend David Norris, has quite literally stayed with Eddie for the rest of his life. Whilst playing submarines, a big rock fell on his little finger and split it quite badly. Eddie was in a lot of pain, but after the bleeding had been stemmed and the trauma over, he was left with a crease on his left finger. He has used it ever since to remind him of his "left" and "right". St. Michael's Kindergarten was a beautiful, loving and positive environment and was the beginning to Eddie's understanding of education and of learning. These attitudes and ideals of the importance of love and a positive outlook have stayed with him throughout his life.

Eddie's formal education began at Wollongong Infants in 1951, followed by Wollongong Primary in 1955. School was a wonderful adventure for him. He was an enthusiastic, energetic and likeable character and had a wide circle of friends who scurried about barefoot playing games of Cowboys and Indians, holding running races, making lunchtime sandwich deals (always vying for the hundreds and thousands varieties if available) and generally enjoying a carefree existence. His ever-caring and willing mother

Ursula was heavily involved in school activities through the Ladies Auxiliary and the P&C. Eddie delighted in having her so involved and nearby, except for the one occasion where he, and the rest of his class, were spotted marching around barefoot by his mother. At home barefoot was forbidden by their short-tempered father. Much to Eddie's embarrassment, his mother approached the teacher, *"Do you mind if I come in with the class?"*

The teacher replied, *"By all means."*

"Eddie, come here," instructed Ursula, who then took Eddie to the back of the class and put his shoes and socks back on, stating, *"Now keep it that way."*

School uniforms, and shoes as it turned out, were fairly casual obligations for the school, except on photo day. What wasn't casual, was the singing standard of the choir! The choirmaster, on listening to them getting ready for a performance on one occasion, identified a "problem" with one the singers. *"Now I want you children to sing individually starting with you, Jane. 'Down yonder green valley where streamlets meander'. David... 'Down yonder green valley where streamlets meander'. Ok now you Eddie, 'Down yonder....' Stop! I think we've found it."*

Eddie looked teary-eyed. His class teacher, noting Eddie's sullen face, consoled him, *"No matter, Eddie. You can turn the pages for Mr Christie, the pianist. You're still part of the group."*

Eddie couldn't read music so he had to wait for Mr Christie's nod to turn the pages. Then came Wollongong Primary Play Day and both his mother and father turned up at the school and Eddie stood there and thought to himself, *"My parents have come to watch me turn the pages!"*

Perhaps it was being asked to refrain from singing that gave

Eddie time to ponder, to sit outside of the "now", and observe what the greater masses were blindly accepting. It is a skill that has followed him throughout his life and career. In 1952 these musings were over an address to the school by headmaster, Mr Mowe, who explained that as the King had died, they would now be singing as the anthem "God Save the Queen". It occurred to five-year-old Eddie that they should probably choose an entirely different song as "God Save the King" had done very little for his late Majesty, so what good would it do the Queen? Academically Eddie did well in mathematics and science as both came naturally to him, but as for reading, writing, and spelling, he really had no mastery of them and was not interested in books. At home, there were only ever a few Golden Books and the German children's stories 'Der Struwwelpeter' (Shock-headed Peter) by Heinrich Hoffmann. These were rhymed moral stories about children that had disastrously exaggerated consequences for those misbehaving. They rather terrified Eddie.

Throughout primary school, he developed a great passion for sport, particularly for playing team sports, cricket and football – his greatest loves. His entire summers were devoted to playing cricket and snatching little bits of professional cricket on the radio at friend's houses. In December 1954 he was up the street at Tony Oyston's place where Tony, his elder brother, father and Eddie were all cheering Neil Harvey on for a last wicket stand with Bill Johnson. Eddie recalled that it was an hour of complete excitement until Harvey was left 92 not-out and Johnson was out 38 runs short of the required runs. Australia lost but it was a great moment. To his disappointment, listening to sport in his own household was unheard of.

In 1954 he had his first taste of rugby league with the Wollongong Police Boys Club and despite a one hundred to nil loss Eddie was hooked. At cricket, he showed similar enjoyment and flair. One day he was fielding in an all-ages playground game of cricket with a hard cricket ball. Needham, the school cricket captain, a large strong lad in sixth class, yelled at Eddie to move away when an extremely high catch with the hard cricket ball was up in the air. There was no way Eddie would move. He dropped the catch but the teacher noted his courage and, to Eddie's surprise, he was selected for the school representative team. In both sports he was identified as having talent beyond his years, being the only 4th class child selected for both the school cricket team and the football 5-stone-7-pounds team. His ability was matched equally by his belief in his invincibility. He was able to distinguish himself as a good player, a try scorer, and a fearless competitor. In 1957, he proudly accepted the Wollongong Primary, five stone seven pounds, rugby league team captaincy.

Bubbling just below the surface of the Price family's seemingly idyllic existence were the professional struggles that Eddie's father, Henry, continually battled at Wollongong Hospital. Echoes of past prejudices ran through the corridors. This self-assured and stubborn German Jew was caught up in an Australia still cloaked in intolerance. Henry also had a brash, no-nonsense approach that included ordering staff to *"Shut up!"* in the operating room. It was not a combination that would endear him to many colleagues and ultimately would see them endeavouring to ban him from working in Wollongong Hospital. Refusing to submit to unfounded claims and restrictions that would have been crippling to his practice, Henry took eleven of the doctors to court on civil conspiracy charges, defamation and libel. In doing so, he made legal and medical history and headlines in the major newspapers of the day. On the 5th of February 1953, crowds flocked around the old stone courthouse in Wollongong intent on watching the on-going drama unfolding inside between Dr Henry Price and the 11 other doctors. Had it not been that the courthouse was located almost opposite Eddie's school, Ursula would have avoided the area entirely, but pass by it she must. Despite her concerted efforts to shield six-year-old Eddie from the pressure the proceedings were having on both of his parents, he was obviously well aware of the stress and strain they were enduring. He comforted her saying, *"Don't worry Mum, God will help Dad."* Indeed, justice and due process were on his side and Dr Price was permitted to operate and he dropped all charges. However, the doctor's sons were unfortunately seen as a way of administering punishment on Henry by the infuriated hospital staff. Michael suffered at the fists of fellow classmates at Wollongong High who were the sons of the eleven doctors. Eddie had a particular teacher at cricket practice who on one occasion pitched the ball towards him at a dangerous speed. Eddie then threw it back as hard as he could at the teacher. This exchange of hard throws lasted some six minutes, much to the amusement of his classmates. Their status as outsiders was also exacerbated and certainly the ill-will was palpable during a hospital visit for Eddie shortly afterwards. He was admitted to Wollongong Hospital to have his adenoids out. He personally didn't have a lot of love for the establishment based on his father's treatment. The rather unfriendly staff weren't shy about showing where their allegiances lay either. Eddie woke feeling ill and crying. His parting gift to the uncivil staff was to, involuntarily, vomit blood all down the corridor as his parents ushered him home. The other body part of Eddie to be removed was a more civil, but certainly a bizarre, affair. He needed two teeth extracted and was given injections for the first time. Throughout the procedure, he did not say a word. At the end he thanked the dentist and said, *"Goodbye,"* and proceeded to walk straight past his mother in the waiting room without saying a word and walked back home - roughly four kilometres. From her bus Ursula saw him walking down the street and had plenty of ice cream waiting for him when he eventually arrived home.

Unbeknown to Eddie, his relatively carefree existence was about to disappear. His mother had made a pact with his father prior to their move to Wollongong that would put an end to the life he knew and loved. Ursula desperately wanted to immigrate to Israel and be near her brother. She had agreed to living in Wollongong for five years in order to establish the family financially, on the proviso that Haifa, Israel would be their ultimate destination. Her conviction was further cemented by her husband's court case and she had said to Henry, *"I've had enough of this, you know. You may want to fight your battles, but I don't want my kids to suffer."* On the 19th of March 1958, nearly eight years on, the family set off on a tour of Europe that was destined to end in Israel.

If one believes in a higher power, or perhaps energies that we cannot see, then perhaps one could be forgiven for thinking that "the universe" was trying to tell the Price family that they should stay on Aussie shores as their departure was an extremely protracted one. Henry Price was nervous about the long flight he and his family would be taking. He had had an excellent experience when flying with

KLM, the Royal Dutch Airlines, from Beirut to Cairo, and so wanted to repay their friendliness by choosing the airline again for their return to Europe. His loyalties and his composure were soon to be tested. The late night flight was having some problems and there was a two-hour wait on the plane, followed by further delays off the plane. After boarding a second time and then eventually taking off, they were notified of more engine trouble and the need to return to Sydney airport. Landing however isn't that simple when you have a plane heavy with fuel so many laps of Sydney were undertaken to burn some of the fuel off. More delays on the ground only heightened the tensions of a now extremely anxious Henry who, much to the embarrassment of Eddie, Michael and Ursula, proceeded to erupt at one of the KLM staff officials. *"Can't you see I've got two children, a wife! Everybody is absolutely nervous. We flew out here by KLM. You were a good airline back then!"* Eventually the plane took off and headed for New Guinea but a little while into the trip, to their annoyance and concern, there was once again engine trouble. In Biak, Dutch New Guinea, they were told their short stopover would now be an overnight stay as a new engine was needed.

The unexpected tropical experience turned out to be a surprisingly enjoyable one. Tours of the lush green jungle teeming with life from the wet season rains were a delightful distraction. The beautiful wooden hotels were primitive but made bearable by warm and friendly hosts. Eddie and Michael played billiards, gorged on delicious tropical fruits and stumbled their way through Pigeon English. After twenty-four hours, their sojourn was over and they were in the air once again. The Presidential Hotel on the Bangkok River made up for the primitive bedding of New Guinea. It was magnificent. The boys particularly delighted in the friendly staff cleaning and polishing their shoes. The hectic hustle and bustle of the city was mesmerising. Even the river was full of life with floating markets, boats, people, produce and Buddha. There was the golden Buddha, the sitting up emerald Buddha, the walking Buddha, the lying down golden Buddha, the longest Buddha... all nestled in the most picturesque scenery. Their hearts, minds and cameras were full.

It was the beginning of 1958 and the Vietnam War had been running for two years, so it was a nervous stopover in Saigon airport for the Price family with Eddie's parents telling he and Michael to *"Stay close and don't wander outside"*. Eddie could feel the tension in the air and wondered why there were soldiers at the airport; his brother explaining to him there was some type of fighting going on. Thankfully, when engine trouble again forced the Price family into another impromptu visit, it was in Karachi, Pakistan and not war torn Vietnam. In Karachi, they were put up in a hotel, given a guided tour, camel rides and generally an entertaining time all at the expense of KLM. The snake charmers they saw in the city plazas seemed to have even bewitched Henry, who had now accepted the delays to their journey as welcome adventures to parts of the world they may not have otherwise visited.

Arriving in Germany was an awkward affair for the Prices. Ursula was not at all comfortable in the country that had claimed her mother's life. For the brothers it was a glimpse of the home country of their parents, a "face to a name". For Henry, who always identified more as German than specifically a Jew, there was a strange mix of emotions from a bitter sense of betrayal to the warm comfort of familiar surrounds. There was a practicality to their stay in Germany and not just nostalgia. The German government were offering financial restitution for complete loss of possessions during the Nazi regime and both parents were submitting claims for their own and their late parents' estates. Henry's father had quite a bit of property and also had had his career and life terminated. Henry explained to his sons, *"Boys, we have to stay here for a while. I know Chancellor Adenaeur is a good German and while he's in power and willing to offer compensation, we have to take it now. It may not be available in the future."* It seems the German government had told Henry that it was not his turn to claim restitution, but they would take his file out of order if he settled for a once-off lump sum for everything. Henry agreed. The family based themselves in Wiesbaden from where they could continue compensation procedures. For some of the time they stayed with Ursula's "Uncle" George and wife "Aunt" Adaila (previously an Italian ballerina). Following the suicide of Ursula's father, George had lived with Ursula's mother when Ursula was a child. There was a cloud of whispers surrounding George as to whether he'd done enough to save Ursula's mother from her horrific end at the hands of the Nazis in Auschwitz, but regardless Ursula and George had remained close.

Compensation from the German government required paperwork, and lots of it, so while the legalities were being processed the family purchased an Opel with a sun roof and toured Europe, visiting Italy, Austria, Switzerland, France and Monaco. For Henry the trip was partly educating his family, partly flirting with the memories of his own youthful travels before he was forced to flee Germany, and savouring his great appreciation of European culture and architecture.

In Florence and Rome, they inspected every church, and in Switzerland, every snow-capped mountain. Not all European traditions were to Eddie's liking. In Avignon he was unable to sleep, frightened by the constant church bells ringing out of unison. They ring every hour, for twenty minutes each, but as they are not in unison, by the time one lot had stopped ringing it was almost time for the next to begin to peal! In Monaco, they had their brush with fame. Demigod of the time, Frank Sinatra, was filming nearby. Michael and Eddie had recently watched his latest film Around the World in 80 days and wanting to say they'd touched their idol, they literally bumped into him. They devised a chasing game; first Eddie would run and be on one side of Frank Sinatra, whilst Michael, chasing him, bumped into him and then it was Eddie's turn to chase Michael and he too managed to bump into him. Henry pretended to discipline the boys but underneath he enjoyed their little game. The French Riviera was paradise for two young, active boys. They hired a small spot of the beach and spent their steamy hot days frolicking in the Mediterranean, swimming or on paddle-boats, playing table tennis or dining from little restaurants right on the beach. One morning on the beach, Henry excitedly motioned for the boys to join him, *"Boys come here. See this?"* He showed them the headlines of a French newspaper with a picture of General de Gaulle. *"Michael and Eddie, this man resisted the Nazis when France fell, despite my efforts in the French Foreign Legion. France is still in a mess and de Gaulle is offering himself at age 67 to again be Prime Minister. This is great news. You need to understand this and celebrate this with the French. We should all sing the Marseillaise. He will fix the French issues in a humane way."* The other people on the Juan-les-Pins beachfront looked equally happy.

Ever the sportsman, Eddie was elated when they were taken to the beautiful little ski resort of Brandt on the Austrian border. It was his first time on the snow and, despite an initial close call with a cliff, grew to enjoy the sport immensely. The family ski trip was so successful that it turned from one week into two. When fatigue and hunger dragged them off the slopes they'd scurry in from the cold into cosy mountain top resorts, to be rejuvenated with hot lemon juice, Apfelsaft (apple cider) and crunchy apples. Unfortunately, a twisted knee and a torn ligament put an abrupt end to Eddie's skiing and he spent the rest of the week soaking up the history of William Tell adventures in the area.

The return to Europe for his parents was also a time of reconnection with family and friends. In Switzerland, it was with a cousin of Henry's, Fred Fischer, on beautiful Lake Lugano, where the brothers messed around on paddle-boats. In Paris Henry reunited with a man whom he had met only briefly whilst fleeing Hitler. This man's actions had enabled Henry to find refuge and register as a doctor in Lebanon and had altered the course of the Price family's life. Raol le Bourgeois in 1933 was a young French diplomat and a member of one of the most prominent families of France. Henry had requested assistance and Raol had dropped all his work to help this young German Jewish doctor whom he had never met before. Prior to departing for Lebanon, Henry asked Raol why he had been so eager to help. His answer had been simple and simply brave, *"You are a victim of persecution. I shall do all for you that I can."*

Leaving Germany on this second occasion should have been a triumphant one for the Prices. They were leaving of their own volition with hopes of restitution and not with nightmares of persecution. Sadly, their months of European bliss ended with a small, hard and dreaded lump in one of Ursula's breasts. They hastened to Israel and to the haven of Herward, Ursula's much loved brother of whom Eddie had heard so much throughout his childhood. Herward and girlfriend Ruth lived in Haifa and from here Henry rushed to have Ursula seen by a doctor. The lump was diagnosed as cancerous and their mother was immediately admitted to the Rothschild hospital in Haifa to have a radical mastectomy. Eddie and Michael were in shock. Their positive and ever present mother was suddenly ripped from their lives and had morphed into a sickly, aged woman they hardly recognised in a hospital bed. They were not told why she was there, only that she was gravely ill and needed her rest. Rather bewilderingly, Ursula was also denied her prognosis. Henry, in a loving attempt to shield his wife emotionally told her that the operation was a success and that she was cancer free, even showing her false records and pathology tests. However, the years of radiation therapy to come surely must have raised this intelligent woman's suspicions.

While their mother was ill and their father pursued employment, the brothers were sent to various summer camps to spend the long warm days playing sport and other games. Eddie managed to foster a love of cricket amongst the local kids and even taught them a little rugby. Uncle Herward and girlfriend Ruth also took the boys spear-fishing at various resorts around Haifa. There was a stream of relatives from both sides of the family for the boys to meet, including a visitor from New York, Ursula's favourite, Aunt Hedy. Unfortunately, Eddie did not share his mother's enthusiasm for Israel. He found the old cities like Nazareth and Acco dirty and unappealing and thought they showed signs of poverty. He preferred modern architecture but most of all he missed the sport at home and his friends in Wollongong. What was also obvious to him was the lower standard of living. He saw that in the way his own family lived. He wanted to return to Australia. He wasn't the only one.

Henry was floundering. He had difficulties with the language. His wife was just out of hospital and was now living with a serious illness. Then Michael became very sick and was diagnosed with glomerulonephritis, a severe kidney disease and was bedridden. He remained fatigued for six months and although some go on to be chronic, Michael made a full recovery.

Henry had gone to work in a hospital in Afula in the north of Israel. The young socialist country certainly wasn't running its medical system to the levels Henry was accustomed to in Australia and Germany. To exacerbate his frustrations, Henry's conservative nature was uncomfortable with the socialist system that saw a highly decorated doctor being treated equally with a gardener and where the secretary of the hospital was afforded bigger and better cars than the doctors. Not only was Henry's pride injured, but the pay was pitiful and their financial hardships were only broken by a lump sum settlement of restitution from the German government. Henry, however, was a surgeon, not a businessman. Not only did he not invest the amount, but his negotiations were, in hindsight, not as lucrative as those who were given a substantial pension for the rest of their lives. Henry was offered a job as a gynaecologist in Eilat, an extremely hot and isolated port on the Red Sea. He felt that restarting their lives in Israel under all these circumstances would be unpleasant, if not impossible, and so he decided to return to Australia – to Sydney - to set up practice there.

Chapter 2

Coming of Age

Returning to Australia in October 1958 was welcomed with much joy and enthusiasm from 11 year-old Eddie. He was going back to the country he knew and the sports he loved, despite having to negotiate a new school, as the Prices were making a fresh start in Sydney. The new boy was received with great interest by his year 6 classmates at Middle Harbour Primary School, particularly by the girls. This was a novelty for Eddie who had only ever had boys in his classes in Wollongong. Much to his further delight his new headmaster was also a cricket enthusiast. At Eddie's suggestion he instigated school cricket matches on a Friday afternoon down at Primrose Park. There was so much interest in the games that the following year the school entered into the inter-school competition.

Not all the family were as happy as Eddie with their return to Australian shores. Ursula had not only been deprived of her opportunity to attempt living in Israel but she'd also been denied her health. Following her mastectomy operation in Haifa she started radiotherapy in Sydney. Despite never being told she had cancer by Henry, as the effects of the illness spread, she gradually realised the gravity of the situation. Regardless of her health battles and lament of leaving her dreams of Israel behind, Ursula never complained and poured all her time and energy, as always, into her family - working at Henry's surgery and being heavily involved with the P&C at the boys' school.

In January 1959 the family purchased a house in a predominantly Jewish area of Dover Heights with views to the ocean that reminded Henry of Mount Carmel, a coastal mountain range in northern Israel stretching from the Mediterranean Sea towards the southeast. The home became affectionately known as Carmel Heights as Henry's way of recognising Ursula's love and longing for Israel. The first few nights in the dark, run-down property were rather unsettling. The large home and gardens needed a lot of attention. Restoration was a family affair, with Michael and Eddie choosing the light turquoise colour for their own bedroom, painting all the front wrought iron work on the verandah and assisting their mother and father with the dreaded gardening while "*Monday is washing day, Tuesday is soup, Wednesday is roast beef, Thursday is Shepherd's Pie, Is everybody happy? You bet your life we are,*" pumped out of the radio from 2UE. Once the weed wrangling was over, the large backyard was the scene of many cricket matches, cubby and tree house building and hours and hours of basketball.

Living in Sydney also meant the family could continue their tradition of trips to the theatre and movies and with greater frequency than when they lived in Wollongong. Most Saturday evenings, after an afternoon at the beach and followed by the compulsory nap, the family would dress up and be entertained by Can Can, West Side Story, South Pacific or any number of Gilbert and Sullivan plays and followed by a meal at a favourite restaurant. On one outing to the Ensemble Theatre to see Between Two Seasons, Eddie had his first experience with interactive theatre. Actors had been planted in the audience and Eddie got so carried away with the conversation they were having, not realising they were indeed actors, he began to interject as well. He was extremely embarrassed when enlightened as to the situation mid-performance by his whispering parents.

Eddie continued to do quite well scholastically on entering Randwick Boys High School. Once settled into the new surrounds and new group of friends, he focused on his studies. Heading towards his first lot of exams he realised his class were far behind other classes in their French. He requested some tutorials from his French-speaking mother and much to the surprise of his classmates, whose marks were dismal, his marks were excellent.

"Eddie, please explain," quizzed his perplexed French teacher, Ms Bonjus.

Eddie, in a soft, somewhat embarrassed voice said, *"My mother speaks French."*

By the end of his first year of high school he was heading for first-in-his-class overall. Only one spelling exam stood in his way where he needed to get at least 26 out of 50 to hold the top rank. Sadly, English never was one of his strengths. His final mark was 6 out of 50 and he had to copy others' work just to get that. Eddie finished the year a respectable fourth. These results saw him move to a higher class with a new cohort of students.

One lesson in particular stayed with Eddie. It was an Ancient History lesson on the life of Jesus Christ and they were taught how the Jewish people appealed to the leaders of Judea to have Jesus killed. Many of Eddie's classmates turned to their Jewish friend. Whether they did so accusingly or just in an instinctual response to acknowledging the Jewish boy in the class, either way he felt terrible. It was an ongoing theme for a Jewish child growing up in a predominantly Christian society. In Wollongong when his class had been told that Jews killed Christ, the god of everyone else in the class, all of his friends had frowned at him and Eddie had felt awful. There was some solidarity in numbers now in Sydney though. Rather than being left to wander the playground alone as was the case during scripture classes in Wollongong, in high school there was Jewish scripture and the room was overcrowded. However, Eddie preferred the playground option. Not long after beginning scripture, the class was being disruptive and the teacher Mr Rothfield explained that there was no obligation to stay and listen. He took his opportunity and left. Only one other child followed, a boy called Bart, previously unknown to Eddie, who soon became his firm friend. Ironically, Eddie's decision to leave scripture, which could have been seen as rebellious or a snub to Judaism, actually played a major part in Eddie's relationship with his Jewish heritage and his loyalty to Israel. Over a game of marbles in the yard outside, Bart Doff told him of a fantastic youth group he was a part of where they played games, met plenty of girls and generally had lots of fun.

"The girls kiss great Eddie," claimed Bart.

The group was called Betar, a Jewish youth group that focused on Jewish identity, culture and the importance of Israel. They believed that Jews had an obligation and duty to help re-build their native land. Henry, recalling his own involvement in the blue-white youth movements back in Germany, was supportive of Eddie's interest in Betar and Ursula was delighted her son wanted to know more about her longed-for Israel, so arrangements were made for him to accompany Bart to the next camp during the Christmas holidays.

Celebrating their Jewish culture and heritage was of high importance for the Price family and part of Eddie's journey as a Jew was to have a Bar-Mitzvah. Bar-Mitzvahs are a coming of age, a Jewish tradition, seen as a rite of passage towards "manhood" and towards accepting responsibility. For Eddie and his family, the process was more a cultural dedication towards keeping four thousand year-old traditions alive, rather than a religious undertaking. In March 1959 he went to the Great Synagogue with Rabbi Porush to be tested to see if they would accept him as a Bar-Mitzvah candidate. He was asked a variety of questions and had to read in Hebrew, all of which he couldn't answer nor do. If Eddie wanted to do his Bar-Mitzvah at the Great Synagogue the Rabbi said he'd need time, and lots of it. Henry decided they'd look elsewhere for more liberal training to expedite the process. The Emanuel Synagogue in Woollahra was much more accepting of Eddie and even questioned, *"Why bring him so early? He's got plenty of time. There's still six months before his Bar-Mitzvah."*

Rabbi Brash, who ran the Bar-Mitzvah, didn't miss an opportunity to spruik three textbooks on Judaism (that he'd written himself) saying to Henry, *"To train for his Bar-Mitzvah, Eddie must have these books on Jewish studies."*

Henry, unwilling to pay for unnecessary books, politely declined with the excuse, *"Oh thank you, thank you, but we already own them."*

Eddie, in his childish honesty refuted his father, *"No we don't dad. We've only got one of them!"*

Henry assured the Rabbi that they certainly did own the books, but Eddie was adamant and insisted, *"Dad, we don't have them!"* Henry was forced to buy autographed copies of the Rabbi's books.

For three months prior to his Bar-Mitzvah, Eddie attended Jewish Sunday school. It was an organised rabble of twelve years-olds mucking around and talking, with the teacher having little authority. There were also private lessons with Reverend Mandel who was a lovely, short, slightly tubby man, with a sincere heart. Mandel had been good friends with one of Eddie's relatives, Gary Price, living together on a Kibbutz in northern Israel many years earlier. The family connection helped begin a warm relationship between Reverend Mandel and Eddie who was told he must attend a Bar-Mitzvah the week before his to see how everything was done correctly. He found himself sitting in the back row of the synagogue next to his scripture-skipping friend, Bart Doff. *"Pricey, what are you doing here?"*

He explained, *"It's my turn next week. What are you doing here? We skip scripture."*

Bart pointed to the boy out the front. *"Leo Rogovin is a family friend, you know. Our families came to Australia via China together."*

As Eddie studied the actions of Leo Rogovin that day he had no inkling of the relationship they'd forge through Betar youth camps and would see them as lifelong friends.

Eddie's Bar-Mitzvah was held on the 12th of September 1959. Reverend Mandel had quickly realised that Eddie, true to form, was no singer and so had organised for him to only sing the introductory prayers and for the rest of his Haftorah to be spoken in English. Ursula cried tears of happiness as this cultural ceremony meant so much to her. The day culminated in a reception at the family home in Dover Heights with speeches and gifts. He received four bedside sit up clocks that would fold over and a total of seventeen pounds which went towards his Betar camp at the end of the year.

It is perhaps no coincidence that Bar-Mitzvahs occur at the age of thirteen, for it was around this time when Eddie did come of age....when he started to think....embracing greater thoughts and thinking beyond his self. Henry's unrelenting standards were embedded into his psyche. He found a social need to help the greater good and perhaps a subconscious influence from the stories that were seeping out of Europe of the horrors that the Jewish people had suffered. Eddie felt a need to bring harmony – to unite people. It was at this time that a dream was born to exact as much impact on as many people in the world as possible and to give a greater quality of life to as many as possible. Such an altruistic goal seemed in need of an esteemed and powerful position. Eddie's dream was to become the Secretary General of the United Nations.

Whilst an ember of fascination towards Israel began to glow deep within him, his outer Aussie shell was still ablaze with an enthusiasm for sport - cricket and football. In his first year of high school he tried out for the school cricket team in a bid to make new friends, but with no one to vouch for his spin bowling prowess, others were given the role and he was left to play house cricket. Representing the school was still a possibility though with football. Eddie excitedly turned up to try out for rugby but was rather disillusioned when he was joined by another one hundred boys also vying for a position on the team. He noted there were only 20 or 30 trying out for soccer so decided he'd have better odds there. That was until he saw the level of skills displayed by those already gathered. They could stop a ball just using their chests, no hands, and when they kicked a ball on the ground, it went straight to its desired destination...their team mates.

Eddie thought, *"My singing is better than my soccer."*

He hated every minute of it and thought it was all too hard and gave up. He quickly returned to the rugby trials. Much to his delight, at a couple of the training sessions he took an intercept and scored a solo try and so was one of the first to be called up for the team. He'd played a lot of rugby league in primary school but this was his first time playing rugby union. He was chosen as Vice-Captain of the team and his teammates became his friends. They included Bobby Cameron, Phil Wade, Kingsley Young and Jimmy Stone. The highlight of their rugby year was playing the revered Sydney High team in the Grand Final. Sydney High boasted players like John Brass and Phil Smith who went on to play first grade and for Australia. They were favoured to win but Eddie's team devised a plan and even though it was not his greatest game, their team won 6-3. Randwick Boys High was ecstatic and Eddie was awarded the Best and Fairest award for the season. The award was only slightly tarnished by his guilt that he'd been the one tallying the weekly awards for the coach to determine the final winner. None the less, he had won the title fairly and was very proud to have it written up in the school magazine.

Saturdays afternoons had always been family time for the Price family but Eddie was also most eager to join his father on a Saturday morning in a regular cricket competition. Henry had decided to make a conscious effort to become a bit more involved in the Maroubra community and as an ex-serviceman himself had joined the local RSL. The club had a cricket team that welcomed sons to play. Eddie was very enthusiastic and as the team didn't have a wicket keeper and, as he was quite adept at catching, he volunteered for the job. It wasn't wicket keeping however where he shone. His understanding of the game meant he was invaluable in assisting and offering advice to the captain Ian Robertson.

The first half of the school holidays at the end of 1959 were filled with hikes, singing, games, lectures, sport, girls and good times at the Betar camp held near Newcastle. Initially lured by the promise of kissing girls, Eddie ended up being indoctrinated by the pro-Israel ideology that Jews must live in Israel, as well as establishing a strong foundation of friendship. He had found his tribe and began attending weekly meetings as well as the regular holiday camps. The second half of the holidays was a bit more subdued. Whilst playing at a friend's home with hoses in the backyard, Eddie had raced underneath the house and had collided with a cross beam which caused a deep cut. He put his finger to his head and could feel bone and blood rushing out. He was raced to the local doctor and his father called. Henry said for the doctors there to do nothing and that he would see to it. The knock had been so hard that Eddie's head was still numb and he was not showing much distress. By the time his father saw him most of the bleeding has stopped and his father smiled and said *"It can't be that bad,"* as he took off the bandages. He was in for a shock. The wound was significant; it had gone straight to his skull. Eddie was taken into theatre under local anaesthetic to be cleaned and have twenty-two stitches in his scalp.

"I must've given it a fair whack. I didn't feel a thing when you were stitching!" exclaimed Eddie to his father.

Henry smiled, *"Eddie, you ratbag. As a loving father I gave you one injection of a small dose of local anaesthetic and when the area next to it was numb I gave you more in sequence all the way along and on both sides. That's why it took so long, other than all the stitches, but that's why you didn't feel anything. It wasn't the extent of the bump!"*

Eddie wasn't a pretty sight the next day when all the kids in the neighbourhood came to visit him. Half his head was shaved around the wound, a big bandage had been applied and his face was terribly swollen. He carries the scars to this day. A few days after surgery his head began bleeding again. On closer inspection it was revealed that there were more cuts that needed dressings applied and, to Eddie's strong objection, the rest of his head had to be shaved. Indeed, it was his baldness that seemed to affect him more than his injury. He covered all the bandages and his baldness, with a red and white Ivy League hat. It looked somewhat outlandish but did the job of disguising his injuries. By the following Sunday afternoon, he was back playing basketball at Betar but when his hat covering his bereft head came off he was mortified and left in tears. On his first day back at school a teacher, Mr Mitchell, belted his head and pulled off his hat saying, "*What do you think you are doing? Cut it out, that's not the school uniform!*" Mr Mitchell was in shock when Eddie's bandages rolled out. He was raced to the sick bay and then allowed to go home.

Head injury or not, Eddie continued his vigorous involvement in sports. He was a leading try scorer for BAYS Rugby Union team near Rose Bay and was also in the Under 14's school basketball team and the Under 14's Maroubra RSL cricket team. Much to his surprise and delight he was asked to play first grade cricket as wicket keeper for Randwick Boys High and in one proud moment was interviewed for the Daily Mirror's school sports column. The write-up espoused great things about Randwick's captain, Geoff Davies, a wily spin bowler who could spin the ball both ways and had a difficult-to-pick wrong-un. What the journalist didn't realise was every time Geoff was to bowl a wrong-un he would give Eddie a sign by rubbing his hand through his hair because Eddie had difficulty picking him. The combination took four wickets. Geoff Davies went on to captain New South Wales and was twelfth man for Australia although he never got a game. Towards the end of high school Eddie's enthusiasm for playing sport began to wane, to be replaced by greater preoccupations.

Who am I? Why am I here? Am I really Australian? What are the important issues?

He felt more of an association with his Jewish Betar friends who offered more intellectual satisfaction than with his "Australian" friends but his Jewish friends didn't share his love of sport. He felt that he didn't entirely belong to one group or the other. He began to divorce himself, little by little, from the other boys at school and started spending more and more time with his Jewish friends. He was getting more involved in debates, taking closer note of the teachings of Betar, as well as showing a greater interest in international affairs and Israel and Australia's respective places in the world.

Socially Betar had a lot to offer Eddie, particularly when it came to meeting girls. There were Saturday night parties, Luna Park dates and long nights of rock'n roll, twisting and stomping at the end-of-year Betar camps. Often in their late teens when their parents would go out on their own, Eddie and his brother would invite a large group from Betar to party at their home. When their mother found out that some social gatherings had taken place she seemed delighted that her sons felt comfortable enough to invite their friends to their home. She may not have been so pleased had she known how friendly they were indeed getting. With the progression of his thoughts, Eddie began to drift a little apart from those more interested in the social side of Betar. Even his personality made a shift. He was less extroverted and more content to think about being Jewish, about Israel and to participate in discussions of philosophy. He sat for exams at Betar that elevated his status within the organisation by demonstrating a high degree of understanding of, and a love and appreciation of Israel, of Israel's history and of the Jewish nationalistic movement. At this stage he was a fairly right-wing radical who saw all Communism as bad. Betar had lit a passionate desire within him to live, as he believed all Jews should, in Israel, and so to be close to the bosom of Judaism, Jerusalem. He came to the conclusion that if their race was to have any chance of survival then Jews needed to be in Israel thus contributing to their cause there. These thoughts presented a dilemma for Eddie. Throughout his youth, and indeed his life, he felt torn between two identities; an Australian exterior with an ethnically Jewish core. He was an enigma. He was neither fully "Australian" nor a Jew living in Israel. He was the outsider.

With such in-depth studies at Betar, at times Eddie found his formal education a little boring. He did reasonably well, particularly in maths, physics and chemistry. He wanted to do well for his leaving certificate, so in 1963, whilst also a prefect at school, he applied himself to the task of studying for honours in maths and honours in physics. His efforts were rewarded with 3rd in his half yearly exam and 2nd in his trial. All that was left to be done were the final exams. After months of hard work and dedicating himself purely to study, Eddie's results were in... but he was out...at the beach when the phone call was received at his home with the scores. His family decided not to pass on the good news but instead took him into the city and let him read it for himself in the paper that came out at midnight. There was much celebrating at Kings Cross that night with his friends from Sydney High, Betar and his brother Michael when it was revealed that he had received four A's -First Class Honours and Second Class Honours. These were much more than he had ever hoped for. With such great results, a position studying medicine at Sydney University was assured. Henry might get his prophesied doctor after all. Studying medicine wasn't something that was decided by Eddie or by his father, but was something that had gradually been assumed over time and through his desire to please his father.

One hundred straight, lazy, sunny days of holidays stretched in front of him before his University studies were to begin. Most of those were at the beautiful, wide Bondi Beach with its soft white sand and natural surrounds. Eddie and friends camped out in the central steps area below the pavilion known as Little Jerusalem as the Jewish youth usually congregated there. On one such day he bumped into an ex-girlfriend, Michelle Kogan, and her friends and began chatting and playing games with one girl in particular. Wearing a white costume with blue dots that complemented her dark complexion, this attractive and well-groomed girl with lovely legs caught Eddie's attention. Not only was she full of life and outgoing, despite being a couple of years his junior, he was able to have serious conversations with her about all manner of things: roles of different people in society, homosexuality, sophisticated versus non-sophisticated people. Her name was Maria Fiszman, known as Mia. At the end of the day they walked to the shops together and Eddie got on a bus and waved goodbye saying that he'd look her up. They met at Bondi Beach on a number of other occasions. He walked Mia home to Rose Bay from time to time. It was on one of these walks that he started to debate with himself, *"When is the right time to hold her hand? Should I or shouldn't I?"*

They did. They held hands and then parted with a kiss.

Chapter 3

Becoming a Doctor

It was 1964 and The Beatles "epidemic" had infected the globe. Internationally it was a time of social upheaval, of civil rights activism, of anarchistic actions that espoused religious and cultural diversity and it was a time of love. Eddie Daniel Price rocked his role in the world as the fun-loving larrikin of the medical faculty at Sydney University. Inwardly, he too, was in a state of emotional turmoil, of grief, of confusion over divided loyalties and injustices, and it was also a time of love. Flowing on from their holiday romance, dating in the 60's for Eddie and Mia consisted of frolicking at the beach by day and frequenting folk singing venues by night. They would squeeze into small, dark, crowded rooms and find a mattress on the floor to sit on and listen to drawn out folk songs. As appealing as that sounds, it wasn't until years later that Eddie found out just how much Mia detested those nights. More to Mia's liking was when they managed to sneak out to be together on sacred Friday evenings. After the family's candle lit blessing of wine and a special loaf of Jewish Challah bread, Eddie would offer to take Susie the Alsatian for a walk and would rendezvous with Mia and her Labrador Troy at the Dover Heights Reservoir and soak up the exquisite view of the Harbour Bridge and the twinkling lights of Sydney at twilight.

Their mutual attraction was heightened by their shared intellect, love of sport, politics and that they were both proudly Jewish. Mia, however, had not come through life quite so unscathed by the generational social implications of the persecution that her parents had experienced at the hands

41

of the Nazis. Her father, Sam Fiszman, was born in Poland. He was a thirteen-year-old student when the Jews were being rounded up and systematically murdered by their own government, including his family. Sam endured a harsh existence in the Warsaw ghetto and then joined the Polish underground and later the Russian army and survived the genocide and war through his wit and "gift of the gab". Mia's mother, Esther, was detained in Auschwitz from age eleven to fifteen. Lying about her age in order to survive the gas chambers, Esther was sent to the factories making arms. She got by on charm and, like her husband to be, her ability to win over people who not only liked her, but loved her, and her ability to talk herself out of dangerous situations. These two survivors met in a displaced person's camp in Poland at the end of the war and married so that Esther, aged fifteen, would not be adopted. Their union soon produced a daughter, Mia, who was born in Paris in a hospital attached to the Notre Dame Cathedral on the 19th of July 1948. Being a Catholic hospital, the nuns rejected the young couple's wishes to name their daughter Malka which means "Queen" in Hebrew, and instead called her Maria. After years of surviving off charm and not "rocking the boat", Maria or "Mia" as she would become known, was accepted. Mia became the "apple of her father's eye". He felt guilty that his mother and sister had not survived and saw Mia as their replacement. In August of 1948, with Mia under one month old, the family immigrated to Australia. Their arduous journey was made famous by Dianne Armstrong's book The Voyage of Their Life which documents the hellish conditions aboard their migrant ship. For three months the passengers who included displaced persons, survivors of death camps, labour camps, and Russian gulags and sixty-one orphans, endured a hellish and traumatic passage. Mia's own father claimed to have been involved in despatching one poor soul overboard during a fight. Their future life in Australia would be defined by their past, recognising that you do whatever is necessary, even lie, to protect your life and your family. "The law doesn't look after you - you make your own rules. Money doesn't protect you – people do." So they made it their habit to know influential people and became influential people. Sam's leftist leanings, shaped by his experiences in Europe, led him to become a dynamic supporter of the Labor Party in Australia. His lateral thinking and business sense made his advice invaluable and called the likes of Graham Richardson and Bob Hawke close friends. When Sam died many Labor Party dignitaries attended his funeral and a park in North Bondi was named after him. The Sam Fiszman Park is a popular whale-watching spot with spectacular views. Eddie would joke to Mia that Sam must have known they spent some Saturday evenings, after having gone out in the car, parking and schmoozing in that exact spot and that Sam was seeking his revenge. But Sam and Esther's ability to win hearts, to talk their way in or out of any situation they chose, set up a childhood of confusion for Mia and her brother Robert. The siblings were further impacted by the lack of discipline from young parents who had experienced "discipline" in-the-extreme at the hands of the Nazis and wanted no part of it in their children's lives. The loss of their entire families added to their desire to please their daughter and to not discipline her. It was a world away from the strict childhood Eddie had experienced. Regardless of their differences of character and upbringing, they were in love.

As one important woman in Eddie's life made her entrance, another was beginning to take her final curtain call. Even though Henry had never explicitly said that his mother had cancer, Eddie knew that her health wasn't good and that despite all the radiotherapy she was receiving, she was getting weaker. His parents' 25th wedding anniversary was coming up and they would be celebrating with a show, How to Succeed in Business without Really Trying, to be followed by dinner at the dimly-lit basement restaurant, St. Georges, run by a Polish fellow down near Circular Quay.

"I want each of you to come with a partner for the evening," instructed Henry to his sons.

There was no alternative. This was a command and Eddie had to bring a girl with him. He wanted to have somebody special as a date for the night, and in particular, he wanted to please his mother. His date had to be someone who could easily converse with his parents, who would be interesting enough and well-groomed enough to look the part and who could deal with a father who wanted to promote analytical thinking in his sons.

"Mia, we will be quizzed on the play. What were the underlying messages? Who was the best actor? Are you up for it?" asked Eddie.

She smiled, *"I'd love to."*

March 19th 1964 would be Eddie and Mia's first official date. Mia looked stunning in a brown dress and felt immediately at ease with the family. The downstairs cellar of the restaurant had a pleasant atmosphere with its soft lighting and diners being serenaded by the live band playing strains of Cha Cha, Bambina, Marina and Autumn Leaves. Henry expected the kids to dance with their partners and so dance they did. It was a very special evening that Eddie's ill mother greatly enjoyed.

Realising the looming inevitability of his wife's illness,

Henry arranged for Ursula to take one final trip to Israel in June of 1964 to visit her brother Herward and his growing family. Her delight only marred by the physicality of her illness. As cancer ravaged her body, it took not just her health, but her looks, disfiguring her face and injuring her pride. With the disintegration of his mother's physical appearance, Eddie became reasonably aware that she was gravely ill and didn't feel that he ought to be happy when his mother was so sick.

He lay awake at night thinking, *"How can I be happy? How can I joke with my friends when I know my mother is dying? This is inappropriate."* He felt guilty every time he laughed or was light-hearted. It was one of the internal dilemmas that gnawed at him throughout his journey into adulthood.

As part of Eddie's baptism into grown up affairs, he needed to learn to drive and his father declared that he would teach him and explained the basics of driving as they entered his old Zephyr. He handed Eddie the keys saying, *"Now drive!"* Eddie put his foot down on the accelerator fairly swiftly and they went hurtling along heading for a cliff. Henry, after the initial shock, somehow managed to get his foot on the brake in between Eddie's feet.

Once they'd stopped Henry yelled, *"You mechanical idiot!"*

There were no more driving lessons from his father. A driving instructor was arranged and even though he passed his test a month later on the first attempt, he's never had a high opinion of himself as a driver. Soon after Henry purchased a new car and the Zephyr became the mode of transport for Michael and Eddie to travel to Sydney University. Michael was studying for a Bachelor of Science and a Bachelor of Engineering which would culminate in a

Masters of Engineering with a thesis on Computers and Computer Controlling Systems. To his father's delight Eddie had won a Commonwealth Scholarship and was enrolled in Medicine. He had greater plans than pure study for his first tertiary year. He wanted to allow time for social activities and he particularly wanted to devote himself to Betar where he was climbing further up the ranks. He'd been elevated to the executive committee and was running the Sydney chapter of the organisation.

The importance of Betar's teachings for him was only enhanced by an article that came out in the University newspaper Honi Soit. In his eyes the editor was wanting to provoke the community's sensibilities and garner attention and so commissioned a pro-NAZI piece that claimed Jews were the criminals of the world. Eddie and his allies retaliated and protested at the anti-Semitism and gross racism that was blatantly expressed. Eddie was appalled that this vitriol came out of the mouths of academics, from people he thought would have known better. Ted Whitgob penned a response in Honi Soit to the original article.

"No one will deny that a Jew is equally capable of committing an economic crime as a gentile. But when it appears that almost all those sentenced to death or paying lesser penalties for economic offences have been Jews or people with Jewish sounding names, Soviet statistics become questionable. Yet these economic criminals received a good deal of publicity, and many Rabbis are said to be involved, with the synagogue being described as a den of iniquity synonymous with the black market. Furthermore, Jews are being labelled with various communist epithets ranging from 'lackeys of the imperialists' to 'Zionist spies' to the unprintable. The situation was further aggravated by the

publication of a book called Judaism without Embellishment which was published under the auspices of the Academy of Science!!! The book will stand comparison with the most virulent anti-Semitic publication of Hitler's heyday. Its contents in both words and caricatures are insulting to an unprecedented degree. Small wonder then, that the situation is viewed with alarm by Jews all over the world. It is in our own lifetime that 6 million of our brethren were eliminated by the Nazis and therefore the situation cannot be allowed to repeat itself ever again. If the Jews are not wanted in Russia, they should be permitted to leave, yet they are not. Instead they are being subjected to intolerable conditions, which in the long run will lead to their elimination. Thus the Sydney Jewish Students Union in conjunction with the other political and religious clubs, calls on you to attend a protest meeting at the Old Geology Theatre on Tuesday, April 21st at 1pm. It is not a protest against the political system of the USSR; the USSR is as entitled to its own political system as we are ourselves; but it is a question of the denial of the basic human rights which are the birthright of every man". Ted Whitgob.

Part of Eddie's Betar teachings, as promoted by the founder, Zeev Jabotinksy, in the 30's, when the pogroms were on against the Jews, stated that they should not take such attacks lying down and that they needed to arm themselves. Jabotinsky's major disciple was Menachem Begin, who is quoted as saying "*I fight, therefore I am*". Eddie felt he had to do something but he hated guns. He conversed with a fellow medical student, David Itzkowic, and they decided that they would learn Judo through the Judo club at Sydney University. Eddie didn't want to go and wasn't keen on judo as a sport but he felt it was better than

47

nothing. Both somehow obtained a yellow belt, but Eddie's confidence in Itzkovic protecting him was probably on par with Itzkovic's confidence in Eddie defending him. He was too much like his father – ever the pacifist. Henry saw war as stupid and futile and thought it crazy that he should be a fighter in the French Foreign Legion. These sentiments he'd passed on to his son. He'd also passed on his tendency to be wary of exposing his Jewishness to the general public. He had told his friends at the RSL that Eddie had gone to Italy, not indeed to Israel, at the end of his studies. Regardless of any stigma, Mia's parents were delighted and relieved that their daughter was dating a Jew, and such a passionate one at that. Eddie and Sam shared not only their love of their Jewish heritage, but of sport. On one evening when he was invited to Mia's home for dinner he confided in the elder Jewish statesman, then aged thirty-seven years, for advice on how to deal with an alarming situation. There was a Nazi party active in Sydney, headed by an Arthur Charles Smith, and they were gaining momentum and publicity in Ashfield. A Four Corners program aired that highlighted Arthur Smith and the Nazi Party rhetoric against blacks, Asians and Jews. They were wearing Nazi uniforms and greeting each other with *"Heil Hitler"*. It was an affront to Eddie and to many others that here was such blatant racism and anti-Semitism right "in their faces". It was in their living rooms and with the law as it stood, the perpetrators had the protection of the police to do this. He began scouting around all the youth movements and senior members associated with the youth movements trying to organise a group to do something about these Nazi supporters. Harnessing physical action against people wasn't Eddie's forte, or even something he felt comfortable with, but he wasn't prepared to sit back and put up with such a group. He felt action was required. When he spoke to Mia's father he was reassured by Sam that, "*We'll do something and don't worry about it. We're getting everything under control.*"

Eddie asked, "*Who is 'we' and what are 'we' doing? What can I do to help?*"

Sam replied, "*Something will be arranged.*"

Shortly after the police raided the Nazi Party and many were arrested and charged with a variety of offences including possession of firearms and other illegal items.

Eddie thought to himself, "*I bet Sam and some of his mates from the racing fraternity had something to do with ensuring illegal items were found in that flat!*"

He had no idea how this was organised. Sam had survived the Polish Underground and the Warsaw ghetto so anything was possible. Arthur Smith was charged in a Sydney court for these offences and when he arrived at court a member of the public leaped out and punched him twice. Sometime later Eddie was driving taxis as a 21-year old medical student and late one night he was parked outside the Latin Quarter Nightclub. He picked up a bouncer by the name of "Jerry". Sam had been known to attend this nightclub occasionally and would take the floor singing his favourite song Sway.

He asked his passenger, "*Jerry, are you the Security here?*"

"*Yes, I am,*" he replied.

"*Maybe you've heard of my father-in-law, Sam Fiszman?*" asked Eddie.

"*Hey, what a great bloke!*" espoused Jerry.

Eddie was intrigued, "*How do you mean?*"

"*Oh, three years ago, he paid me fifty dollars for throwing two punches at that Nazi guy when he went into court,*" grinned Jerry.

Eddie shook his head in wonder at his father-in-law and thought, *"You have to be street smart and I'm certainly not that."*

Nevertheless, it would be an ongoing battle to keep these fanatics at bay and their shadows still smoulder today.

In Eddie's second year of medicine in 1965 his mother took a turn for the worse. She was becoming weaker and weaker. On his regular walks with his mother and their dog Susie, Ursula had to make frequent stops to catch her breath. Her facial disfigurement became even more horrifying to her and her stomach began to swell with fluid. Ursula's visits to hospital became more and more frequent with severe kidney colic and other side effects of the cancer as it ate away at her diminishing body. Still refusing to be a burden on her family she struggled through her work and even arranged a hugely successful 21st birthday party for Michael. Ursula swallowed her pride and the embarrassment of her physical appearance in order to celebrate with her son and family and share one last milestone. The evening was wonderful and joyous, full of singing and dancing. One song in particular that was played that night would illustrate their mood, *"Domani, forget Domani - Let's Forget about Tomorrow"*.

In April of 1965 Henry finally divulged the true cause of Ursula's illness to Eddie and Michael, that indeed she had cancer and he did not expect her to live for much longer. Ursula was mostly house-bound at this stage with long rest periods during the day. Henry made it clear that the boys needed to share in the care of their mother, often bedridden, especially on Saturday nights. He would be keeping up his social engagements to maintain his sanity. Eddie was on duty one Saturday evening when an inebriated Michael and Henry stumbled home at 3am. They were met by an irate Eddie who was sick with worry as to their whereabouts. His rare display of anger towards his domineering father was as much of a release to him as the imbibed spirits had been to Michael and Henry. Eddie's life had become preoccupied by his mother's health. He spent hours and hours by her bedside or in the family home endeavouring to buoy spirits. When his mother required orange juice he would throw a serviette over his arm and pretend to be a waiter, *"Yes madam. What can I get for you, please madam?"* and put on a whole show. *"Would you like me to squeeze the oranges at the table or in the kitchen?"*

The act gave Ursula so much pleasure and welcome laughter that Eddie, even in the company of Mia, would continue with the fun role-play overcoming his embarrassment in front of his girlfriend. He was not the only one attempting to lift spirits as Ursula herself was continuously trying to cheer everyone up and Henry had arranged for Herward to send a continual stream of letters that would arrive every two to three days.

By early July Ursula was so sick and weak she dropped down to 25 kilos and was hospitalised when she began vomiting continuously. She begged Henry to, *"Take the boys out; they shouldn't see their mother vomiting like this."* As always, she was thinking of others.

Eddie spent sleepless nights shortly before his mother's death crying in bed, thinking to himself, *"Why her? She had always been such a good person. Why not somebody like myself who is less meritorious and more deserving! She doesn't deserve to die young and certainly not in such a cruel way and feeling so distant from the Israel that she loves."*

One day at university he couldn't concentrate on his work at all. At lunchtime he returned home....his mother had died.

It was the 6th of July 1965. She was 54 years old.

As with Jewish tradition the family lit a candle and remembered the wonderful, loving, self-sacrificing person that was Ursula Josepha Price. Everyone who had met her loved her and appreciated the kind-heartedness and warmth she emitted. She didn't go out of her way to be popular; she was sincerely interested, empathetic, sympathetic and understanding. She was a joy. Henry recounted to his sons that, *"When she was on the boat on her way to Israel, people were taking on Hebrew names. The group stated that her name should be Ora, for the 'light', because she had lit up everybody on the boat."*

His mother loved life itself and taught her sons the value of life and of making the best of *"nothing"*. She didn't need anything to be happy and that's the way she had lived and enjoyed life. Eddie recalls her saying to the boys, *"You can make a party out of nothing. Just find a spare bit of wood. You can put cardboard around it or paper and make it into a cupboard or a kite. You can have fun. That is a party with nothing."*

The day after his mother died and the day before her funeral, Eddie had his largest exam in second year medicine – biochemistry. It counted for a large percentage of final marks. Second year medicine is renowned as the hardest year with half of the year usually failing. Sitting for the exam in the fog of grief, surprisingly, he managed to achieve a Distinction. During all those nights prior to his mother's death Eddie had sought solace and distraction in his studies and they had been the key to his success. It was his marks after this exam that suffered the brunt of his circumstances as he could no longer concentrate nor find purpose in his studies. He began philosophising about life and what it was all about and what was medicine for if it couldn't save his mother. He began to question why he was even studying medicine. He was designing a life where he would be surrounded by sick people when he didn't particularly like sick people! He sought the advice of a faculty counsellor regarding his ill-ease with hospitalised patients but was advised to continue with medicine as there was a very wide field of roles in which he would surely find his niche.

Within a few short months of Ursula's death, much to the horror of Eddie and Michael, the ever-social Henry began dating once more. A few failed romances passed until one particularly glamorous Hungarian hairdresser caught his eye. Henry was again in love, or perhaps lust, with Kathy Popper whom the boys secretly labelled a spicy "Paprika". They were married, albeit shortly, just long enough for Henry to be relieved of some of his hard-earned cash. One very big positive did come out of the relationship though.

"She saved my life you know Eddie," recalled Henry.

Eddie was intrigued, *"What do you mean?"*

"We had an agreement that if the marriage didn't last, then she would be entitled to my life insurance money for five years. I went swimming in Tamarama and it was a bit rough and I was pulled out to sea. I had to be rescued by the lifesavers."

"Yes, so what?" said Eddie.

"Well," explained Henry, *"There was no way I was going to drown 'cause I still had another half a year to go to get out of that arrangement. I was determined that there was no way that I would go!"*

A close friend and confidante was Bernie Kresner. Bernie and Eddie had met at Betar when they were 13 years old and went through Randwick High School together. The two gravitated towards each other as they both were very much "Aussie" Jews and a firm camaraderie was formed. In 1966 Bernie proposed that through the summer holidays they both take a road trip up the east coast of Australia and back. Much to Mia's consternation and resistance, Eddie eagerly agreed and the two set off in an old grey and pink Holden borrowed from Bernie's elder sister, fuelled by testosterone, and a little cash gathered from labouring jobs. From Port Macquarie to Proserpine the boys explored the golden beaches, the bars, the beautiful scenery and the beautiful girls. Not all they witnessed was quite so beautiful. At a bar in Surfer's Paradise a group of men and women had had their fair share of beer and were shaking bottles and spritzing the beer over each other. Unwisely they then sprayed the heavy-set Maori band. Eddie recalls they were playing Hang On Sloopy, Sloopy Hang On when all hell broke loose. The band put down their guitars and suggested the patrons leave, which they didn't. One of the women removed her high heels and started hitting the band members with them. The owner of the bar locked the till. Tables and chairs were flying, glass was broken, windows shattered and blood splattered on the floor. Bernie and Eddie quickly skirted the melee and continued their coastal adventure.

By the time they neared northern Queensland their financial situation was dire and the radio sound track of the time, heralding the change from Pounds to Dollars, certainly summed up their problems (to the tune of Click Go the Shears) *"Quick go the coins, quick, quick, quick"*. After several purchases, at kiosks and other shops, and after counting their change, both of them realised that they had actually paid them for their custom. These Queensland shopkeepers were still trying to understand the new coinage.

The boys were coming out positively. Their budgets were running low but they, courtesy of Queensland hospitality, had another two or three days of funding. They really started to enjoy the new dollar currency. At their most northerly destination, on an idyllic cruise to South Mole Island where Eddie should have been playing in nets off the back of the boat and soaking up the sun under tropical palm trees, he became delirious with fever. Back in Rockhampton, Eddie decided he should take himself to the Emergency Department of Rockhampton Hospital. He made the mistake of telling the registrar that he was a medical student and was travelling and sleeping in a tent.

The registrar exclaimed, *"We must look after our own. I'll get you better in 24 hours. You're being hospitalised and will be given large doses of intramuscular penicillin."*

He was diagnosed with tonsillitis, a complaint that had afflicted him throughout his life. Suddenly the medical student who disliked sick people was stuck in a remote hospital, far from everything and everyone familiar, surrounded by patients coughing and spluttering, vomiting, some with strokes and paralysis.....and in the geriatric ward to boot. He counted eleven of his fellow patients walking around with urine bags and catheters in situ.

He thought to himself, *"What happens if I fall asleep? I might end up with one of those."*

Eddie wanted out, and fast. The doctor desperate to help the restless young traveller recover dosed Eddie up with large penicillin injections every two to three hours for the twenty-four hours he was in his care. By the next morning Bernie and Eddie were on their way home.

He commented to Bernie, *"Mate, you're lucky you're not holding a bag with my urine in it."*

Bernie retorted with a friendly warning of his own, *"Ed, it was great to be able to stretch out in the tent. Maybe tonight I can find another hospital accommodation for you."*

With finances now extremely low, their stomachs were empty, but their hearts and minds were full of interesting stories and memories to be treasured forever.

On returning to Sydney, they both wanted to invest time in ventures outside of Betar. Bernie was increasingly studious with his university Building Degree and Eddie was thinking of a comeback to rugby with the university under-21 team. When Leo Rogovin suggested that Betar put on a play day festival he recruited Bernie to be the show's production manager and Eddie to be the MC. Bernie with a reputation for playing a major role in Randwick Boys High School's production of Oklahoma and being instrumental in many camp productions had difficulty saying *"No"* to Leo. In August, 1966 a sequence of short plays and skits from different age groups was presented to a most receptive audience. Eddie used all the records he'd heard for years and years from his father's collection of Victor Borge and Dr Murray Banks. Everyone agreed it was a great evening and even went down in Betar history. In 2017 Peter Keeda saw their one-page program on display in the Jabotinsky Museum in Israel.

Like his father, Eddie's brother Michael was to experience a short nuptial period with his long-term girlfriend Shula. They married at the Great Synagogue on Ursula's birthday, 15th of January 1967, but the marriage only lasted six months with Michael claiming he was too immature. Eddie suspected it was possibly more accurate that Shula just wasn't the right girl and that Michael had used the marriage as a way to get away from his domineering father. The breakdown of

Michael's marriage did however divulge a poorly-kept family secret. In comforting his son in his relationship woes, Henry explained that getting divorced wasn't the worst thing in the world. "*It's not so bad. It's actually happened to me too.*" He explained to Michael that he'd been previously married and had a son who was a half-brother to Eddie and Michael. Prior to meeting Ursula in the Middle East, Henry had married Ilse Szamatolski, an attractive tall blonde he had met in Berlin prior to fleeing Germany and whom he invited, on a whim, to join him in Lebanon. She agreed. Only a few months after the birth of their son she demanded a divorce and immigrated to America with her family who were fleeing Nazi Germany. At the time Henry was devastated and longed for his infant son.

Henry explained to Michael, "*Look, it wasn't simple. Ilse had suffered from typhoid in Lebanon and her family had made it to New York and they insisted Ilse and I come to the United States. Michael, you understand, who was running my family? Me and Ilse, or her parents? I was well-established in Lebanon at the time. I loved the life there. This was a town that you could ski in the morning and in the afternoon you could head down to the beach for a swim. I was recognised as a doctor. It may not have been so in the USA. Ilse was dictated to by her family who applied maximum pressure that she get out of Lebanon. Then Ilse found a new partner who was happy to marry her and adopt Peter. Your mother and I were equally happy to adopt him but it would not have been in the child's best interest to suddenly uproot him from all of his connections to a new family and home. We also felt it wasn't in the child's interests to have two families fighting over him. Michael, your mother would have happily adopted him and been a wonderful mother to him as she was to you and Eddie."*

At the time Henry's distress was amplified when Ilse's family blackmailed him to approve the adoption of his son by her new husband and insisted he cut off all communication. They threatened to disclose the whereabouts of his sister to the Nazis if he did not comply. This traumatic first attempt at family life had never been discussed previously by Henry, but Ursula had alluded to the situation to Shula, Michael's then-girlfriend, prior to her passing. The revelation to Michael and Eddie that they had a half-brother somewhere on the other side of the world was met with a genuine interest.

"What do you think Eddie? We may have a half-brother somewhere on the other side of the world!" exclaimed Michael.

"Wow. That's interesting. I'd love to meet him someday," replied Eddie.

He recalled, *"Michael, do you remember in Wollongong, your friend Sue Green, amongst others, asking us if our father married before because he seemed somewhat older than other people's fathers? I continually said no. Well, it seems they were right!"*

Both of the brothers had reservations of whether it would be difficult to track down their half-brother, if it would be appropriate and if they would really have anything to say to each other. This and their desires to get their own lives together delayed any attempt of contact at the time.

Eddie's wish to do well in his studies was tempered by his desire to have a full social life and that needed funding. So through the university holiday periods he and Bernie would earn their money by being builders' labourers....Bernie often having to re-align part of Eddie's work! On one occasion

Bernie was not available to go job-seeking so Eddie enlisted another medical school friend, Anthony Frumar, to join him at 5:30am to go to job sites. Anthony (Tony) turned up in a suit.

"This is not an interview situation. You come in your roughest gear, heavy boots and you sit and wait, and the general Aussie rule is first cabbie off the rank!" Eddie cried incredulously to Tony who had gone to a private school and obviously needed some real education. *"Here, take this and this,"* Eddie said as he gave him some of his roughest clothing. It didn't help. By the time they had visited three building sites, they still had no job.

"Perhaps we can get a job as a bus conductor," suggested Eddie.

Tony was horrified, *"Are you kidding? Somebody might see me!"*

Tony left the job-seeking up to Bernie and Eddie from then on.

For his birthday that year Mia gave Eddie a present of three month's weight training at Paul Graham's gym in Coogee. He initially was quite enthused about the possibility of building up his physique although perhaps not quite to the extent of his fellow gym goers entering the Mr Universe muscle building competition. To his surprise and enjoyment, they sang opera whilst training. His gym days were quickly abandoned however when a fellow medical student, Richard Martin, commented that Eddie's neck resembled a condition they were studying called 'bull-neck'. Mia concurred and weight training ceased.

Eddie was now 21 and could get a taxi drivers licence. It was the ideal job. He was now more flush with money and he could join Michael in renting an apartment in Glenmore

Road, Paddington. It was a small apartment with one bedroom and one lounge/bedroom, Michael's, which led to a kitchen. Both had settled into university life and Eddie knew that if he heard the theme song from Man and a Woman playing in the lounge/bedroom it was Michael's message that under no conditions could he enter the room. Fortunately, the bathroom separated their rooms. The apartment block was also home to members of a band called Tully, famed for their role in the music for Hair. Unsurprisingly the foyer of the building had a distinct smell of a particular strain of "incense". Eddie's personal extracurricular activities continued to be dominated by sport, playing under-21 Rugby and interfaculty cricket.

In the lecture halls and medical wards Eddie became more and more disillusioned about becoming a doctor. He really did not enjoy being around sick people. Whilst attending classes near Royal Prince Alfred Hospital at lunch time, rather than walk the most direct route through the wards to get to the kiosk, he would happily circumnavigate the entire hospital. This aversion to illness was to later inform his ideas and theories for turning the medical system on its head and creating a system that focused on true HEALTH care as opposed to just caring for those already sick. But first he had to survive medical school. Eddie's first time assisting in theatre was for a gall bladder operation and his role was to hold the liver out of the surgeon's way. This was a surprisingly arduous and physical job under the hot lights.

After about three-quarters of an hour, Eddie said to the surgeon, "*Excuse me, things are going a little blurred. I can see two of you.*"

The surgeon quickly instructed, "*Sister you'd better take over from the doctor.*"

The assisting nurse took over and the anaesthetist Dr Clifton, a friendly, outgoing fellow, said to Eddie, *"Gorgeous, you're going all white. You'd better lie down on the floor."*

He sat down and only just avoided fainting. He was about to get back up when the anaesthetist insisted, *"No gorgeous, you look lovely down there. You stay on the floor."*

So Eddie put his head down on the floor in the operating theatre for half an hour on his first operation. He knew immediately he wasn't cut out to be a surgeon!

If he wasn't to be a surgeon, then where was his role in the medical world? He wasn't interested in being an academic and tied to a university. For him universities were too dissociated from the "real world". Eddie and his close university friends at RPA spent their lunchtimes brainstorming and debating. All of them shared the common goal of wanting to make some sort of contribution to the world. The others seemed to find their niche and did very well for themselves. Richard Martin became a professor of Neonatology in Cleveland and edited an internationally-acclaimed book in the field. Henry Brodaty became Professor Brodaty and was one of the initiators of the Alzheimer's support movement. He was awarded an AO for his work. Graeme Stewart, a professor of Immunology at Westmead, was also decorated with an AM. That left Eddie. He was fumbling to establish himself in a particular field and grappling with a system that he refused to accept as the only way to operate. He wanted to run his own course. He was viewed as the slightly eccentric outsider. It was a position he was familiar with religiously, culturally and it now seemed professionally.

He was even starting to find himself on the outer when it

came to his beloved Betar. His personal views began to deviate from their hard line messages. In particular, he felt their political teachings outside of Israel weren't appropriate and were far too right-wing. Eddie was now becoming more and more socialist in his world views. He intended to go and live in Israel after he finished Medical school so he felt there was no great need to continue with the youth movement and he made his exit from Betar. However, world events intervened and he was soon called back to help run the organisation when The Six-Day War broke out. Tensions had been escalating in the months prior to fighting with the Egyptian President Nasser closing the Straits of Tiran to Israel and blocking access to Israel's only Red Sea port, Eilat. At the time 90% of Israeli oil passed through the Straits and Time Magazine questioned whether Israel could survive surrounded, as they were, with unaccepting Arab nations. Cutting Israel off was a brazen move and the Israeli government retaliated with unrelenting force. On the 5th of June 1967 Israel launched what they claimed were pre-emptive strikes on the Egyptian airfields. They destroyed nearly the entire Egyptian air force. At the same time a ground offensive into the Gaza strip and the Sinai was carried out and despite initial resistance the Sinai was soon conquered. Many Israeli civilians were mobilised by the army and there was a shortage of people to run the economy and keep the country functioning. Australian Jews and particularly those in the Zionist youth organisations were volunteering to fill these positions. The Jewish communal centres in Sydney were signing up volunteers and Mia had offered to go. This gesture in Eddie's eyes was motivated not only by her love of Israel but her desire to prove to him that their feelings for Israel were mutual. In the aftermath of those six days, Israel had crippled the Egyptian, Syrian and Jordanian militaries and on June 11 a ceasefire was signed. Israel seized the Gaza strip, the Sinai Peninsula, the West Bank and the Golan Heights. Despite the end to the fighting Israel still needed all the volunteers they could get and on the 19th of June a large group departed from Sydney, including all of Eddie's Betar friends. The group lived on a Kibbutz called Kissufim on the border with Gaza. Mia would be overseas for around five months. Even though she and Eddie were officially "apart", she wrote to him every two to three days. He enjoyed receiving these romantic gestures but loved his romantic freedom even more. The Betar exodus had left the organisation without leadership and a special request was extended to Eddie to come back and help while the others were away. He was to become President of The State Zionist Youth Council at the time which was an umbrella organisation that oversaw all Jewish youth groups in NSW.

In 1968, in fifth year medicine, Eddie embarked on an elective term in Indonesia with a group from Sydney University. They were to do unpaid medical work in Indonesia and were billeted with local families, often in the homes of Indonesian army generals. The main financial outlay was that they had to self-fund their tickets to get there. One of Eddie's ingenious friends, Peter Fletcher, decided that as the group was volunteering, he would write to organisations - such as large pharmaceutical companies – and ask for donations to help them in their venture to rehabilitate Indonesian patients. Peter also wrote to the RSL, a rather unlikely benefactor at the time, as the Vietnam War was going on and students were generally the most vocal in anti-war protests. The relationship between the RSL and students was one of adversaries. Nevertheless, Peter sent his letter. The timing could not have been better for the medical students as the RSL was desperate to mend public relations Australia-wide after one of the Heads of the RSL, Sir William Yeo, had called members of the British Commonwealth a *"polyglot lot of wogs, bogs, logs and dogs"*. National media coverage harshly condemned Yeo, and by association, the RSL, as out-of-touch with contemporary Australian society and called him a "sabre-rattling war monger". The image of the RSL was damaged and needed repair.

Peter Fletcher received a call from the RSL. *"Peter, how much money do you need?"*

Peter replied, *"The airfares for seven medical students, back and forth."*

"Are the students willing to pose for a photo and have some publicity?"

"No problem," assured Peter.

A General from South Vietnam was coming to visit Australia and the students were asked to pose for a photo that appeared on the front of the Sydney Morning Herald with the article claiming the RSL were helping Asia by sponsoring medical students to go and work in rehabilitation centres in Indonesia. The arrangement suited both parties. The students had free flights and the RSL were able to leverage off these willing students some publicity that promoted the RSL as not only being supportive of Australian students, but also, investing in and supporting Asia.

Eddie was based in Solo in Central Java at Dr Soeharso's Rehabilitation Centre with seven other trainee doctors. The young medical students were there to learn all about the rehabilitation done at the centre. They assisted the physiotherapists with their patients, many of whom had paraplegia, mainly caused from falling out of coconut trees. When they were not working the medical students visited surrounding villages which often drew large crowds of local children fascinated by the strange foreigners.

To celebrate New Year's, the students decided to spend three or four days in Bali. Eddie wanting to spend the evening in style invited one of the two girls in their group, Mary Gillam, to join him for dinner and dancing at the top restaurant of the Bali Beach Hotel. He ordered a bottle of white wine and the waiter placed it on a stand in an ice bucket some metre and a half from their table. A different waiter appeared and took their bottle of wine and poured it into the glasses of the four people at the next table. He watched his investment disappear but chose not to say anything to the management as he and Mary considered that the waiter, in all likelihood, would lose his job. They drank water but enjoyed New Year anyway. They celebrated into the early morning and then the students went their separate ways. Eddie had a bus to catch in only a few hours' time and elected to get his belongings, go to the bus stop directly and wait there for the bus. He lay down on the only bench at the bus stop and went to sleep. At approximately 6:00am, when the bus had arrived, he awoke to find himself surrounded by thirty Balinese passengers who were all enjoying the shock on this bleary-eyed foreigner's face.

The entire trip for Eddie was a fantastic experience, not only of travelling and working with doctors in a foreign country, but also seeing and understanding more about extreme poverty and the squalor in which some families were forced to live. Eddie and fellow medical student Peter Fletcher were able to experience some of the opulence on offer as well. In mid-January, Peter rang the Australian embassy in Jakarta and explained that they were Australian students in Indonesia, volunteering in hospitals, and suggested that he and Eddie be extended an invitation to the Embassy's Australia Day celebrations. The Embassy declined their suggestion so Peter, who was determined to attend, contacted the wife of the Ambassador directly, *"Mrs Loveday, we are two medical students who have been working as volunteers in a rehabilitation centre in Central Java in Solo helping to rehabilitate the Indonesians and we would love to celebrate Australia Day at the Embassy."*

"Certainly Peter. What are your names?" was Mrs Loveday's reply.

"Eddie Price and Peter Fletcher," said Peter.

"Sure. We will send an embassy car to pick you up. Just give us your address."

So they arrived by Mercedes at the door of the Australian Embassy.

The doorman called out, *"Introducing Mr Fletcher and Mr Price. This is Mrs Loveday and the Ambassador."*

The two unlikely guests joined an array of highly esteemed Australians who were working or residing in Indonesia at the time. Gough Whitlam was in attendance (this being prior to his PM days) and rather unexpectedly, so was Eddie's former French teacher from Randwick Boys High School. Mr Savey had become Australia's UNESCO representative in Indonesia and was with a small group of other dignitaries when Eddie made his presence known. *"Hello, Mr Savey. You recall you taught me French at Randwick Boys High School and you also had me write out 100 lines, 'French class is not a shoe shop, I should not try on my football boots'. You recall I did that 100 times for you?"* Mr Savey wasn't overly impressed with Eddie announcing his recollections of their time together.

Spending three months in Indonesia gave Eddie the opportunity to break up with Mia once again and with his final year of study ahead of him he decided to create some space in his life and free himself from the supposed monogamy of dating. He ended their relationship. After watching his brother's marriage fail he didn't want to make, what he saw as the same mistake, of marrying too young. Mia was not happy, and endeavoured to reverse Eddie's decision but to no avail.

Whilst study took precedence in his life once back in Australia, he also needed to support himself and his dreams of relocating overseas so he continued his job as a taxi driver. The nights driving around Sydney certainly opened his eyes to a very different world. At the time American GI's were coming to Australia for a week of R&R from the Vietnam War. One evening at Kings Cross a GI accompanied by a young lady who Eddie soon learned was a 'lady of the night' was conversing in the back of the cab. The lady said, *"Stop here driver,"* and said to the GI, *"Up those stairs there is a bottle shop. If you pay me now and then we get some beer it will make for a much cosier atmosphere."* The GI eagerly obliged. He paid her and hopped out of the cab and ran upstairs. The young lady quickly said to Eddie, *"Driver, drive!"*

He hesitated, *"Driver, I've got the money. I will pay you. Drive!"* the lady insisted.

He drove away but continued to worry about that incident. On another evening he recalls dropping one passenger at Whisky Au Go Go with the American giving him a $100 bill, thinking it was $20. Eddie, realising the mistake, hopped out of his cab and ran into the club to find the young GI.

Thinking their fellow driver had been scammed a host of other cabbies leapt from their cars and raced inside in his support. Eddie gave the change to the GI but then had the embarrassing job of explaining to the other five or six drivers what had indeed happened.

At the end of 1969 Eddie's medical studies were complete and he awaited his results....they came whilst he was in his taxi and in his excitement he collided with a parked car. Being an honest fellow he left a note to apologise and stated his name and taxi number. About one hour later his boss was yelling through the radio network to immediately bring his taxi in and return to Head Office. As Eddie hopped out of the car, the boss yelled at him, *"You're sacked!"*

He calmly retorted, *"You mean, 'You're sacked' DOCTOR!"*

He would no longer need to drive others around to make ends meet. He could drive in his own direction. The Sydney University Medical School Yearbook, honoured Eddie's time at the University with the following composition....

" '....take off your trousers before getting violent'. Yoko Ono. This Paddingtonian taxi-driver and gold medallist at the '69 R.P.A.H. Face Hair Olympics presents with an unremittent history of pig-headed individualism. Apart from occasional inter-faculty debating and cricket, one presumptuous attempt at Med. Society election and an upper percentile academic career, he had little to look back upon with regret. Amongst his close friends must rank Balinese, Mrs Doff, N.R.M.A. Servicemen and Sir William Yeo. His time-consuming interests embrace most of the non-medical Sydney from second-rate football teams to first-rate fornication. Most would foresee a 'good medical career' for Ed....When he 'buckles down.' Hope not, it sure don't need* *papier-mache physician No. 3526."* How prophetic of the author, for Eddie certainly would prove not to be a doctor to fit into anyone's mould.

Eddie obtained early registration work at Fairfield Hospital to earn some money but this was only a temporary means to an end. Endeavouring to find his way, his place in society, it was to Israel that he went to do his internship at Tel Hashomer hospital in Tel Aviv with a desire to eventually settle there.

Chapter 4

Finding the path

Like many youth, Eddie was trying to find his way in the world – ethnically he felt a strong pull towards Israel, but would this Aussie-raised young man find his true home in a country he had glorified and worshipped from a distance? Whilst culturally floundering, he was also floundering professionally. He still did not fit the standard mould of what a doctor should do or should become. What part of the medical field would placate his aversion to sick people and enable him to practise without having to deal with blood or the emotional trauma of seeing people in distress? Whilst training and working at the Tel Hashomer Hospital (now the Sheba Medical Centre) in Tel Aviv, his experiences corroborated his concerns that indeed he was not cut out to be a doctor. This was particularly evident when he was treating a lady with breast cancer. Overcome with painful memories of his mother Eddie had to rush out of the room in tears.

Socialising was certainly an area he had always excelled at and in Israel it was no different. Together with two Mexican Jewish doctors, Alejandro Berenstein and Mario Rosenberg and another Australian surgeon, Sam Slutsky, they formed a strong friendship that involved lots of discos, lots of women and little study. The regular nightclub of choice in Tel Aviv was Mandy's. Owner Mandy Rice-Davies, was made infamous by her associations with the UK political scandal the 'Profumo Affair'. A model was caught in romantic liaisons with both conservative John Profumo, the State Secretary for War, and a Soviet naval attaché causing concerns of a possible security breach. Eddie's liberal approach to socialising and to girls continued on what was meant to be a cheap $12 return trip to Athens for him and Mario on Turkish Airlines. The trip ended rather differently than expected. The boys had met two Irish girls and all four were absorbing the very lively atmosphere of the Athen's suburb of Plaka with its small alleys and vibrant night life. They entered a Greek taverna enticed in by the jovial music playing on the outside patio. The locals demonstrated a tradition that the boys thought was great fun with smashing their plates on the concrete corner of the patio. Unfortunately for the cash-strapped Mario and Eddie every plate cost them a dollar. The boys' bill soared from $20 to over $100! Regardless of expenses, Eddie planned another boys' adventure to Cyprus with friend Sam Slutsky but he was to have a visitor prior to departure. When he left Australian shores he and Mia were no longer an item. They had remained in close contact with Eddie reminding the young beauty that if she was serious about settling down with him she needed to understand that he intended to live in Israel. There was no planned reunion whilst Eddie was overseas but Mia saw an opportunity to visit. While she was working at Qantas Mia learned that a young child required an escort to travel to Israel. Mia volunteered for the job and arrived on Eddie's doorstop. Her mother, Esther, and father, Sam, were also to visit Eddie at varying times. Mia's current, non-Jewish, Qantas boyfriend didn't compare in their eyes to the young Jewish Doctor. They were prepared to accept Eddie's edict that, *"I want you to understand that if we do get married and I haven't found anyone else that I prefer at this stage, you have got to accept that I will be living in Israel."* Mia departed with the understanding that he would probably be back by the end of the year and they would probably get back together then.

For now, Eddie was off to explore Cyprus with his mate Slutsky. Their trip had an interesting start with Slutsky held in Customs due to an expired visa for half an hour for which he was fined 150 shekels. The financial hit was no deterrent to his duty-free spending spree however. Sam instructed the sales lady, *"I'll have one of these and three of those and four little radios and these as well."*

"Sam, they've just called our flight," urged Eddie.

"Yeah, yeah," acknowledged Sam.

Eddie was insistent, *"Sam, that's the second call. Come on or we'll miss the plane!"*

Sam seemed quite relaxed, *"Don't worry. Settle down."*

"I'll carry some of your bags," said Eddie as he rushed ahead. *"My friend is just coming."*

But the steward had bad news, *"Sorry, it's too late. We've closed the flight."*

Sam then sidled up to the counter and looked at the steward. *"Dr Slutsky! How are you?"*

"Oh, how is your mother doing? I trust she's doing well after that operation," said Sam.

"Dr Slutsky, let me carry your bags and accompany you to the steps," effused the steward.

Eddie could not stop shaking his head, first from worry, then relief and finally laughter. Sam continued to surprise him with his contacts in Cyprus when he entered the supermarket in Nicosia. Seeing Sam, the shop owner's face lit up, *"Sam, you were here a year ago. You're still my best customer!"* Apparently Sam had come by car last time and had filled it with Duty Free goods that he then took back to tax-burdened Israel where he made a pretty profit. It paid for his trip and the following. Travelling with Sam would never be dull.

It was a mid-morning operation in Tel Hashomer Hospital. The surgeon's focus on the task was as refined and as honed as the instruments in his gloved hand. It was the anaesthetist who after a few minutes of observation said to the surgeon, "*DIESE STAGEUR SCHLUFT! - Your intern is standing there asleep!*" After a late night at Mandy's, a severely hung-over Eddie, was swaying on his feet and wafting in and out of consciousness.

"*GET OUT OF MY THEATRE!*" demanded the surgeon and kicked Eddie out of the room for lack of responsibility. It was literally a wakeup call and he realised his reputation was on the line. From that day on he dedicated his time wholeheartedly to his work as an intern and for his need to address the ever-present dilemma of where in the medical world he would find his nirvana. His professional epiphany came when he volunteered for a special and very dangerous mission with a small group of young doctors. They were sent from Tel Hashomer Hospital to El Arish to resurrect an abandoned Egyptian hospital. The seven young medical graduates were faced with all of the ingredients of a basic hospital and medical centre but without any sense of order or management. Eddie stepped into the void.

Dusty El Arish lies on the Mediterranean in the north of the Sinai Peninsula next to the Gaza Strip. The coastal desert city, abundant in palm trees, had been under Israeli military occupation since the Six-Day War and nearly four years later tensions were still perilously high for the young Jewish doctors. Their safety was always in question. On being supplied with a gun for his own protection Eddie claimed, "*You're wasting your time giving me a gun; I'm not going to take it."*

"*You have to take it,*" was the response.

He insisted, *"It'll stay in the locker!"* It did.

Eddie the pacifist, had no intention of ever hurting someone else and thought the more likely scenario would be him accidentally shooting himself. He didn't, however, reject the presence of army ambulance escorts when travelling throughout the Peninsula to visit remote Bedouin villages in their desert oases – a small clump of palm trees and a cluster of thatched houses. When the ambulance arrived, the villagers and particularly the children ran out enthusiastically to greet them. There was no shortage of patients. It was here that Eddie encountered communities that had no understanding or experience of modern medicine.

"*What is the problem?*" Eddie asked a young mother through his Hebrew-Arabic interpreter.

"*The baby is not doing well. He has difficulty breathing and is short of breath and is not growing as one might expect,*" replied the mother.

He then saw some deep burns on the child's torso, "*And what are these marks on his chest?*"

The local nurse answered, "*Oh, they are from hot irons that have been applied to the area of the chest where the baby has difficulty breathing in order to help expel the evil spirits.*"

Eddie diagnosed the child with congenital heart disease and he was referred to Tel-Hashomer Hospital for corrective surgery. This most basic level of local medical knowledge continued when he had to appoint and train some locals as nursing staff in El Arish. One morning on his rounds he, and the registered nurses who came down with him from Tel-Hashomer, came upon a patient's records that showed regular monitoring of pulse rate as had been instructed. The pulse had been recorded as plummeting through the night from eighty, to sixty and then to zero... and for each subsequent hour it had again been recorded at zero. The inexperienced "nurses" had been taking the pulse of a dead person and had diligently recorded it for about six hours. Eddie turned to his registered nurse colleagues, *"We have messed up in our training of these temporary nurses. What we neglected to tell them, while getting them to diligently measure the pulse, was that if the pulse rate dropped below 60, they had to call the doctor immediately."* This was a lesson on better communication and training. Their fast-tracked training had neglected the vital, yet seemingly obvious, detail. Regardless of this, and many other glitches, Eddie thrived on the organisational structure that he was having in managing the hospital, the hiring of staff, the acquisition of medications and the allocation of doctors. He essentially built a hospital and medical centre from scratch. Their presence in the region was greatly rewarding for he and his colleagues in seeing how much of a positive impact they were able to have on the health of the population. Once a month specialists from the main hospital in Tel Aviv would come down to treat those in need. On one occasion a paediatric surgeon came and attended to a child with hydrocephalus, a condition which results in severe fluid retention and a swollen head. After the standard procedure of inserting a cerebral 'shunt' the child had been cured. The head size had been reduced thus averting further brain-damage. The next month word had spread that "The Big Head Doctor" was coming and there was a line-up of children all with the same swollen head complaint. Eddie commented to one of the nurses, *"It's amazing. You don't see this in Western countries such as Australia where these problems are picked up shortly after birth and are corrected before they do damage."*

It wasn't just the infirm that benefited from the resurrection of El Arish Hospital; the local fishermen were also enjoying the benefits. Staff at the hospital had noted that the Mercurochrome, which has a distinctly red colour, was disappearing and it was traced back to a local pharmacist who worked in the hospital and who was selling the tincture to fishermen to put on the gills of day-old fish to make them look fresher for sale. The same entrepreneurial chemist was also only giving patients half the prescribed quantity of medicine at the hospital and was selling the other half from his private pharmacy in town. When this discrepancy was picked up Eddie turned to another young doctor, Dr Avner Remu, and stated, *"Avner, you realise our patients are receiving half their proper dosage of medication?"*

Avner replied, "Yes. I noticed that. Did you notice that nobody is coming back sicker due to the lack of medicine?" Could it be that half the dosage would suffice or was this the placebo effect in full swing?

Eddie's constant and most valuable companion during his four months in El Arish was an Arabic-to-Hebrew interpreter. Achmed's knowledge of the Jewish tongue had been learned while he was a prisoner of Israel on charges of terrorism. It wasn't till the very end of his stay in El Arish that Eddie realised how fragile their presence in the area was and how close to harm they had come. He asked Achmed, *"I'm your mate now. If the situation reverses and you come to power, how will you treat me?"*

With a calm, steely regard Achmed said, *"You see that sea over there? After I cut your throat, I will toss you into there."* Eddie quietly left... but not filled with fear. He was filled with excitement for what his time of building this hospital had given him. It was at this posting that he realised that through hospital management he could practice in the medical field without seeing blood. More importantly, the work he did could have an impact far greater than on a small group of patients seen by a single doctor. He had influence over an entire hospital. What if that influence could extend to an entire health care system and in his wildest dreams....to the way the world practised medicine? He had found his calling. He now knew he wanted to study Health Management and so needed to experience more forms of healthcare and various health care systems to broaden his knowledge. He applied for a job as a Kibbutz doctor on Israel's northern borders. He would spend the next four months there.

Kibbutz Yiftach is perched on a green hill in the Upper Galilee of Northern Israel near the Lebanese border. Its clear skies and fields of cows and chickens were an idyllic reprieve from the dusty streets of El Arish. Eddie's clinic was set up in the weatherboard and yellow brick army barrack style buildings that housed the small left-wing community. Their ideals were so far to the left they were almost communists. They observed a strictly communal lifestyle where families were separated to have all of the children living together. As part of his employment he would visit four surrounding areas in his Fiat 600, other Kibbutz and "Moshavs"- privately owned farming villages, in the zone. For a young doctor the work was an incredible learning curve. One day he would be caring for a chronically-ill elderly patient and the next he would be treating multiple children with allergic reactions after a tractor transporting bees rolled in front of the school just as school was let out. He was also required to do regional work up into the Golan

Heights. He conducted clinics with the Druze communities of Majdal Shams (Village of the Sun), a town in the southern foothills of Mt Herman in the north of the Golan Heights on the Syrian border. Since the Six-Day War it had been controlled by Israel under martial law and Eddie bravely entered to do his duty. The Druze, an Islamic sect with contributions from other faiths such as Gnosticism, neo-Platonism, Pythagoreanism and Hinduism, has a distinct and secretive theology. They are known to form close-knit, cohesive communities which do not embrace outsiders. Their goodwill towards the young doctor was tested when the brother of one of Eddie's nurses was arrested for spying for Syria. It was the occasional night visits to Israel's most northerly town, Kiryat Shemona (The Village of Eight), with guards wary of terrorists crossing the nearby fence from Lebanon, that were the most perilous for Eddie. He would travel in convoy with an army truck in front and an army truck behind and his little Fiat 600 in the middle. His fears, however, were not for the Lebanese militia in the mountains....he was more scared of the apprehensive Kibbutz guards shooting him on his return. Indeed, the only gunshot wound he attended to in his entire time in Israel was that of a Kibbutz guard accidentally shooting himself in the thigh.

He wasn't the only Australian looking for something in this small Kibbutz in the far north of Israel. While Eddie was looking for medical experience Jimmy Driscoll was looking for mainstream seclusion and concealment. The pleasant and highly regarded laundry worker first met Eddie when he presented with an ear complaint. The two Australians ended up back in Jimmy's hut where he showed Eddie clippings from Australian newspapers that claimed Jimmy had investments in, or was "head of security" for Sydney's

Whiskey Au Go Go nightclub. Eddie thought nothing more of the articles from the land he had left behind and he and Jimmy enjoyed a friendship and their Kibbutz life together. Jimmy had such a good reputation as a valuable worker that when his girlfriend Judy came to visit, the Kibbutz gave them a rare gift of a weekend away in Jerusalem.

Later in 1974 and back in Sydney, on the front of the Australian newspaper Eddie saw a picture of his mate Jimmy, identified as Linus O'Driscoll, the head of the Toe-cutter Gang - wanted for the Whisky Au Go Go fire in Brisbane. In 1973 a fire had ripped through the Whiskey Au Go Go discotheque in Fortitude Valley, Queensland, taking the lives of two men and five women. The leader of the notorious Toe-cutter Gang, Jimmy, was their main suspect. Jimmy briefly returned to Australia and he, his girlfriend Judy and a group of his friends bumped into Eddie and Mia in Double Bay just prior to their wedding. Eddie excitedly proclaimed, *"Why don't you come to our wedding? Here is the address!"*

Judy hurriedly tried to hide the wedding details from their "friends". The naïve Eddie did not understand he was mixing with an international group of gangsters. On a visit to Kibbutz Yiftach many years later he noticed the library full of books donated by Jimmy and Judy.

The kibbutz members said to him, *"Do you know that Interpol came here looking for Jimmy?"*

Eddie replied, *"I was wondering why he was staying here back in 1971 and when I saw his picture on the front of a paper in Australia, I thought to myself, 'I know where he is'."*

The kibbutz member continued, *"Interpol came with many questions and told us many stories."*

"I can tell you a story or two as well," said Eddie. *"One day I came to use the phone at the kibbutz and Jimmy was on the line to Australia. I said, 'How long will you be?' Jimmy said, 'I'll probably be another hour'. I said, 'Jimmy that'll cost you a fortune'. Jimmy replied 'Eddie, I'm not stupid. It's a reverse charges call and Judy is sitting house for somebody else'."*

He had decided it was probably prudent to wait the hour and a half before the phone freed up. The story was that Interpol had finally caught up with Jimmy for other crimes and he spent most of the remainder of his life in prison.

Eddie's new found enthusiasm for Health Management wasn't shared by his father. He was disappointed that Eddie wouldn't be a "real" doctor and even wrote letters to contacts in Israel championing his son's abilities and sensibilities with children and claiming he would make an ideal paediatrician. Eddie could only think of one group of patients he'd rather not treat than sick people and that was sick children – especially children with cancer or other terminal illnesses. His father would have to face disappointment as he pursued health management wanting to broaden his understanding of medical systems further. He had been impressed with what he knew of the English NHS, so he decided to further familiarise himself with it by applying for work in London.

Initially he obtained employment in the UK as a resident in Edgware General Hospital. He also briefly enrolled in Kings Fund College that ran courses on Health Management. After a day at the course the organisers realised that no one was paying the £20,000 tuition fees for this Aussie and so terminated his tenure. During that day Eddie soaked up the wisdom of the main lecturer and one line in particular, *"We all should take a lesson from the turtle who never gets anywhere without sticking his neck out."* It's a sentiment that he would carry with him throughout his life. After seeing how the NHS was run from a hospital point-of-view he then wanted to experience it from a GP's perspective and took a locum position in the historic market town of Godalming in Surrey. Usually a locum is called in when a GP is on leave, but Dr Richard Lyne-Pirkis, part of the landed gentry as Earls of Liverpool, was doing some extra study and needed Eddie to fill in while he was ensconced in his books. Rather than a small, dismal doctor's residence at the top of the practice in town, his accommodation was to be in Dr P Lyne-Pirkis' own home which was a large manor house in the country with a long drive and imposing reception hall. He was greeted by the Maltese nanny who was a short, squat lady with several teeth missing. Behind her, on her hands and knees, cleaning the carpet was Mrs Lyne-Pirkis cursing to nobody in particular that, *"Oh this shag carpet is absolutely, absolutely terrible!"* The eccentric family included a couple of sons, one off at Eton, a grandmother that walked around with two Siamese cats on her shoulder, and a daughter, Rosemary, who had designs on this handsome Australian doctor staying in her home. Eddie was invited every Saturday to the family dinner and on one occasion was asked to carve the turkey dish that had been presented to the table. Lacking in carving expertise he sent the golden turkey sailing down the other end of the table where it was caught. The whole matter seemingly was dropped by this well-groomed aristocratic mob who hardly drew breath between, *"Would you like some peas Mrs Lyne-Pirkis?"* and *"What about some carrots Mr Lyne-Pirkis?"*

He entertained a number of guests whilst in Godalming including his cousin Dinah who was living in London at the time and friend Brian Hillman. Brian was working as a lawyer in the neighbouring town of Haslemere. With no phone number nor address to connect his friend, Eddie drove to the small community and yelled out of his car window, *"BRIAN HILLMAN GET FUCKED!"* His tactic worked and a bewildered Brian Hillman emerged from a nearby building. They then spent many a weekend together in the local university town of Guildford getting to know popular nightspots and the female students there. While his GP work was largely uneventful during his three-month stay there was one episode that stood out. He was visited by a patient complaining of varicose veins and when Eddie examined her he asked if she'd been putting on weight as she was wearing a tight corset that could not have been helping her varicose veins.

The girl replied, *"For about the last eight months."*

He gingerly enlightened her as to her situation, *"I think you're about 8 months pregnant."*

As he had been the one to diagnose the pregnancy he was then expected to deliver the baby. A healthy boy called Felix was born. This gave him a total of 12½ deliveries in his career. At medical school there was a requirement for twelve but at his last delivery Eddie said to the nurse, *"Would you like to deliver the placenta?"*

The nurse said, *"Certainly."*

He thought little of it until it came to his exam. He was asked how it was that he had only completed 11½ deliveries. He had to convince the examiner that the nurse had been very keen to deliver the placenta herself and that he had been there overseeing the procedure. Nevertheless, Felix was born without a hitch in a country hospital in Surrey. Eddie was also ready to embark on a new life. He now felt equipped with enough understanding of various health systems to reinvent himself in the medical field and retrain in Medical Administration.

Chapter 5

The healthcare system is "naked"!

It was a matured and enlightened Eddie who returned to Australian shores in 1972. He had a clear understanding of where his position in the medical world lay. Having determined that management was his path he pursued studies in a Diploma of Health Administration at UNSW. He'd now found the niche where "this doctor who hated blood" could thrive. Retraining in health and hospital management in Australia confirmed his trajectory. His passion, enthusiasm and talents were rewarded with various opportunities and positions. Eddie, the philosopher, was forming strong ideas on how the health care system was seriously flawed and how he believed it could be entirely reformed for the greater health of the nation and world.

What brought him back to earth drastically from his grand visions was his need to make ends meet. During his nights he earned "blood money" as an emergency doctor covering for general practitioners' out-of-hours doing house calls. He also worked part-time at the Veterans' Affairs Department assessing veterans for pensions. The experiences he gained from these work placements proved valuable in exposing the flaws and faults in the current health care system. One veteran from the First World War was requesting a pension for tinea that he had suffered on his left leg during his army service.

Eddie said, *"Okay, show me your left leg."*

The veteran replied, *"Oh no Doc. I've got a prosthesis. The leg has been amputated."*

Eddie suggested, *"Perhaps you might like to consider*

84

claiming for tinea on your right leg as the department only pays pensions for ongoing war problems."

The veteran insisted, *"I do not have tinea on my right leg. It was on the left leg and that's the leg I wish to claim on!"*

He called for assistance from the senior medical assessor who concluded that the patient really wanted to claim for the amputation of his left leg, a claim already rejected, but that he wished to appeal this matter. The system wasn't treating the veteran as a whole functioning person but rather assessed a specific ailment or injury with little regard to the impact on a person's functionality and ultimate health. Eddie did note that for assessing the pension there was a small lifestyle section that measured the functioning of the whole person. Some claims were tied to the environment of the claimant. If a professional pianist lost a finger or a hand it would be a bigger impairment than if the person was not dependent on the use of a finger or a hand for an income. Eddie determined that there was a need to start measuring the improvement in functionality to the eventual 100%. He read voraciously and came across the writings of A.J. Culyer "Measuring Health" and also those of Dr Eric Cassell who looked at the role of a carer. The realisation that Eddie had at this time was to define his future. He determined that improving patients' health functions and relieving their distress were the two main aims of medical care; neither of these aims was at the time being measured. One essential piece of wisdom was from his idol Peter Drucker who claimed one needed to measure any objective in quantity and time to achieve effective management. In Eddie's experience this was not happening in healthcare. How could the health system possibly know if they were doing things correctly, or in the best possible way, if they weren't measuring the outcomes of a patient's treatment? Was the entire medical world blind to this problem? Was he the only one who could see this flaw? He felt like the little boy in the Emperor's New Clothes. He saw that the "healthcare emperor" – the healthcare system - was "naked".

In his busy schedule of full time studies and evening work his relationship with Mia was also thriving. Much to Mia's father's consternation, Eddie moved in with Mia and her two Qantas girlfriends at 13 New Street, Bondi. Despite the unacceptability of co-habiting prior to marriage at that time, he felt they needed to live together first in order to ascertain whether or not they could exist cohesively. In reality it wasn't always amicable. According to one of Mia's friends who lived with the couple, the relationship was reminiscent of The Taming of the Shrew and, in fact, Eddie packed his bags to leave on a number of occasions. However, there was a great chemical attraction between the two. They were in love and shared a love of sports, politics, their Jewish heritage and the joy of life itself. An agreement was made that at the end of his studies in 1972 they would wed. No fancy engagement rings, no financial pre-nup, but there was an arrangement. Eddie still felt that at 26 he was too young to settle down with one person sexually and wanted to be honest with Mia saying, *"I am only going into this marriage if you understand that I am not going to be faithful at this age."*

A loyal Mia retorted, *"Well I will be."*

He claimed, *"If I play around I will do it with respect and not in your face or anything like that."* Mia agreed to accept him on his terms. It was a shaky foundation from which to launch a relationship which was to be essentially, nowadays, an open marriage.

On the 17th of December, 1972, Mia floated down the aisle of the Central Synagogue in a simple white dress to Katushka, a favourite Russian song of her father's. At her side was her father. Her best friend Janey Barber walked in front as her bridesmaid. She joined Eddie and his best man, Michael, at the chuppah and they were married. The reception was in Mia's parents' backyard in Vaucluse with a dance floor over the top of the in-ground swimming pool. The guests were a colourful assembly of family, friends and acquaintances of their parents. There were a few of Henry's old European friends, Betar and University friends and one hospital teacher that he was particularly fond of, Dr Steve Mistilis. One of Steve's lessons will stay with Eddie forever.

"Well, tell me what do you see? What can you diagnose from a distance?" asked Dr. Mistilis to his class as they gathered around a patient in her hospital bed. The students offered various suggestions when Dr Mistilis said, *"Isn't she particularly ugly?"* Eddie and his fellow students went white. *"Please describe her. What do you think you see?"* urged the Dr Mistilis.

One student observed, *"She has an enlarged chin."*

"Her face is very broad," said another.

Someone chimed in with, *"She has a large tongue."*

And another with, *"Her chin juts out."*

"So students," said Dr Mistilis, *"what do you think the diagnosis might be?"*

Finally, one student suggested it might be acromegaly.

"Correct", said Dr Mistilis. He went on to explain, *"Acromegaly is caused by a tumour of the pituitary gland and this has occurred late in life and it has over-produced growth hormone. Hence, the changes in her facial features.....What else can you tell me about the patient?"*

asked Dr Mistilis. *"Where does the pituitary gland sit in the brain?"*

The students replied, *"It's at the base of the brain."*

"That is right and when it enlarges, as in her case, it presses against the auditory nerve making her completely deaf."

The students breathed a sigh of relief. They would never forget that deafness was a side symptom of patients presenting with acromegaly. At the time of Eddie's wedding Steve was going through a tough time as he was being kicked out of Prince Alfred Hospital due to politics. He was devastated that he would have to abandon his liver research. During the reception Eddie reassured a depressed Steve with an old saying of his mother's, *"Out of all the bad things, there will be something good."* Steve replied doubtfully, *"There's a saying in Greek that 'if a pigeon shits on you it's good luck', but you know what? If a pigeon shits on you, a pigeon shits on you!"*

But Eddie would prove him wrong. Shortly after the wedding he was to get a job at Sydney Hospital and he went "into bat" to get Steve a job there also with, the then, Superintendent Bruce Herriot. Steve was employed and a year or two later as a Specialist in Macquarie Street told Eddie, *"I'm earning a lot more money. The bottom fell out of research and research funding. It's the best thing that has ever happened."*

Alongside the doctors at the wedding were quite a large group of Sam's Aussie friends including several of the Rosenberg brothers who were all great drinkers and gamblers. Neville Rosenberg was asked to give the toast to the Queen as he was the only person who'd spent time at the Queen's leisure (in jail) for going AWOL and visiting his girlfriend whilst in the army. In the midst of the lively

Jewish gathering was an auditor to ensure all was Kosher. Mia's father Sam was kept busy keeping the gentleman well plied with scotch so any slight indiscretions might be overlooked. Mia was hoping the wedding "cake" might be overlooked too or at least presented in poor light. The day before she and her bridesmaid had gone to the Carmel cake shop to collect the croquembouche that would be their "cake". It had proven somewhat difficult to obtain with all the kosher requirements but the end result of the plump pastries glistening under the thin and crispy veil of toffee was a visual delight....that was until Mia, on her way to the car with the precarious edifice, tripped and the mass of sticky balls collapsed on the ground rolling in every direction.

"Oh no! What are we going to do?!" the girls cried.

Later they gingerly reassembled the dessert with homemade toffee and hoped the guests wouldn't notice the small particles of dirt stuck to the hastily brushed off profiteroles. While Mia's mind was on her guests' constitutions, Eddie spent a lot of time thinking about his speech and crafted it to honour his beautiful new bride and their plans for the future. He began with Abraham Lincoln's Gettysburg address, *"Four score and seven years ago..."* alluding to their long courtship which had been on and off for 9 years. He then morphed into Hebrew secretly decreeing, as most were not fluent, his intentions to live in Israel. He then went on to describe Mia as having a vibrancy, a unique quality of being able to look at the world so differently to others saying, *"You don't find many girls like Mia. There is a certain something about her; an unpredictability. Take a sign at a beach for example. If the sign says 'PRIVATE BEACH – NO SWIMMING ALLOWED', Mia will interpret it as 'Private beach? NO! Swimming allowed!'"*

The celebrations continued all though the night with Sam challenging revellers to *"break the dance floor!"* An "agreement" was made with the police to not shut the party down. By 5am the last stragglers left the dance floor.

After a night at the Sebel Townhouse in Elizabeth Bay the couple flew out on their honeymoon to San Francisco. Mia was working for Qantas at the time so their stand-by flights were very cheap but also unpredictable. The newlyweds were seated apart. Before take-off, however, an announcement crackled through the plane, *"Could Mr Eddie Price please make yourself known to flight staff. We at Qantas believe you're on your honeymoon and we can't have you separated from your bride!"*

The plane erupted into cheers and *"Congratulations!"* In San Francisco and LA, they enjoyed their time together, but their final US destination was to be a shared experience. Mia's parents were very friendly with Don Lane and he had invited them to Las Vegas as a wedding present. They joined him and his mother Dolly for a couple of wonderful nights enjoying good food, good wine and great nightclub shows. Eddie rolled with laughter through the Don Rickles show and also enjoyed Louis Prima performing. An amusing incident occurred when they were at a plush restaurant for dinner and Eddie's wine glass was filled with crushed ice. The boy from Wollongong did not know what to do. The ice appeared very appealing to him and he wished to sip it. However, he waited to take cues from Dolly who did not touch hers. Eventually, the waiter returned and took the crushed ice and threw it into a bucket. It was just a matter of chilling the glass!

Eddie said to Mia, *"They didn't teach me that in*

Wollongong."

On the way back to Australia Mia had booked them a few days on the tropical Etai Island in Fiji. This wasn't designed to be as crowded as Las Vegas but the dormitory sleeping arrangements they shared with 80 Girl Guides certainly wasn't conducive to the romantic island retreat Eddie had envisaged with his new bride.

Back at home and with the one-year Diploma of Health Administration course now complete, he was interested in embarking on a Masters course. It would only involve two extra years of part-time study and a thesis as he already held the Diploma. With this in mind he began to look for a full-time job in Health Management in a smaller hospital and applied to Canterbury first. They were delighted and offered him the job. In the meantime, Henry had seen an ad in the newspaper from Sydney Hospital, looking for a doctor to join their Management Development Unit. Henry called him and said, *"Why are you not going for this? It is good for your career. It's a teaching hospital. It sounds like an interesting job. You should apply."*

Eddie thought, *"Only a father's love would find an ad like that and know that was a job his son would love."* He got the job.

It was April 1973 and a meeting was taking place in the elegant Honoraries Room of the colonial "Rum Hospital" (now Sydney Hospital). It was given its original name because when it was constructed in 1816 the funding had come from private individuals. In exchange for their investment they were given a monopoly on the importation of 45,000 gallons of rum to the colony. At the meeting were Ron Beer, CEO of the Sydney Hospital, Dr Bruce Herriott, Medical Superintendent, Deputy Matron Shaw, Len E

Crawford, the Divisional Director for PA Management Consultants Pty Ltd, and Dr Eddie Price, Assistant Superintendent, Sydney Hospital and Medical Representative in Sydney Hospitals Internal Management Development Unit. They were present to hear Len Crawford present the results of three years of work at Sydney Hospital devising a quality measurement system to determine if the hospital was offering good patient care. At the time Sydney Hospital was under threat of closure and Ron Beer, CEO, needed to prove that he ran a quality service. He had hired PA Management Consultants who set up their program based on the latest management principles. For the previous three years PA Management Consultants had trialled a Patient Care Index categorising patients' care under five headings:

1. Patient Welfare and Safety.
2. Patient Comfort.
3. Medical Records.
4. The Ward.
5. The Nursing Unit.

The development of this index had been reported in the Medical Journal of Australia (December 18, 1971, L E Crawford et al) and was probably one of the first PREMs (Patient-Reported Experience Measures) in operation. There was a great deal of pride in showing that they could now measure quality hospital care. PA Consultants claimed there was proof through their use of the Patient Care Index that the quality of service at Sydney Hospital had been improved. The figures showed that 20% more patients had been treated than ever before in the hospital's history and that the cost of patient treatment had reduced but nursing staff levels had remained constant. The company was now handing over their program to a team of internal hospital managers and they were keen to have the medical staff involved so Dr Eddie Price had been recruited. When he reviewed the questions in the Patient Care Index he intuitively felt something was wrong. It seemed the questions were only really looking at whether or not a patient was happy with how they'd been treated and whether or not their food had been served cold.

He wondered, *"Wasn't medicine more than patient satisfaction for a service? Wasn't the real aim to improve the patient's health?"* He then asked himself the next question, *"What is health?"* and *"What part of the patient's health status do these questionnaires measure?"*

He had his own ideas on how the hospital should be measuring its quality of health care. His recent studies into the management theories of Peter Drucker had piqued his interest, particularly the ideas on starting with an objective or a target. He felt that each patient during admission into hospital should be asked: What was their objective? If the hospital was able to meet the patient's objective, then that would be real quality care. At the time there was a move, championed by Lawrence Weed, to complete Medical Records that were problem-oriented so that each specific problem for each patient was isolated. Eddie believed this should be medical records by objectives or by what was soon to be known as Desired Health Outcomes. He felt that something significant was being missed by the Patient Care Index, or as he called it the "Patient Satisfaction Index", although he acknowledged it may certainly be a part of the Health Care mix. He saw medicine as "patient management" but felt that as a science it should have defined goals or its own objectives in order to determine whether these were being achieved by the medical system. So began a time of intense research and reflection for Eddie. Some of his thoughts of the time were written down in a paper for Sydney Hospital in May of 1973 and followed by a second, more expanded exploration of the ideas, in a published paper called "Health Outcomes" in July of 1973.

It was one Friday night family dinner at Mia's parents' house when they were joined, rather unusually, by Henry. In the interests of dinner conversation and as was his habit whilst Eddie was growing up, Henry asked how his week had been. Eddie knew from years of experience that he wanted detail and so detail is what he would get! He had just spent an amazing week on a course presented by Len Crawford of PA Management for internal management consultants. Joining him were an eclectic group including a delegate from the Hydro Electric Commission in Hobart, people from ICI Australia in Melbourne and personnel from the Government Aircraft Factory in Port Melbourne, Victoria. Eddie reported that the course was fascinating and Henry wanted to know more. He explained that the course was centred on a case study of a man called Victor Stone who worked at a Royal Palace and he outlined the premise that they had worked with.

"There was a king who ruled over a small kingdom. The cost of running the King's palace was paid for out of the Royal purse administered by the Royal Treasurer. Once a year the Royal Treasurer filled the purse with money levied from the Barons. Each Baron paid according to the size of his domain to a formula worked out by the Royal Treasurer. The Barons in their turn taxed the common people. A year came with scarcely any rain and the harvest throughout the kingdom

was so bad that all the people were very poor. The king, who was sorry for the plight of the common people, impulsively proclaimed that taxes would be reduced without consulting his Royal Treasurer. He, himself, would set an example by spending less at the Royal Palace. The Barons were very angry indeed at this proclamation as they grew rich by putting into their pockets taxes raised for the king. Fewer taxes for the king would mean less money for the Barons. The Royal Treasurer was also vexed because the king had made an important proclamation without seeking his professional advice first. He was secretly glad for an excuse to curb the extravagance of the Royal Palace. Realising what he had done the king was aghast. In a panic he went to the Royal Treasurer. The Royal Treasurer, a wise old man, listened with a long face to the king. Finally he said gravely, it was a very serious matter for the king to make proclamations without consulting him first. It could easily lead to serious trouble with the Barons and they were difficult enough as it was. After speaking in this vein for a long time to impress the king he said, 'There is only one thing to do. It is unthinkable merely to cut the Palace budget. That would force his majesty to tighten his Royal belt and be both uncomfortable for his majesty and bad for the prestige of the kingdom. We need to be cleverer than that. We have to find ways to improve the value obtained for the money spent at the Palace.' The relieved king asked how this could be done. 'Send for Victor Stone, your Majesty,' said the Treasurer. Victor Stone had previously been in charge of roadworks of the kingdom and was paid a small stipend to administer the roadworks. The scheme worked well and the king had formed a very favourable impression of Victor but he could not see how Victor's skill at road-mending could save money at the Royal Palace. However, the king knew he was in no position to argue so he summoned Victor. 'Victor,' said the king, 'the Royal Treasurer wants you to fix up the Palace to save money. Do what he tells you but I don't want any trouble.' The Royal Treasurer told Victor what he wanted. He explained that the Palace was run by the Royal Chamberlain, a very dignified and very old man who had been there since the time of the King's late grandfather. It was clear to Victor that the Royal Treasurer disliked the Royal Chamberlain and thought him as a tiresome old muddler. The Royal Treasurer told Victor there were three departments inside the Palace – the Royal Butler who looked after the Royal Footman, the Royal Chef had charge of the kitchen and the Royal Housekeeper, a widow, looked after the Royal Maids. The Royal Treasurer stressed that it was very important for Victor to be accepted by the Palace staff. To do this, the King had agreed to Victor staying as a guest at the Palace."

Henry became concerned at the lengthy story going nowhere.

Eddie retorted, *"Victor Stone was a Management Consultant Dad. The management changes that had fixed the roads would work in other environments. Since I did that case study I have realised the importance of control statements and of assessing the situation and how any organisation is to someone their kingdom and they object to outsiders coming into their 'palace' and telling them what to do. The Barons at Sydney Hospital are the Visiting Medical Officers (they were called Honoraries), and the 'Royal' Managers of each department feel it is their domain over which to rule and they are not keen on any interference."* He extrapolated that this also fitted with the Pareto Principle, the 20/80 Rule that PA management's consultants espoused. 20%

of the causes had 80% of the effects, or, if you have influence over 20% of a specific empowered group (like doctors or Barons) they will then produce 80% of the effects. Eddie was able to garner from this that if he was to establish his ideas for the health system broadly and have the most widespread effect on the health of the nation he needed the support of that 20% of the system - the doctors. He thought that this was different from the physics he was taught where every cause had proportional effects. *"Some causes have a much larger effect than other causes. That is interesting".* He also noted that Victor Stone had cautioned him to tread carefully for a GP's practice was his kingdom and a specialist's practice was his kingdom and they may not take an outsider's advice readily.

"But what did you do in the course?!" His father implored, *"How did you help the king at the Royal Palace?"*

Eddie explained, *"It was a five-day course and it will take too long to detail all the programs we initiated at the Royal Palace. For an example, in the Royal Kitchen we found there were huge amounts of waste that went to the royal pigs. The average pig's meal was more costly than the average guests at the Royal Palace because the Royal Kitchen did not know in advance how many royal guests were coming and they purchased excess to make sure they did not run out. They employed more royal kitchen maids to ensure that there was adequate labour to cover the needs of the cook. Victor designed what we learned were control statements so they could prudently ensure the correct quantity of food was ordered and then different and appropriate food for the pigs could be ordered at a much cheaper rate."* By this stage, everyone at the Shabbas Table was interjecting and laughing at the Royal Chef's problem. Esther volunteered to bring some Jewish food to the Royal Kitchen and that would solve the problem. Eddie explained to his father that this was the issue with the health service for most things they were trying to achieve were not measured. There were no proper and effective "control statements" (that described the actual quality) for the meals in the Royal Kitchen just as there were no control statements as to the quality of the health services or hospital services. Henry concluded by saying, *"You're good with kids. It's not too late to specialise in paediatrics rather than worrying about the Royal Kitchen!"*

Once the hilarity subsided Eddie remained inspired by the course and was even more determined to figure out how the health system might benefit from quality measurement and management practices. He also recognised that in order to gain access to, and traction in the system for his ideas, he needed as much gravitas and prestige that he could manifest. He felt it important that he become a Fellow of the Royal Australian College of Medical Administrators. In order to be accepted as a Fellow Eddie had to prepare a written paper. It was not particularly difficult as most of the detail had been covered in his health management training. He would also have to pass an oral examination of two hours at the Heidelberg Hospital in Melbourne, Victoria. Eddie went to Melbourne where he stayed with his good Israeli friend Edju who was living with his Australian wife Betty. Whilst re-connecting with Edju and enlightening him on his most recent studies, Eddie again enthusiastically explained the story of Victor Stone and the Royal Kitchen. Edju, who had trained as an engineer was managing a main road development project in Victoria for a private enterprise. He insisted that Eddie copy him the notes from the course. He had his own issues with the "not-so-royal kitchen". Edju had learnt that in managing road projects out in the countryside of Victoria, the main requirement to keep his workers happy was to have meat pie warmers available. Eddie said, *"The Royal labourers!"*

Edju explained that once these warmers were in place he got the job done much more readily. They discussed behavioural change and how important it was in any managerial situation. Edju dropped Eddie off one day later at the Heidelberg Hospital for his oral examination.

Here he was faced with a panel of seven senior health managers for his two-hour inquisition. Dr Ian Brand, CEO of the Alfred Hospital, asked several questions regarding the details of management. *"Dr Price, if I pay for the hospital pharmacy deliveries and this is a double entry accounting system, what is the other account that I debit when I pay out each many thousands of dollars?"*

Eddie answered, *"Thank you. Your double entry is against the bank."*

He was then asked about the petty cash system and how Eddie would implement controls so that the petty cash could be readily available, yet appropriately monitored, so the medical administrative staff were not wasting their money. Other similar questions came from Dr Brand. The newly-appointed Chairman of the NSW Health Commission, Dr Roderick McEwin, asked more along the lines of, *"What is your vision for the future of health services and how can we improve them? What techniques would you use?"*

Eddie was delighted to have the opportunity to share his ideas and go into the detail of his recently-completed course.

After passing his examinations Eddie returned to training staff at Sydney Hospital in the implementation of management techniques whilst all the time thinking about how medicine could better define its objectives. Close to the end of the year a memo was circulated around the Sydney Hospital that the Health Commission and Public Administration Group would be running a two-day training course for health managers at the Institute of Public Administration at Prince Henry Hospital. Keen to learn and lap up more knowledge on management theory and how health services operated, Eddie jumped at the chance. The training was divided up into small groups of eight to ten people from assorted areas of the health service. Various health management problems were provided to the groups to be solved. Eddie was enthusiastically involved in discussions when Dr Bill Barclay, one of the five Commissioners of the newly-formed NSW Health Commission that managed health services in NSW, sat in on the group for approximately an hour. Eddie took no notice of this until months later when Ron Beer, CEO of Sydney Hospital, called him to his office. *"Eddie, I've been approached by the Health Commission on behalf of the NSW Royal Australian College of General Practitioners. They submitted an application for funding for a new training program for GPs and have been awarded a million dollars by the Whitlam government. The College has to spend this money and establish their program by the 30th of June next year and have appealed for help from the NSW Health Commission. Dr Barclay has contacted me and suggested that you might work with them for a three-month period to help them set up the program."* Eddie was thrilled by the opportunity and enthusiastically agreed.

January 1974 was a time of new beginnings. Not only would he be starting a new role, but socially he and Mia were about to join a gathering that would become a tradition for them that continues to this day. On the 26th of January, Australia Day, a group of their friends came together for lunch in Centennial Park and "The Famous Picnic" was born. The group included Hedi and Thomas Atkinson, Ross and Judy Matthews, Hal McAvoy, Janette Kingsbury and Arch Nicholson, Ana and Kerry Wanka and Malcolm and Janet Smith. In later years this group would form the backbone for another gathering; a scientific one that would support Eddie and his philosophies about medicine, science and life.

Professionally Eddie was now a fully-fledged Fellow of the 'Royal' Australian College of Medical Administrators and was working with the NSW Royal Australian College of General Practitioners. He was still receiving his salary via Sydney Hospital but for the next three months would be working for the NSW Health Department. On the 2nd January 1974 he turned up to work at the plush new offices of the Family Medicine Program at 80 Alfred Street, Milsons Point, to be greeted by Mr Des Lamcraft, the National Administrative Director and the Executive Assistant, Pekita Kellaway. Des explained that they had just appointed a State Director for establishing the Family Medicine Program in NSW, Dr John Dowsett, who would join them shortly. The GP training program was designed to attract more doctors to the role of General Practitioner, rather than being drawn to the specialties, and it needed to be up and running by the 1st of April, in three short months' time. It was important that the program be established by that date as they would then be reviewed and if it could be shown that they had provided an effective solution, further Commonwealth budgets would be available in future years. Eddie thought of Victor Stone at the Royal Palace and likened himself to working for the

101

Kingdom (the State of NSW). Unlike Victor's problem where he had to cut costs, the College was flush with money thanks to the Whitlam government's million-dollar grant. The resource that was limited in his case was time. When he came home and mentioned to Mia that his problem was to spend $1 million dollars in three months, she assured him that she could not only help, but could achieve that with ease.

It was time to assess the problem. In the past, doctors were trained during a six-year course and a one-year hospital internship. After this they were able to be licensed to work as a general practitioner. Specialists had to train for another five years in their particular specialty. General practice was viewed by many young doctors as the job you took when you missed out on specialty programs. General practitioners, for some time, had felt that this was inappropriate and in 1958 the Royal Australian College of General Practitioners (RACGP) was set up and they had their own postgraduate training program established. It was also a five-year training program and the Royal Australian College of General Practitioners had established an excellent system of training known as The Check Program under the auspices of Dr Wesley Fabb. Young doctors completing their internship usually associated with a particular teaching hospital. Then they would go onto a residency program, also within the hospital, before choosing a specialty and becoming a registrar in a particular specialty. The major problem was that no GPs were appointed to the large teaching hospitals where the majority of medical graduates were training. There was always a race from each of the specialities to get the best graduates and for the graduates to get into their specialty of choice....however General Practice was not seen as a desirable option. It was often left with the doctors who had been denied access to the specialties.

The issues were fervently discussed in management meetings with Dr Dowsett, Pekita Kellaway, Des Lamcraft and Eddie. A strategy was established to communicate that they had potential training roles for residents not accepted into specialty programs. The group determined they needed to work fast as it was a crucial time of the year. In mid-January there was a rollover from the previous year when interns would become residents and jobs were sought in the teaching and peripheral hospitals. Discussions were had, not only with residents, but also with the medical administration of the various hospitals. Functions for residents were held and brochures were produced to immediately spread the news of their project far and wide. Pekita and her staff were extremely competent administrators and in today's world would probably be executives themselves, a position not readily thought of for young women at that time. The workload was such that within a couple of days Pekita had to hire another executive assistant.

Eddie was restless. He pondered over whether there was more that they could do to ensure these GP positions were validated and were given as much support as other specialty areas. Then he had an idea. The RACGP and the Commonwealth could pay for trainees to spend three-month terms in a GP practice. That would mean that within one calendar year, four doctors could rotate through. He asked for a meeting with Dr Barclay and put the proposition to him, *"To join the other specialities, you need to go and do a term of this and a term of that but there is no general practice term. It doesn't exist. We've got to put hospital residents out for a general practice term in a GP practice as part of their normal rotation. At no cost to the State, the teaching hospitals can add another doctor to their establishment, usually a second-year resident, and then with that one hospital position, there would be four new trainees within a training program."*

Dr Barclay concurred and applauded the concept, *"I think that is a good idea and I think we could probably get the Feds to pay for it IF you can get the permission of each of the teaching hospitals."*

When Eddie rang the medical administration of each hospital he was surprised at their response. They were all delighted to have another established position on their books, another doctor, and if they found enough young residents who were interested then they could establish two new positions. This allowed them to boast larger staff and so they jumped at the possibility. The new positions had to be determined by late-January and needed approval by the Health Commissioners themselves. Eddie and the team had to work furiously but all was completed by the end of the month.

During this time the Executive Assistants were writing training programs based on the check program and having regular contact with the National Office of the College of General Practitioners in Jolimont, Victoria. The pot of money was finally being dipped into and a portion allocated to supplementing the GPs "training in practices" salaries. Pekita's administration team grew with three more senior executive assistants and the premises at Alfred Street were becoming overcrowded. They looked for bigger offices and soon moved the Family Medicine Program into 55 Lavender Street, Milson's Point; offices with amazing harbour views.

Mr Lamcraft, the National Administrative Director, recognised the success and potential of the program. He quickly advised the other states around the country which started to implement similar programs, adding establishment positions to the teaching hospitals and gaining for each position, not one, but four, potential trainees. This system would later become a College of GP program that was set up across Australia and gave the role of the GP more prestige. No longer were they viewed as second class doctors.

Six weeks into the job, Eddie was delighted to receive from Roderick McEwin, Chairman of the Health Commission, the following memo:

"Placement and Training of RMOs. Please note paragraph 12.0. I was very pleased to hear of this. Thank you for it. Dr Roderick McEwin," and he attached the report of the HASAC Postgraduate Accreditation Committee Meeting with the Combined Education Committee of the Royal Colleges Melbourne, from the 6th of February 1974. Under Point 12 of the minutes of the Academy of General Practice, Dr Robert Harbison paid special tribute to the Health Commission of NSW for their efforts in establishing the new program and specifically to the work of Dr Eddie Price. The program has never looked back from that point.

Towards the end of his three-months, Eddie was invited to run some of the group training sessions at the National Symposium of all State Directors of the Family Medicine Program. He facilitated the classes with ideas gained from his management training and formulated games and various other interactive strategies to give the groups some general administrative skills. Soon after his tenure ended he headed back to Sydney Hospital. On leaving the program, Eddie asked for a reference from Desmond Lamcraft who indicated he wished to determine the ongoing progress before he would provide Eddie with this reference. In the reference,

February, 1975, he stated that Eddie had worked there in the creative phase of an operation which was now on or ahead of target in all States of Australia. He was to receive various commendations for his assistance in setting up the Family Medicine Program and the GP training program.

He returned to Sydney Hospital pleased that he had managed to spend the $1 million. He was more satisfied that he had played such an integral part in improving the health care of the nation by encouraging higher calibre candidates to the role of the General Practitioner. His position at Sydney Hospital producing courses continued, but he struggled to involve the medical staff and residents and was dismayed that most of the work he was doing was with the nurses and administrative staff only. He determined to return to his cultural homeland, to Israel, and attempt to implement his management theories on their relatively new and hopefully more flexible medical system. Eddie was to have one more exciting opportunity presented to him prior to his departure. Rocky McEwin, the Chairman for the NSW Health Commission, approached him with an offer to work in a consultative capacity for the Commission as his Special Projects Officer aimed at developing a Management by Objectives program through the health services. Eddie was ecstatic that his ideas seemed to be gaining traction and was eager to obtain a position of influence as well as great experience. He happily accepted on the understanding that it would only be for six months as he would then be heading back to the Middle East. McEwin agreed and encouraged him to implement his ideas on setting targets and outcome measures for the Commission for all the various health regions in terms of mortality rates and the number of admissions.

He reluctantly wrote to Mr Beer, the CEO of Sydney Hospital, to advise him of his resignation. Eddie greatly admired Mr Beer for his visionary activities but also his ability to have adapted and thrived in his role as Chief Executive Officer after having started his life as an upholsterer. In his resignation letter he wrote, *"In resigning. I feel sad and excited. I feel sad to be leaving the hospital which has given me the opportunities to work in a consultative capacity, an ability which I feel I'm just now mastering. However, I'm excited by the challenge of my new position."*

In his new role, Eddie familiarised himself with people in Head Office and then was dispatched to talk to the Directors of all the health regions to assist them in formulating their objectives. Having the authority of the Chairman (the King) of the NSW Health Commission helped considerably in this endeavour. What he found, through his research with the Directors, was that many senior administrators had been deployed to manage the regions from Sydney, often against their will. He was surprised to find that now the majority said the move was the best thing that they had done as they were so much more content in the country regions.

Even though he was the educator in many of his interactions with the regions he also had a lot to learn about stepping into "Royal Palaces". The Southeast Sydney Regional Director had called a meeting to discuss a variety of issues including how they were to go about setting objectives, setting targets and generally how to implement these new management techniques. He invited all the CEOs of the various hospitals in that region to the meeting. Eddie was to present how the Commission wished the regions to implement the Management by Objectives program, but it was to be given his own interpretation. On this occasion, he became carried away suggesting that the Pareto Principle, when applied to costly supplies (i.e. 20% of the supplies cause 80% of the costs) and that this was the area they should concentrate on when looking at cost-cutting. Many of the hospitals' CEOs strongly rejected his position. They all understood this principle but what really mattered was the overall culture of not over-spending and that this could be achieved by closely monitoring the lesser-expensive items. Eddie had to agree and to admit that he was only commencing his journey into the real life medical system away from the freedoms to theorise in academia. He thought to himself, *"Interesting....Paretos' concept, that not all causes have proportional effects, is opposite to and opposes what was demonstrated by the CEOs, that all causes have effects....but both I see as correct."* He determined to ponder this conclusion further.

He reported regularly to Dr Rocky McEwin and at one of the early reviews suggested that if Management by Objectives was to be effective at the regional levels, the Health Commission and the health commissioners themselves must have their own objectives quantified including timelines. Rocky said to him, *"I am happy for you to put this to a meeting of the Commission but what is your equanimity like?"*

He had no idea what this word meant. Nevertheless, he said it was okay and then Rocky warned, *"If you do come to a meeting you understand I will not be able to defend you or come to your assistance in any way."*

He understood and went home to look up what the word equanimity meant. (Equanimity - a state of psychological stability and composure, which is undisturbed by experience of, or exposure to, emotions, pain or other phenomena that may cause others to lose the balance of their mind.) He now understood that by suggesting to the commissioners that perhaps they change what they were doing carried an implied criticism of what they were doing now and this was coming from a young upstart! Eddie prepared for the meeting and, in doing so, read up on what he had learned regarding behavioural change in group processes. His research showed that in any group situation there will be in general terms, a persecutor, a victim, and a rescuer. He inherently knew that he would be the victim and attacked viciously. The relatively-inexperienced twenty-eight-year-old bravely presented his objectives and suggestions for change to the Commission. *"We have got to start by setting our targets and we have got to start at the top."*

At Eddie's conclusion Dr Barclay, his previous direct boss, started the relentless attack. *"You have no experience in the health services. These are areas where you need lengthy experience in managing such broad systems."*

Then the other three commissioners took it in turn to barrage the young Dr Price. Rocky, true to his warning, did not come in and assist. Eddie kept mumbling to himself, *"Do not defend yourself. Stay quiet, agree or keep quiet."*

After approximately half of an hour of the ruthless onslaught one of the other commissioners, Dr David Storey, the Deputy Chairman, eventually said that perhaps there may be some minor benefits to the Commission. It was at least worth taking a look at the suggestions. The whole tone of the meeting began to change. They started to debate some of the objectives. Dr Price was amazed. What he had learned regarding behavioural change and group processes had worked. Dr Storey became his rescuer. The meeting concluded with the assessment that the Commission would look at Eddie's suggestions in a future meeting without his presence.

It is easy to forget that all the while he was broadening his experience in the world of Health Management he had also kept up his Master's schedule of research and exams. At the end of his three years of study he was due to end up with two degrees, one for the Diploma of Health Administration and one for the Masters of Health Administration. This was "double dipping" and "unfair" according to many of his fellow Master's graduates who were only eligible for one degree. *"How come he is going to get two degrees and we are only going to get one!"*

Despite two years of additional part time studies, sitting all the exams and working on a thesis on medical records by objectives relating to outcomes medicine, Eddie relinquished the title of Masters and settled for one degree with the Diploma. He claimed, *"I don't care about the degree. I have enough degrees. I just won't hand my thesis in."*

For him the task of completing the work was becoming onerous anyway and in his mind all he was losing was a few letters after his name. What was really important was all that he had learned in those years and how he was now planning on implementing his grand ideas.

When he finally stepped away from his consulting role for the NSW Health Commission to travel to Israel he was leaving with high accolades as demonstrated in an excerpt from the letter of recommendation from Dr Rocky McEwin:

"Dr E.D. Price....a young man of outstanding intellect, together with the energy and enterprise which should enable him to challenge accepted concepts and with a high degree of ability to innovate within the health services. He is an

extremely hard worker with a highly superior intellect; highly motivated towards change. I believe he has a valuable contribution to make to health administration.

Dr Rocky McEwin, Chairman of the NSW Health Commission, December 1974."

When Eddie showed his father the reference Henry said, *"Are you ok? You don't get a reference like this unless you are sleeping with the guy!"*

A proud father, Dr Henry Price would have welcomed the news that his son was rising to such illustrious heights in his chosen medical field and was being commended so highly for his work. It had been a difficult year for the ageing German doctor with a diagnosis of Lymphosarcoma cancer and given only one year to live. Against this backdrop of finality and fear a letter arrived that gifted Henry not only some happiness in his final days, but it gave him back a son.

"It is now 36 years since I was born Peter Edward Price and it would help me understand myself a little better if I could meet my natural father."

Henry quickly replied:

DR. H. M. Price
Unit 4. Yuruga
2 Oak St. Clovelly HSW 2001
Tel 665 7803

April, 21, 1974

Dear Peter,

Your letter of April 10th 74 was "the" surprise of my life, quite a happy surprise, because I took it for most likely – in view of the attitude of the Szamatolskis to me – that you were brought up and indoctrinated with the conviction that I am a bad character. – The very fact that you are writing to me, giving me some information about yourself and that you wish to meet me, seems to be evidence of your independent mind.

I got remarried and had an utterly happy and ideal married life until 1965, when my wife died from secondaries of a breast carcinoma, (Inspite of an immediate mastectomy with the first symptom in 1958). I got 2 sons, 30 and 28 years, the older a highly qualified Electrical Engineer and manager of a computer team, the younger a doctor with postgrad. degrees in Health Administration and Asst. Superintendent of a large teaching hospital; both married, both at present in Sydney.

I would be glad to meet you: the trouble is that I got suddenly ill last September: Lymphosarcoma , allegedly

Stage IV. I had a rather risky Spleenectomy of a grossly enlarged spleen on 10th Sept. and recovered fully, but there was no chance to remove the tumor in the mesenterium of the transverse colon. I am kept in a fair general condition with regular injections of Cyclophosphamide i.v. Although I am (still) living a normal full life, I get easily tired. I had to give up working after this operation and I am unfit to travel overseas in view of my health and my treatment. Therefore the only possibility to meet each other would be that you are visiting me in Sydney. Of course you are cordially invited to be my guest here and you would have only to worry about your travel expenses and ararngements.

According to my physician my life-expectancy is approx. 18 months but with such an abdominal tumor any acute illness could reduce this time.

Please let me know what you decide. In case you make up your mind to come to Sydney, it would be better not to delay this trip.

I do appreciate how hard it must have been for you to find my (previous) address and to overcome your inhibition to write to me.

My best wishes to your 36th birthday.

Yours very sincerely

P.S.

I apologize for writing by typewriter, but my handwriting is so difficult to read that "typing" seems to be the "lesser evil." There is a postal strike here with several thousand mailbags unopened at post offices; that could delay our correspondence.

It was thirty-six years since Peter Edward Price had been born to Dr Henry Price in his own private hospital in Lebanon just as Michael and Eddie had been some years later. Peter was requesting to make contact with his natural father. To Eddie, Henry commented that he was sure Peter had marital problems, *"Why else would he suddenly need to know more about me after all these years?"*

He also confided that meeting the child who was ripped from his life so long ago would be difficult for him. Peter's early years had been fractured ones. New York City in 1938 was not an ideal place for a single mother seeking a new life and a new life partner so Ilse had relinquished her baby into the care of foster homes. He'd been bundled from one home to another and when he asked after his birth father he was fed stories of a soldier in a far-off war, at first fighting for the French. A three-year old Peter would cheer for the French Army, only to become bemused when suddenly the story changed and it was the English Army he should now be barracking for. When the war ended and there was no sign of this longed-for father the true tale of separation and divorce could no longer be denied and a little boy was left confused and wounded. After some eight years of fluctuating between being cared-for and then being abandoned by his working mother a new husband had been found who offered to adopt Peter, so he was returned to his mother's care. With the adoption came a change of name and the request to Dr H. Price in Lebanon to relinquish his parentage (or face the horror that his sister's whereabouts in Germany would be disclosed to the Nazis). So Peter Price became Peter Schrag, son to reserved German-born American painter and printmaker - Karl Schrag.

Stepping off the plane at Sydney International Airport and into the arms of two emotional, and unknown, half-brothers was a highly emotive moment for Peter. His reserved facade portrayed none of his internal turmoil. For five nights he resided with Eddie and Mia but his days were spent making up for wasted time with his once-fabled father. Henry Price had been correct in his summation of his long lost son; he was indeed having marital problems. The two formed what bond they could. They knew much had passed that could never be returned and one of them would soon be passing. Peter, a specialist physician at Columbia Presbyterian Hospital in America, had picked up on the Price family "gene" or inherent expectation to study medicine. There were other family similarities. Whilst on a night out together Peter noted to Eddie, *"By the looks of things none of the Price brothers ever had a problem with girls."*

Knowing he had limited time, and wanting to show his love and support for this newly acquired son and his family, Henry requested the approval from Michael and Eddie that after his death some of his estate would be left for Peter's children's education. The suggestion was greeted warmly by both boys. For Peter what brought solace to the reality that he would not spend much time with his father was that he would now have a relationship with two half-brothers on the other side of the world. There maintained a close relationship over the years between the three families.

Jonathan, one of Peter's sons, later came and lived in Sydney near Eddie and Mia whilst studying at the University of NSW and went home with an Aussie bride. Eddie and his family visited Peter's other children, Daniel and Deborah, on a number of occasions when they travelled in the US. The splintered Price family was being put back together....but fractures were forming elsewhere in Eddie's private life.

Since his marriage to Mia he had felt a shift in their home atmosphere that he didn't fully understand. Despite being social and gregarious they were no longer socialising with their Betar friends. They spent less time with his brother Michael. Earlier displays of affection and professions of love had dissolved into a stilted awkwardness in expressing their feelings. It was similar to that between both Mia and her parents and Eddie and his. Undoubtedly a strong love was felt but this was not necessarily expressed outwardly. Mia's demeanour would often manifest in outbursts of frustration and anger towards him. They both reflected that Mia had perhaps married her mother, a martyr and self-sacrificing, and that Eddie had in fact married his volatile father. The attraction of choosing partners who mirrored their childhood home life was a form of security, of safety and the comfort in a known paradigm.

Eddie was restless. Again the pull of Israel was strong and with Mia in tow, he returned.

Chapter 6

The long way to Jerusalem

Eddie faced a number of conundrums at the beginning of 1975. He wanted to trial living in Israel but his father had been diagnosed with Lymphosarcoma. Henry had always expressed his belief that children shouldn't sacrifice their own lives to look after their ageing parents. He continued to support both of his sons' careers abroad even if those were not in his own best interests. Eddie also recognised that if he were to put his career on hold to care for his father, he may find himself waiting for his father to die when really he wanted his father to live for as long as possible. His internal dilemma was compounded by the guilt of asking Mia to leave her parents in Australia while he was also tormented by the decision of leaving his father. Mia's agreement to share their married life in Israel had been difficult for her. Esther and Sam Fiszman had already lost their family once in the Holocaust and Mia and Eddie's move to Israel would be like losing their family again.

Despite these strong family ties the young couple decided to follow their hearts and their dreams and set off for their beloved Israel. Mia resigned from her job at Qantas so they wanted to take advantage of her staff travel allowances one last time and on the way to Israel took the trip of a lifetime to parts of the world they were unlikely to see or may never have the opportunity of visiting again. Michael was living in Hong Kong, establishing his computer software business, so their first stop was to visit him and then went on to see their newly-found half brother Peter in New York. Dr Peter Schrag was a specialist in internal medicine at the Columbia

117

Presbyterian Hospital. His wife Minna was a lawyer with the New York Prosecution Section often looking into cases of persecution by the Nazi regime. Having met Peter in Australia this was the first time meeting the rest of his family. The families clicked. Peter took Eddie on a ward round of his patients at the Columbia Presbyterian Hospital and delighted in introducing his brother Dr Price. Peter also introduced Eddie and Mia to his mother, Ilse, and her husband Karl. The meeting was very pleasant. Ilse approved Eddie's looks and then spent the rest of the time engaged with Mia. Karl Schrag was a soft, gentle man and Eddie sensed that Ilse's second husband's personality was diametrically opposite to that of his father.

After the family visits they were off on the real adventure to Brazil, Argentina, Chile and then East Africa. For Eddie the colourful and effervescent energy of Rio was a reflection of the true personality of his beautiful bride. Her vibrant and happy disposition was right at home here and they had many fun-filled days on sunny beaches. He observed that Mia's olive complexion with some sun had turned rather dark and channelling Frank Sinatra he called her the "*not so tall girl from Ipanema*". In Buenos Aires they enjoyed the elegant nightlife that the port side suburb and tango hub of La Bocca had to offer. One evening they were in conversation with a fellow guest at their hotel. Mia asked about the person's necklace that displayed an extremely large Star of David. The guest turned his necklace around to reveal on the other side an equally large crucifix.

"*It depends who I'm talking to*," he said, as to which side he displayed.

Mia continued their conversation, "*And so what are you doing here in Buenos Aires?*"

The man replied, *"I'm a journalist and I'm working on a documentary called 'Miracle of the Andes'. I'm following up the story of the Uruguayan Air force Flight 571 plane crash in 1972. You may recall that after 72 days in the snow-covered Andes passengers emerged with incredible stories of survival by eating their deceased fellow passengers. I was awestruck by their personalities and I feel they gained a special strength through eating other human beings."*

There were to be further Jewish connections on their journey. They tangoed from the streets of Buenos Aires to the dining room of the Sheraton hotel in Santiago Chile where Mia approached a lady at the next table. *"Forgive me, but are you Lilli Palmer?"*

"Yes, I am," she replied. They conversed about their mutual Jewish origins, after which Lilli returned to her handsome male companion, who appeared to be at least 20 years younger than she. Eddie whispered to Mia, *"Who's Lilli Palmer?"*

Mia responded that, *"She was a German Jewish actress who fled Germany to Paris like your father did in 1933 but she was spotted by talent scouts in Hollywood."* Mia then whispered, *"She was married to Rex Harrison and starred opposite Fred Astaire and Debbie Reynolds in 'The Pleasure of His Company.' Eddie, she's a big star. My father loves her and I think she may have won a Golden Globe Award. It's like you meeting your idol Ritchie Benaud!"*

After this brush with fame, they decided to hire a car and drive to Vina del Mar on the Chilean Riviera. Passing through one small village Mia said, *"Eddie, stop. Go back. We passed a beautiful-looking cake shop."*

They stopped. The cake shop displayed apple strudels and had a Konditorei feel about it. The shop owner was an 80-

year-old lady who noted Mia's Star of David on her necklace.

"You're Jewish?" she asked. *"Vee hav a small community here and tonight vee hav Shabbas night and we have a small service. You would be most welcome to attend."*

Despite such a generous and enticing offer they only had limited time and had to get to the Chilean Riviera. They took their strudels and set off.

Eddie said to Mia, *"I don't think we'll find such cake shops in Nairobi, Kenya or in the next destination, Dar es Salaam in Tanzania."*

Africa didn't disappoint. There were encounters with a vast array of wildlife. In Nairobi they saw giraffes, zebras and lions, some in parks and others by the roadside on their way to Nakuru to see the migratory birds. Eddie was given an education in street sense as well as zoology. In Nairobi, they were approached by young men holding wads of Kenyan shillings and offering money exchange rates better than those of the banks.

Ever-trusting, he exclaimed to Mia, *"This looks good. We can get a much better rate."*

Mia dubiously replied, *"I'm not so sure."*

But he was willing to give it a go, *"I'll try with ten dollars."*

As soon as he handed over the money the young man promptly sprinted away with it. Eddie gave chase with Mia close behind yelling, *"Stop, stop, stop!"* The young man ran into a shopping arcade and Eddie suddenly came face to face with a group of ten similar young men. He quickly decided Mia was right and retreated. Nairobi soon paid them back however. When their hotel dining room presented them with the check the waiter come running out apologising that he had to take away the bill as he'd omitted the 10% surcharge. There was no room on the handwritten bill for the addition so the whole bill had to be re-written but this time they forgot to include the main course! Even with the 10% surcharge their bill was now some $20 cheaper! In the neighbouring bar were a host of English Royal Air force personnel who had told them that they were doing aerial mapping of the area for the government. Eddie and Mia relayed the 10% bill saga and they laughed. They claimed that they had enjoyed many free beers over the last two weeks. They weren't sure whether it was because the staff members were inadequately trained or if it was their way of getting back at the extremely pushy managers.

Dar es Salaam, Tanzania was of great interest to Eddie and Mia as it was a socialist country and they wanted to see this ideology in action. When they landed there were no advertising signs; no evidence of Coca Cola or vodka. They also had no hotel booking so went looking for somewhere to stay. They entered a modern looking hotel and eventually found a receptionist who advised them that the hotel was full. After requesting a tour of the hotel and finding many empty rooms they were accommodated after all. Following a day of sightseeing they returned to the hotel dining room for dinner only to find it padlocked and told it was closed after 8:30pm. Their idealistic view of socialism was starting to wane with the obvious lack of work ethic failing in the basic functioning of the country. All was not lost however. After a transfer to the Kunduchi Beach Hotel and Resort they enjoyed the relaxed atmosphere and the beautiful beach with stunning white sand.

Their round-the-world tour continued and they arrived in Rome where they hoped to buy a car to take by boat to

Israel. At that time there was a new model Fiat coming off the production line, the Fiat 131 Mirafiori. They had a five-day wait for the car to be ready so Mia said, *"We should look up my parents' best friend Jhony who helped them escape Poland. He lives in Munich."*

They arrived at the door of this family saviour and Eddie in his broken German explained to Anusch, Jhony's wife, who they were.

"Aber nein. But, no," said Anusch, *"Jhony is in Napoli buying shoes for my shoe shop."*

They rang Jhony who insisted they must come to his hotel in Napoli as he had one more day of purchasing shoes at an exhibition. When they arrived on the hotel balcony waiting for them was an elegant man with a coat slung over his shoulders pacing up and down and Mia said straight away *"That is Jhony."* They were greeted with great fanfare and excitement and were shouted a wonderful Italian meal. Their Fiat 131 was then ready and Eddie drove it cautiously across Italy to Bari to load it onto the Adriatic shipping line ferry that would take them to Haifa in Israel. The journey was shared with an eclectic bunch of passengers who soon became friends; a philosophical fellow they called Socrates, Hussein – a young Turk leaving Cyprus for Israel as he felt it was safer than being amongst the warring Greeks and Turks and a young German student going to Israel to study Keno. The boat stopped at Rhodes and a wine-filled night was had by all. There was a stop in Athens followed by the most beautiful sight; Haifa, Israel with its glistening golden dome of the Bahá'í temple. The ancient stone roads winding through the tree-lined streets and the slopes of Mount Carmel sliding down the city's three tiers into Haifa Bay were like a welcoming embrace for Eddie and Mia. As soon as they cleared Customs Eddie decided to drive straight to his Uncle Herward Rosenberg's insurance assessing office near the Haifa Port.

Their elation on arrival in Israel was short lived. Eddie excitedly entered his uncle's office claiming, *"I'm Herward's nephew from Australia."* The staff soberly informed them that Herward was seriously ill at home on Mount Carmel. Shocked, they immediately drove to 101 Hatisbi Street, where Eddie had stayed many nights during his two years of internship and residency only to be advised that his uncle had metastatic kidney disease. Herward's illness had left him confused so that he often called his wife, Ruth, by his sister's name, Ursula. Herward and Ruth had two young children, Shlom aged 11 years, and his younger sister, Orna, aged seven years. Eddie and Mia offered what they could do to help and then drove down the coastal road to their absorption centre for new immigrants, Ulpan Ben Yehuda. The centre was located just outside the town of Netanya, close to the picturesque Green Beach. Here they were to take Hebrew classes and were given temporary accommodation until they settled into life in Israel. Herward sadly passed away some weeks later and Mia and Eddie attended the funeral on Mount Carmel. Following his uncle's passing Eddie drove from Netanya to Haifa on a number of occasions to offer assistance to Ruth. These drives always took longer than expected as every twenty minutes a car enthusiast would hail him down and ask to look at the Fiat 131 as this model was yet to arrive in Israel. He could never say no as it seemed to give them great joy. When he drove the car into the Fiat workshop in Tel Aviv for its first service the staff were bowing as this was the first of the revered model they had seen. The car was a mini celebrity. Scarcity in "the market" was also to aid in Eddie's job hunting prospects in health management. Even though Israel had a plethora of doctors only few had degrees in health management. Eddie was afforded the luxury of choice. His preference was in community based primary care medicine and he was interviewed by Dr Spearman at Clalit Health Fund in Beer Sheva - Beer Sheva Medical School. Eddie was not only impressed by the attitude of this Medical School and their inclination towards community-based care, but he also gained the impression that Dr Spearman was a very competent medical administrator. Despite the allure of an area that he felt he had much to contribute to and that was more in alignment to his own ideology and theories, he made a difficult decision and sought a medical administration role at the Hadassah Hospital. Its international reputation as a large teaching hospital in the Middle East would give much prestige to his CV.

Life in the Ulpan offered Mia and Eddie a number of interesting opportunities and also presented some limitations. They were able to enjoy the friendship of fellow immigrants. Eddie enjoyed fantastic horse-riding along Green Beach and they were close to Mia's mother's cousins in Netanya. Mia was struggling through her Hebrew lessons, claiming that all she saw in the Hebrew writings were ants dancing on the page. For not the first time in his experience in Israel, they were given guns to defend themselves. His misgivings that the possession of guns by untrained people was more of a risk than any outside attack proved correct when one immigrant's gun misfired with the bullet sailing right through one of the flimsy Ulpan buildings. Thankfully no inhabitants were harmed. The basic fibro shacks that were the provided accommodation were clean and adequate for two. Things got a little cosier when Michael and his wife Penny came to visit with Eddie and Mia having to sleep on the kitchen floor each night. During their stay the two couples enjoyed touring around the area and visiting many of the local attractions and beautiful beaches. Mia's mood was elevated considerably by the presence of familiar faces plus family. Mia's longing for her family back in Australia required an agreement between the couple.

Mia proposed, *"If I'm leaving my family, I want to start a family."*

It was of no great surprise that soon after the visit of Michael and Penny that Mia began to feel unwell and frequently fell asleep in the car. Mia was expecting their first child. The news was met with much happiness and the usual apprehension for a new father with worries about providing for his family. For Eddie there was also the added concern that perhaps their marriage wasn't solid enough to withstand the rigours of child rearing. He also understood that family would now need to come first and that may imply a return to Australian shores and the end of his dream to settle in Israel.

As with the circle of existence, as one new life was beginning, another was nearing its end. Henry was struggling and before commencing at Hadassah in mid-August, Eddie and Mia returned to Australia to spend some quality time with him. Henry had just celebrated his 71st birthday. He was without his sons but had his wonderfully supportive partner, Erica Rosen, by his side as he threw himself his last birthday party. At the celebration Erica read to Henry a poem she had written about him. This poem concluded his memoirs when they were published in 1982.

"The Artist.

... Unsung, uncrowned in his day-to-day strife
The best artist of all – the artist of life!
To master the hardest, the art of living,
To enjoy every moment of taking and giving,
To share with your friends, to laugh and to dance -
I'll be blowed if I can do it like Hans!

...I'll be most offended and certainly vexed,
If I'm not invited next year, and the next
And the next..."

The final days spent with Henry were not as one would expect. He was no bedridden invalid. Henry was as active as always going out to the theatre and restaurants, socialising with Erica and his son for the final time. He didn't allow himself to be "sick" even if he was in a lot of distress. There were also no big goodbyes.

Back in Israel, in a white coat at Hadassah Hospital in Jerusalem, Eddie eagerly joined the overloaded hospital management team run by Professor Mann. Eddie had a collaborative and supportive relationship with the Professor, almost a father-son rapport, which was unlike any of his previous roles. Much to his frustration and despite his protestations, he was not permitted to commence work until he'd completed a six-week orientation to familiarise himself with the hospital. After Eddie's stint with the Family Medicine Program and his role at the NSW Health Commission he found this slow start extremely frustrating. One day whilst walking the corridors of Hadassah somebody asked him for directions in English. He turned around and to his surprise saw his friend, Dr Sam Perla, who had completed Medicine after Eddie. He was also a colleague from the Betar Youth Group and a friendly face on the other side of the world.

After only four weeks of orientation on the 2nd of September (his birthday) Eddie and Mia left Israel urgently. Eddie had been in frequent contact with Professor Penny, his father's treating haematologist, who advised him that his father's condition had deteriorated and he should return home. Henry was in St Vincent's Hospital, determined to stay alive until he could say goodbye to his sons and tell them that they were his greatest achievements. Henry pointed to Mia's growing belly, *"Will you name him after me?"* In Jewish religion you can't name someone after a living relative so the gifting of the name wouldn't be an issue. The baby would have Henry as its middle name.

Henry Michael Price, born as Hans Manfred Preiss, died on the 5th of September 1975.

Eddie would not return to complete his six-week orientation at Hadassah Hospital.

Chapter 7

The birth of PROMs

Eddie was now an orphan, not an abandoned child, but a young man with a mountain of responsibilities on his shoulders. His brother Michael had an established business in Hong Kong to return to so it was Eddie who took on the job of sorting out their father's small estate which took the best part of a year to complete. He also felt his paltry salary in Israel was not adequate to build the life he and Mia now desired. Living in Australia seemed like the logical way to proceed. He made plans and a promise to himself that he would work diligently to accumulate a substantial amount of money as quickly as possible and so facilitate a return to his beloved Israel. At the time new immigrants to Israel were offered considerable tax concessions but he and Mia would need to remain out of Israel for five years in order to be classified as new immigrants again. So it was that their Israeli settlement was reversed and the only parts of the "Price Establishment" to become permanent Israeli residents were Israel's first yellow Fiat 131, some Jerusalem crockery Mia had purchased meticulously in the markets in Old Jerusalem and a good deal of their clothing which was stored at Hadassah Hospital until their return.

The move back to Australia at this time also presented Eddie with another opportunity. He would have the ability to do more research to further justify his own thoughts on what quality health care was and what it took to be a "good" doctor.

They stayed with Mia's parents before moving into Henry's flat at Unit 4, 2 Oak Street, Clovelly, with a view over the picturesque Gordon's Bay. Other unit holders were very welcoming and had even named their brick wall leading to the underground garages "Price's Jericho Wall" after Henry. Apparently, in the later stages of Henry's illness, whilst driving his old and battered Valiant, he had managed to knock down the wall on three occasions. It had been repaired twice, but after the third incident it was decided to leave it until Henry had departed. All their offers to pay for repairs were declined. *"Only in Australia,"* commented Mia.

Eddie had no problem finding work as a locum on his return to Australia. The Whitlam government had just put into operation the Universal Health Insurance Bill and Medibank. This allowed all patients to be bulk-billed and full fees were now, for the first time, paid for pensioners. The public was taking advantage of this generosity and business was booming in general practices. Eddie was offered a position working in nearby Rose Bay for a good friend of Mia's parents "Uncle" Ivan Davis. Not only had the Whitlam government's health policies assured him a job but they had partially delivered the reform Eddie felt was needed through Universal Health Insurance. He acknowledged it had its flaws. It was a very expensive, disorganised system, but it was certainly beginning the journey of what he saw as a positive future for the Australian health system. This seemingly inspired vision was to be short-lived.

On the 11th of November 1975 the Australian Governor General, Sir John Kerr, dismissed the Labor Whitlam government to the shock of Eddie, Mia and Mia's parents. Eddie was outraged at this attack on democracy. The existence of the Australian democracy had given his parents a new life and, for Jews, was a bulwark against what had happened in the very sophisticated and cultured Germany. It should and could not occur again in a democracy where every citizen was to be equal. He immediately joined a group of like-minded, socialist-leaning, well-educated intellectuals that included lawyers, small business owners and doctors to assist in righting this wrong. They called themselves Citizens For Democracy (CFD). They charged themselves with restoring democracy, which in their opinion meant rectifying the wrong done to the Labor Party. Their subsequent support through the following election campaign was not unwelcome by Labor. It was not Eddie's first foray into citizen's movements. He had been a founding member in 1973 of the Doctors Reform Society. The Society promoted measures to improve health for all in a socially just and equitable way and supported a proposal for a publicly funded universal health insurance system. The Liberals, under Fraser, went on to win the election on the 13th of December 1975, which Eddie and the rest of the Citizens For Democracy saw as another major blow to democracy. With the elections over, the CFD ended and Eddie and Mia were invited to a wind-up party in Paddington. The hosting couple advised that guests were invited so that business relationships would not be affected by relationships between couples.

Eddie twigged that this was a wife-swapping party and said, *"But Mia is very pregnant."*

"All the better," was the response, *"that makes her especially appealing."*

Despite their trepidation, they attended and found that the only party unsettled by the unorthodox coupling arrangements seemed to be the hosts' dog. When the hosts were on opposite sides of the room in romantic liaisons with other partners the dog ran, barking, back and forth between both involved couples. Soon he advised the hosts that they had to leave as Mia was feeling tired and the retort was, *"Well you should be able to stay on yourself."*

He declined and accompanied Mia home. Despite their discomfort with the social implications of the CFD, their time with the group illuminates Eddie's drive and determination to stand up to a system or organisation that he sees as in the wrong, to stand in defiance for basic human rights – whether those be democratic rights or the right to the best health care system.

Ever present in his mind was his desire to make significant health care reform. After two years of intense research, including studies of both the NHS in the UK and the Israeli Cooperative Health Fund System, Eddie felt on his return to Australia that he had found a measure of what constitutes an individual's health. It was made up of four elements.

1. Restoring patients' health-related functioning.
2. Relieving their distress.
3. Prolonging their life,
4. Preventing disease and disability. He was most concerned that medicine was doing little in this area.

At the end of 1975 he attended the Australian Hospital Association Conference in Canberra at which the Commonwealth Minister for Health, Ralph Hunt, was speaking. Eddie felt compelled to give what he saw as revolutionary and common sense ideas to the Minister so that they could be implemented by the government. The Minister had just stated in his presentation that all ministers need to be like bank robbers and find the money. For Ralph Hunt the big money in the health system was in hospitals where excessive spending had to cease. Eddie was granted an audience with the Minister. Despite his protestations that measuring what really mattered in health would not only improve health care, it would save money; the Minister stared blankly, not understanding Eddie's ideas at all. This was to be the first of many rejections and disappointments. He needed more fuel to back his theories and decided to work as a GP in the heart of the health care system and apply Drucker's theory to every consultation. He determined to keep records of what each patient saw as their objectives for that consultation and what he, as the treating general practitioner, felt the objective of the consultation was.

As a locum he was already earning three times more than he would have done in Israel. He felt that owning his own practice would not only aid his research it would also enable him to accumulate money more rapidly. He originally searched for a practice in Western Sydney. Mia claimed, *"I'd rather live in Jerusalem."* Soon he stumbled across a practice for sale in the inner city suburb of Redfern. He understood immediately that with the advent of Medibank, pensioners who previously paid doctors approximately a third of the consultation fee were now full fee-paying patients. Redfern was full of pensioners and people on social security. The practice would have great potential. It was also close to the city and to Mia's parents and there was an upstairs flat where they could live. He purchased the practice and the terrace house at 100 Redfern Street, Redfern in February of 1976. They set to work to ready the terrace house for how they would like to work and live by renovating the upstairs living quarters and reconfiguring entrances and layouts. The scheduled opening day was set for the 8th of March 1976.

On the evening of the 7th of March 1976 Mia yelled, *"Something's happening!"*

"What?" asked Eddie.

"Something's come away," replied Mia.

He quickly opened his huge obstetric book that he had sparingly read as a medical student.

"It's a show. It may be a show," suggested Mia.

He asked, *"Has anything else happened?"*

Mia replied, *"Yes, I think there's some water or fluid."*

"Are you getting any contractions and pain?"

"Yes, there is a bit of pain just now," confirmed Mia.

They waited another ten minutes and there was a further contraction. He bundled Mia into his father's old beaten-up Valiant and drove cautiously to St Margaret's Private Hospital. On arrival at the Labour Ward, Mia let everyone know that if she was having a baby in the 70's she wanted to benefit from modern medical technology. She was definitely having an epidural. Whilst supporting his wife in labour and preparing himself to meet his first child, Eddie was also facing the reality that in a few short hours his first general practice was due to open its doors. A few late night calls enlisted the help of a doctor to cover any patients that may present themselves in the morning. Little sleep was had. Mia's obstetrician, Dr Bobby Diamond, came in early and said he was operating in the hospital and he would be available for the delivery when it occurred but he felt it was some time off. Contractions were becoming more frequent and Eddie was surprised when he received a call to go the nurses' station. Dr Diamond was on the line. A patient of his, post-cancer operation, had had a cardiac arrest and Dr Diamond was asking him to assist. He raced down.

Dr Diamond said, *"This is not my area."*

Four simple instructions raced through Eddie's head from his training....ABCD. Bang on the chest, open the **A**irway, start **B**reathing, start **C**ompression and then administer appropriate **D**rugs. He followed this routine while Dr Diamond took a back seat.

Within 15 minutes there was a pulse again. Dr Diamond went back into the operating theatre and Eddie went back to sit by Mia's bedside. At 12:30 on the 8th of March 1976, without a hitch and with much joy, Tull Henry Price arrived into the world.

The euphoria of childbirth continued as Eddie rushed back to his practice later that afternoon and enthusiastically ordered champagne and cigars for the staff and those in the waiting room. It didn't take long for word to spread 100m down the street to the Redfern pub, *"Free champagne and cigars down at the doctors!"* The bar clientele moved down en masse. Eddie's practice did not look back from that day on and Tull had his first marketing coup at three hours old. Sadly, the patient Eddie had helped resuscitate only survived a further two days.

Having his new business with a young family was gruelling. He insisted on keeping the doors open from 7:00am to 9:00pm and Saturday and Sunday to 1:00pm. Having the autonomy of his own practice enabled Eddie the opportunity to keep meticulous records on each of his patients and as such carry out research on his theory that there were four objectives of health care: Prolonging Life, Restoring Function, Relieving Distress and Preventing Disease and Disability. The importance of record keeping was realised through his studies of Peter Drucker's Management Theory. That showed that you must have an objective, you need to set a target and know the outcome you want, and then this outcome needs to be measurable in quantity and time in order to determine whether or not you have been able to successfully achieve your goals. Drucker also explained that if you don't currently know your objective then you need to analyse what you are doing day-to-day. The objectives should present themselves. He kept handwritten notes on every patient that he saw including the patient's aim or objective of that particular consultation, the doctor's aim, (i.e. Eddie's aim on behalf of the patient), and then he would work out what percentage of patients were seeking which of the four objectives of health care. Shortly into this research he realised that 58% of what he did was trying to restore people's functioning, i.e. improving their health-related quality of life and another 30% was to offer reassurance and relieving distress, i.e. to be a carer, offering real health CARE. He continued his research on his own with no backing of a university or organisation. He managed to compile records of 5,000 consultations in only one year. After four years those numbers were 20,000 and all of the results supported his original findings.

It was at this point that he had an epiphany. The effectiveness of medical care was traditionally measured by death rates and life expectancies and yet 88% of the health work Eddie was doing wasn't able to be categorised in these terms. Giving reassurance or improving someone's quality of life through increased function doesn't fit in with statistics of life expectancies or death rates. He had exposed a great deficiency. He'd caught the medical "emperor without his clothes on". Eighty-eight percent (88%) of a GPs work was NOT being measured. If something is not measured, how can one tell if it needs improvement or which forms of treatment are more beneficial? What Eddie recognised was that the measurement of functional ability or quality of life was not as simple or classically scientific as tallying the numbers of those departing our world. He came up with an effective, but not psychometrically validated, means of measuring the parameters of the 88% that was currently seen as subjective and perhaps, in some eyes, not even the role of a medical practitioner. Most importantly, he felt that what he had proven over many years to be the most effective form of treatment, health promotion or prevention, was not being prescribed by thousands of treating doctors, both GPs and specialists. Finally, he decided that the power of modern management had failed in the health care industry as there was a dichotomy between two of the goals, that of caring (relieving distress) and that of preventing disease and disability. For him all of these systems needed changing. His research suggested to him that "Lifestyle Prescriptions", together with other preventive techniques, like immunisations, should make up 20% of what GPs do, with restoring function at 40%, caring at 30% and prolonging life at 10%.

After much research Eddie found that the parameters of health care could be measured using questionnaires that focused on a patient's functional health status. Importantly, they could be scored using a highly structured and proven system of patient questioning, labelled Patient Reported Outcome Measures (PROMs). PROMs could accurately and reliably measure a patient's progress to total well-being. Eddie believed that using PROMs would be the catalyst to help restore patients in the quickest time possible to their best quality of life. It was fortunate timing for Eddie that computers had started to play more significant roles in everyday business at this time. He saw what a beneficial tool they would be in conducting and measuring questionnaires quickly and efficiently.

From 1st of October 1976, less than six months after Eddie opened his practice, the Fraser government privatised Medibank which meant that some bills had to be billed to the patient. Eddie didn't have a good billing system. His brother Michael and his partners at CPS had excellent accounting systems that were computerised. Eddie saw an opportunity to develop a computerised billing system that would also act as the first step towards computerisation of the health outcomes he was desperately wanting to measure. He commissioned Michael's partners' software developers to write accounting programs for doctors' billing of their private patients. He set up the company Computerised Medical Systems Pty Ltd (CMS) with the long term plan of using this knowledge to help computerise "health outcomes". This would later be called PROMs (Patient Reported Outcome Measures). At great expense the initial doctors' billing program was established and ten clients found. Mia and her friends were recruited to do a lot of the time-consuming data entry work. However, CMS was haemorrhaging money and the plug was pulled on this project after ten months. His first foray into building his wealth had not ended well. Losing money was not part of Eddie's plan. He wanted to make money, and fast. Not one to be put off by a small set back, he continued with his busy practice continually flexing his entrepreneurial muscles into a number of, what he saw, as promising ventures.

On Redfern Street Eddie and Mia were being woken daily at 6am by patients rather than by their infant son. Unsurprisingly Mia suggested they move out. Their new abode was 25 Lawson St Bondi. The move gave an opportunity for Eddie to rent out the space above his practise. As the building was close to Royal Prince Alfred hospital it was the ideal location for young specialists to rent the rooms for their private patient consultations. Soon there were doctors offering internal medicine, endocrinology and dermatology. One robust young obstetrician and gynaecologist was Dr Richard Reid. Richard was a larger-than-life character and an innovative and lateral thinker. He had an idea that appealed to Eddie's problem-solving psyche as well as to his inner investor. Richard had been using a CO_2 laser at Royal Prince Alfred Hospital to assist in treating abnormal pap smears by removing lesions and it was highly successful. He suggested that this could also be used to remove tattoos. Eddie remembered the 'Sharplan' laser (also known as a CO_2 laser) from his time in Israel that was used for treating skin conditions. After detailed research Richard and Eddie proposed that if the laser were used in conjunction with a Zeiss microscope that was used in microsurgery and, if the surgeon didn't go below the root of the hair follicle layer, then this technology could remove tattoos without scarring. A specialist surgeon was included to oversee the project and a CO_2 laser tattoo removal practice was opened in the upstairs rooms at Redfern that also housed the specialists. Although the laser practice grew rapidly, the doctors were all of the opinion that this may initially be better done at a hospital so the laser surgeon and the laser were moved to a private hospital in Kogarah. Shortly thereafter, Medibank ruled this service ineligible for a rebate; it being "cosmetic surgery". Many of the cheques the practice accepted from patients for treatments began bouncing so the policy changed to cash up-front only. Despite publishing a paper on their research in the Journal of Plastic and Reconstructive Surgery, the practice only limped along and was eventually incorporated as part of the specialist surgeon's own practice.

After another less-than-fruitful investment Eddie decided to take the sage advice of his accountant, *"Eddie, any spare dollar you have should be invested in real estate."*

He invested extremely well in small terrace houses in the Redfern/Alexandria area and accumulated a significant portfolio of around twenty properties.

One gleans from these early endeavours trialled by Eddie to support his family and their dreams, that he would not be discouraged by the collapse of a venture or denial of an idea. He would bounce back and be eager to launch himself and his finances into the next big opportunity to present itself. This determined character trait would serve him well throughout his life. He was knocked back time and time again as he strived to illustrate to the medical world what he believed to be his great ideas that he knew could revolutionise health care. Sadly, it also seems this open enthusiasm and, perhaps, naïve trust that the general populace desired to "do good", made for a recurring theme where individuals were attracted who aimed to take advantage of his finances and his ideas.

Ideas. Ideas. So many ideas. Eddie needed an outlet to show the world what had been whirling around in his head for so long. How could he educate the masses and start his medical revolution? He'd been inspired by his father's memoirs, yet to be published, and decided he too should write a book. The meticulous notes he'd been taking of his own patients in order to substantiate his ideas formed the basis of his book. Its final chapters were to be solutions, remedies, and what needed to be done to improve the health of each individual patient and the nation as a whole. The book's publication would surely help improve many people's health and reform the system. Between patients he started to write his book in one of the upstairs offices. As he was writing his first case studies Mia advised she was pregnant again and the baby would be due in July of 1979. At a time in his life when most would feel overwhelmed, between running a busy doctors' surgery, writing a book and being a father of almost two, he began studying Arabic at Macquarie University. A high number of his patients were Lebanese and he felt that he would be able to fulfil a much more caring role if he knew a few words in their language and could bond further with them. With a possible return to Israel always present in his decision-making, he knew Arabic would also be very useful for any future work there. He was also dabbling in some of his theories about how health practitioners (GPs) should be advocating and educating patients about healthy living and lifestyle choices, rather than just prescribing drugs. He would take some patients for walks and established a few educational groups to teach people preventative measures that could be taken. Generally speaking, these sessions were more farcical than fantastic but it was an opportunity for Eddie to trial his theories on the public.

Josh Remi Price was born to great celebration on the 23rd of July 1979, a brother for Tull. Eddie, now experienced, delayed driving Mia to hospital until well into labour. Mia missed out on her epidural but she was pleased she'd avoided the baby having to share her birthday, four days earlier.

Along with his family, business at the practice was also expanding and Eddie required an assistant. Consistent with his open persona and desire to help others he befriended an old acquaintance, Dr Igo Fisher, whom he had first played rugby against when playing for Sydney Hospital. Igo had gone on to play rugby for Australia and for the renowned Randwick Rugby Union Club but had had some hard emotional times. Eddie was drawn to Igo's quiet, caring nature and saw this as a wonderful trait to have for his patients. He also wanted to help Igo personally. Igo's nature was a magnet for clients and the practice grew even more rapidly. Sadly, Igo's rugby career had stalled and his anxiety and depression worsened. He would need to seek small episodes away from the practice for treatment.

Whilst balancing his own frustrations of the health system and his wife's desire to live in Australia with his own conviction that they must live in Israel, Eddie questioned his life and his place in the working world.

He wrote down these thoughts on the 7th of April, 1980. *"I am a doctor in general practice... however, I don't feel that would be an apt description of what I, in fact, was trained to do, planned to do or wanted to do. So why is it that I, who have had all the opportunities I would think in the world particularly, compared with my father's life where there were opportunities, denied. .... I'm not in the work that I really want to do. I feel a bit like Woody Allen in 'Manhattan'."*

It was almost five years since he and Mia had returned from Israel. Their five-year plan to go back there to take advantage of tax concessions for returning immigrants was dashed when Israel changed the law. After protests from the Israeli citizens the taxation rights were no longer applicable. Despite not being as financially lucrative as before the desire to return to Israel was still great for Eddie. His prospering business and property portfolio would ensure a comfortable life for him and his family once relocated. Before making the big move again, Mia wanted more physical security in

Australia with a new home that catered for their young boys with a larger backyard. This was something she felt every Aussie kid should have. They purchased 60 Queens Park Road, Queens Park, on the proviso that it would not interfere with their move to Israel. This large and beautiful home in such a desirable location would also be a great rental once they were in Israel for the now experienced landlord. It was the biggest property in his portfolio. The move to Queens Park in July of 1980 will be forever remembered as the time when the avid sports fans watched with great interest the Moscow Olympics in defiance of the partial Australian boycott. Eddie's plan was not to become ensconced in this Federation home. Despite Mia's earlier agreement that they would return to Israel, when the time came for Eddie to talk specifically to her about the move she stormed out of the room. Regardless of his wife's great desire to remain in Australia and be near her family, he insisted they go. He orchestrated with friends Betty and Edju for Tull to be enrolled in a kindergarten and for a home in the salubrious suburb of Herzliya Pituah, next to Herzliya Beach, to be rented in anticipation of their arrival.

To maintain some income whilst in Israel and also enable Dr Igo Fischer to work on in the practice, Eddie decided to find a partner to buy 50% of his business. He located another party and signed contracts but Eddie's practice manager and other staff expressed concerns that the other practitioner would very likely cease Igo's employment due to his personal struggles. Realising this would probably be the case, Eddie paid to break the contact and maintained 100% ownership of the business and continued Igo's employment. He hired Dr Sanger to be his replacement GP and left his very organised and efficient bookkeeper managing the practice and his property portfolio.

In November 1980, the Price family left for Israel.

Chapter 8

Homeland

"*Eddie!*" an excited Mia yelled, "*This is the one I organised. See this!*" Mia showed him her purchase. It was a black box measuring approximately 35 x 35cm and weighing 12 kilograms with an arm strap and an electric cord attached to a rather bulky video camera.

"*This is the new video camera! And you see those two boxes over there? They're video playback systems, one for us and one for Mummy and Daddy. Now we can make movies of the kids in Israel and we can send copies to Mummy and Daddy so they can see the kids as they grow up!*"

He eyed the new equipment rather suspiciously and despondently. He quite rightly presumed that his new career as a cameraman was not something for which he was entirely well suited. The multiple videos of the passing ground confirmed his reservations. Years later he would curse this machine when he was physically racked with muscle damage, and its referred pain, from years of traipsing around the Israeli countryside documenting his family's adventures. This mechanical addition to their Israeli lives was another way to placate Mia's concerns about living so far from her parents. Mia was tormented by her own love of Israel and the emotional guilt at having abandoned Sam and Esther (now known to their grandchildren as Zeida and Booba) who had been orphaned through the Holocaust.

She insisted, "*We've got to minimise their losing a second family after they lost their first. The arrangement is that Zeida will come for Tull's birthday and Booba will come for Josh's birthday. Of course, we will ring weekly as well.*"

Eddie also ensured they would have a home with a yard close to her dear friend Betty and they would have outings together. They moved into a house off a street known as Itzak Mangar in the picturesque neighbourhood of Herzliya Pituah. They were living well beyond their means but Eddie wanted Mia to love life in Israel.

He searched for a job nearby. To follow his own convictions and principles he wanted to immerse himself in community medicine away from the hospitals that he referred to as the "temples of science". Working in health administration in the emerging nation of Israel was where he could impart all his experience and knowledge. He saw his ground-breaking theories could make a mark on the health of the entire country. To Eddie's delight one of the several interviews he attended was for a position at the local health district of Clalit, the biggest health maintenance organisation. His interviewer was none other than their regional director Dr Spearman. Dr Spearman had interviewed him five years earlier in Beer Sheva where they had discussed their shared beliefs of how health services should be run in a community based context. The two reignited their mutual admiration and Eddie immediately joined the region's medical administrative staff. With Dr Spearman there was no six-week orientation program. It was into work immediately. Initially Eddie was commissioned to do some clinical GP work helping him understand the system and to be a local back-up should one of the many primary care physicians become ill. Eddie was allocated relieving sessions in three different communities: an old established kibbutz 'Glalil Yam' that had been taken over by the city's Tel Aviv development, a local Arab village, and a small settlement just the other side of the 1967 border where the

West Bank took a huge bite out of the waist of Israel. They were three entirely different populations – the first, the oldest, and the last, the youngest. At the middle one he had to balance relationships with the Arabs who, in Eddie's experience, were, at least at that time, rather carefree and disinterested in political activity and more concerned with their health and that of their families.

He moved around the region from clinic to clinic, meeting the practice managers and primary care physicians, noting an extremely dedicated small percentage were using paper-based recordings to gather research data on their patients. From these records they could see the diagnoses and the main reason for visits. They were measuring processes and these results were being correlated by Dr Aviva Ron at the Head Office R&D department. Eddie was delighted to see "process outcomes" already being measured. Together with Dr Spearman and Dr Ron he organised to have all doctors at two or three large primary health clinics completing these forms. Dr Ron's department was able to have the data entered onto computers and then produced population-related data on bulky old computer paper printouts. Eddie took advantage of Dr Spearman's excitement for population analysis and suggested they introduce the concept of Management by Objectives and also the idea of using a patient-reported outcome comprehensive measure that he had devised. Eddie could implement this into one clinic only, as a pilot project, and he would process the results with Dr Ron. Dr Spearman also endorsed the idea of having Eddie teach the medical directors and the practice managers of each of the major clinics Management by Objectives. This was a crucial breakthrough in the development of Eddie's ideas. He had created a questionnaire that was scored but up until now he had not been able to test it out on a patient body. Israel was giving him that opportunity.

To help in the effective communication of his ideas to the clinics he enlisted the help of one of Dr Spearman's executive assistants, Raquel, who spoke five languages. Raquel translated into Hebrew Eddie's "Comprehensive PROM" - a Comprehensive Health Index (CHI) that Eddie had created as well as his Management by Objectives course that he planned to present to the medical directors. He personally administered the first comprehensive PROM (CHI) covering the four areas of an individual's health: Quality of Life, Quantity of Life, Cared-For Status and Preventive Health to one hundred patients over sixteen years of age. Finally, he was putting his process ideas into practice.

Raquel also proved invaluable with assisting Eddie to compose a report to the Israeli Parliament that offered his – unsolicited – comments on what he saw as the strengths and weaknesses of a new National Health Act that he deemed was moving in the right direction. Such was his conviction that he had much to offer in the interests of public health that he felt little inhibition in expressing his opinions and ideas to those in power. It was to be a recurring theme in Eddie's quest to be heard throughout the years. Despite his attempts to gain an audience with the Israeli Health Minister to present his report, no appointment was made available. Instead he tried his luck with the Shadow Health Minister, Haika Grossman, and received an immediate appointment. Raquel, in her small yellow Renault, drove him to his meeting. Whilst the car putted up the major hills leading to the Israeli Parliament, the Knesset in Jerusalem, Raquel instructed on his Hebrew pronunciation. *"'Objective' is 'Ya-ad' not 'Yad', Eddie!"* A more informed Eddie alighted from the car and excitedly entered the Knesset. It was a great moment and a great honour for this Lebanon-born, Aussie-bred young doctor who felt his real home was here in the Jewish motherland. His euphoric bubble would soon deflate. It became evident that Grossman had little interest or understanding in his proposals. The only consolation to his disappointment was a chance encounter as he exited Grossman's office. *"Sholom"*. *"Sholom"*. A firm hand was plunged into Eddie's and then four bulky bodyguards manoeuvred Menachem Begin, the Israeli Prime Minister, on his way. It was an excited Eddie that curled himself back into Raquel's petite yellow car.

"How did it go?" She excitedly enquired on seeing the smile spread across his face.

"It was wonderful. I got to shake his hand. Begin was my idol you know when I was a young Betari!"

A bewildered Raquel further enquired, *"But how did the presentation go?"*

He replied, *"Oh that? Oh, no good. There was little understanding."*

What one should do with his disappointment? He decided that the new Act was at least moving in the right direction and although he saw many pitfalls he would send his thoughts in a telegram to the Minister of Health. With Eddie's guidance and Raquel's assistance, they worded a short telegram which he decided to sign "Dr Eddie Price from Clalit." Clalit - one little word, but it was to cause much drama.

There was an uncomfortable silence as Eddie entered the regional health head office two days later. All eyes were on him and the most enraged eyes were those of Dr Spearman. After careful enquiry, Eddie discovered that the Minister for

Health in the Israeli parliament had held up Eddie's telegram in front of the opposition and workers' union saying that Clalit (a left-leaning organisation on the "other side" of politics to the government) agreed with the new Health Act that the opposition was strenuously opposing. He recognised his faux pas and requested to speak with Dr Spearman.

"*I may have made a mistake. I'm sorry I sent this telegram,*" said Eddie.

Dr Spearman spat back, "*As a private citizen you can do whatever you like. Sign it as Dr Eddie Price, but not as part of Clalit. That's not your authority. You've created great embarrassment and issues for Professor Chaim Doron, the head of Clalit who had to deny that Clalit supported this legislation.*" Eddie's name was now well-known at Head Office. His endeavours were eventually put down to "over-enthusiasm from a young and caring doctor", a generous outcome for which Eddie presumed he had to thank Dr Spearman. Despite the drama that had been caused he was not unhappy that his name had been mentioned in the Israeli parliament.

Whilst professionally Eddie felt he was in a supportive environment that embraced his philosophies on how health care could be conducted, and where he could have a significant impact, so too was his home life equally enriching. He was a lighter character as he strode the streets of Israel, almost euphoric in his existence and his family's found happiness. Fridays and Saturdays were spent with their friends Edju and Betty and Eric and Myrna and all the children. The colourful party were loaded into Edju's "magic" yellow kombi van as they explored Israel....Eddie schlepping his 12-kilogram video recorder and Tull schlepping Luke Skywalker on a string over various ruins and through the old Crusader castle of Caesarea, over 3,000-year-old floors of an ancient synagogue. Australian-style picnics were had in all these historic places including the Gan Hashlosha. This beautiful and lush parkland was often referred to as "The Garden of Eden". It is cradled between two kibbutzim and fed by natural hot spring waters that gush over an old water-powered mill. The garden's name translates to "The Garden of Three" and is in commemoration of three Israeli pioneers who were exploring the area and were killed by land mines in 1938. Eddie felt much pride and joy watching his young boys play in the dirt of areas that held such importance to their Jewish heritage. From one week to the next they would mingle with the Jewish ghosts of modern history and those of ancient times.

In the hot summer months the expeditions were abandoned in favour of frolicking in the pool of the local country club, Dan Accadia Hotel in Herzliya Pituah, which overlooked the picturesque Herzliya Beach with its refreshing sea breezes. The Australian trained Tull and Josh, aged five and two, delighted fellow hotel guests with their swimming proficiency and abilities on the pool's diving board. Once a week the children were also entertained with an evening movie in the same room that was converted to a synagogue on Yom Kippur – the Jewish fast day. It was on one such day that the whole congregation heard Josh cry out, "*Mamma Mia, I don't like this movie!*"

Bringing much happiness and injecting excitement into their Israeli lives was the stream of visitors that they entertained from Australia, none more so than Mia's father Sam. Tull was skipping with excitement as they entered Ben Gurion Airport to await the arrival of his Zeida (grandfather) who was coming to help celebrate his fifth birthday. Tull spotted Sam through the glass before he came through immigration and he called out, *"Do I look nice to you? Cause you sure look nice to me!"*

Living in Israel also gave the Price family the opportunity to connect with broader family members. Gary (now Gershon) Price had migrated to Israel from Australia in 1949 and settled in Kibbutz Ein Dor. Unfortunately, whilst guarding and helping to clean up the swamps in the north of Israel, Gary had contracted polio which saw him hospitalised and left with a limp for life. He had gone on to become a music therapist and, in Price tradition, wrote a book in Hebrew on music therapy. His children, Eliav and Avidan, continue his tradition of the kibbutz life today. One afternoon when Mia and Betty were at home playing Scrabble they had a surprise drop-in visit from Heinz Leibrecht. Heinz, whom Eddie's father described in his book as his "spoilt cousin", lived nearby and had decided to pop in. Mia answered the door and after brief introductions explained that they had one more move to go in their game of Scrabble and asked Heinz if he would mind. At this Heinz stood up and stated, *"Although I have lived in Israel for a long time, I have never met such rude people,"* and went to walk out just as Eddie was approaching the front door. Heinz, at a brisk pace, walked down the street with Eddie trailing, apologising for his wife's behaviour. At that moment the dog across the road that belonged to the daughter of Flato Sharon took umbrage at Heinz's quick walk and attempted to bite Heinz on the leg, tearing his trousers. (Flato Sharon was an Israeli member of parliament who left France to escape some debts and gained immunity by getting himself voted into the Israeli parliament.) Eddie explained the dog's ownership at which Heinz retorted, *"The apple doesn't fall far from the tree."* He could not be placated. Eddie explained to Mia that they would have to invite him over for a good steak dinner to make amends.

Back at work Eddie continued with his management consulting role. He was pushing for all the Clalit's Sharon region to measure what are now known as Patient-Reported Outcomes or the Patient's Functional Health Status and having reports done with Dr Aviva Ron. As agreed, Eddie invited the medical directors and practice managers from the 16 clinics in the region to a training program that he would run on "Management by Health Outcomes". Prior to the training program, Mia presented with an abnormal pap smear and the Friday before Eddie was due to run his Sunday course she underwent a cone biopsy at Assuta Private Hospital. Mia's gynaecologist told her to *"expect a good deal of bleeding".* Ever the entertainers and generous hosts, the next day they had a house guest, another Australian resident of Jerusalem, Ilona Hahn. Ilona was an actress who Mia and Eddie referred to as "The Voice of Israel". One of her jobs was to read the English news on the Israeli radio entitled The Voice of Israel. Eddie took advantage of his guest's talents and practiced his Hebrew presentation with Ilona, who herself had limited Hebrew. She advised him on how to undulate the pitches of his voice. At one point in the evening Mia complained she was bleeding a little and being one-day post-operation was summarily advised to elevate her legs by Ilona and Eddie and to concentrate on the task at hand. The voice lessons continued. According to Eddie the scene could have been out of One Flew over the Cuckoo's Nest. Late that night Mia woke him. *"Eddie! I'm passing clots. I'm losing a lot of blood!"*

He took her pulse and went into a panic. With a pulse rate

of 120 she was sweating and becoming pale. He immediately rang Dr Ross, the gynaecologist, *"A stitch must have come undone. Get her to hospital immediately!"* he instructed.

At the hospital they reported that Mia's haemoglobin was 7g/L. She was significantly anaemic and was raced into theatre to replace the stitch and be given two bags of blood. Mia, aware of the gravity of the situation, made Eddie promise that if anything happened to her that he would return with the children to Australia to be with her parents. The surgeon apologised to Mia. He would never again advise somebody that there may just be *"a good deal of bleeding"* as this had been a very serious situation. Mia recovered but it was already late Sunday morning and thirty people had gathered for Eddie's training course. Dr Spearman's secretaries were frantically ringing him and he arrived late to face a crowd of annoyed medical directors and practice managers. His lack of sleep, the delayed start, the foreign nature of the subject matter to his audience and his broken Hebrew (despite his honed pitch, tone and undulations) conspired against a successful presentation – nevertheless, it was delivered.

Soon after he began working with Dr Silverberg, originally from Canada, who was Clalit's Director of National Clinical Projects at Head Office. This involved a nationwide hypertension control program with the up-skilling of GP practice nurses to monitor GPs' patients on a monthly basis to ensure their blood pressure was controlled. To his surprise Dr Karnovich in Clalit's Head Office offered him a job. Although Dr Karnovich ran Human Resources which was not an area of particular interest to Eddie, the position was at Head Office of Clalit, the biggest Health Maintenance Organisation in Israel. He saw that working at Head Office would be his opportunity to have significant influence over policy. He agreed to work there two days a week and continue his work with Dr Spearman on the other three days so that he might be able to introduce the management changes at Head Office as well as in the Sharon region. This was an ideal opportunity to influence both.

Whilst his work in Israel was going from strength to strength, Eddie was still juggling issues with his practice back in Redfern. Dr Igo Fischer was working alongside Dr Sanger. Eddie's staff called to inform him that Sanger was setting up his own practice down the road in Botany and was shifting patients over. Eddie had to get rid of him, and fast. Igo found another doctor, Dr Adrian Jones, to fill the void. Dr Jones was a first grade rugby union Randwick colleague of Igo's who had also captained Eastwood. The two of them appeared to work cohesively, but sadly, during Eddie's second year in Israel, Igo succumbed to his mental health issues and took his own life.

On the 6th of October 1981 a bullet ripped through Anwar Sadat, the President of Egypt, and Israel's best and dearest Arab neighbour and friend. The shockwaves ricocheted around the Jewish nation. The fanatics of his own country (The Egyptian Islamic Jihad) who had assassinated him felt betrayed by the peace deal he had established with Israel. The echo of fractured peace resounded through the Price household too. Mia and Eddie's relationship had become extremely strained. Mia was homesick and longed for her children to spend quality time with her parents. The pull between her love of Israel and Eddie and that of her devotion to her parents and her guilt at taking away their precious family was too great. However, Eddie was devoted to his career trajectory in Israel. For the next three Israeli winters

Mia took Tull and Josh back to Australia for a three-month period. The time spent apart took its toll on Eddie and Mia's relationship.

With his family away for the winter he filled his weekends with his beloved sport. He joined a small rugby union competition (pronounced "*roogby*") as part of the Tel Aviv University team, known as Tel Aviv Maccabi. He was (at thirty-five) one of the oldest but he knew how to tackle. There were a few other expat players from New Zealand, England and South Africa. The majority of the team were Israelis who were gutsy (some say, mad) players with no knowledge of the fundamentals of the game. The team travelled by bus to all parts of Israel. They were journeys full of sing-a-longs and spirited fun. One memorable match was held at the Hebrew University of Jerusalem against the Fijian United Nations troops who were stationed on the various borders. The size difference was as amazing as their skill set. Eddie thought, "*This is David vs Goliath again,*" but on this occasion Goliath won. Rather fittingly, it was his love of playing sport that produced a rather poignant moment for Eddie and set him on his trajectory of viewing the human body as more than a mere biomedical machine. He noticed the bruises on his body following a rugby match were getting larger and larger with every game. Then, following hair transplant surgery, he failed to stop bleeding from one of the hair follicles. He was diagnosed with "increased fibrinolysis", a process that prevents natural clotting of the blood. The only cause that could be attributed to his sudden acquisition of the condition was the stress surrounding his family situation. The diagnosis ended his rugby days but it opened his eyes to the impact ones' psychology can have on one physically.

In March of 1982 he returned to Australia to see Mia and the kids and took the opportunity to launch his father's life story The Doctor Who Dared. Henry had been meticulously writing his memoirs when he died and Eddie had commissioned author Joan Clarke to finish the manuscript. The book was to be launched by an aspiring politician and new parliamentarian and a good friend of Eddie's father-in-law Sam, Mr Bob Hawke. The Hakoah Club book launch was a fascinating event. Two hundred and fifty people from all areas of Dr Henry Price's life attended.

"Mr Hawke if you don't mind, I'd be most grateful of a signature in my copy of the book. My name is Mary Shijewski. I was Dr Price's secretary in Wollongong."

Mary proffered him the book. *"I'd be happy to Ms Shijewski, or should I say 'stupid goose'."*

Mr Hawke had only three hours in which to read the book himself yet he was correctly referring to what Henry Price had always called Mary - 'bleude gans' or 'stupid goose' in German.

He signed, *"To the stupid goose"*.

Eddie was suitably impressed by the intellect, recognition and recollection of this young "pollie". The book made the top ten bestsellers for one week and its success inspired him.

"It's not that difficult to write a book," he thought, especially now that he had records on twenty thousand consultations to corroborate his findings. The basis of his first book was complete. It also appeared his time living and working in Israel had also ended. Mia wanted a permanent return to Australia and Eddie acknowledged that family was more important than following his career goals so the decision was made to return. Mia and the children left first, in November of 1982, and he followed some months later in

March of 1983. Eddie's dreams of a life in Israel and a career in sculpting a true health system in the Jewish homeland....were over.

Chapter 9

Is Medicine Really Necessary?

Doctors and dignitaries dressed in their finery, gathered in a small, beautiful old sandstone convict jail perched on top of a hill at the centre of Cockatoo Island. The cool evening air carried the sounds of merriment and idle laughs scattering across Sydney harbour to melt into the hum of the busy city. Eddie hoped that the contents of his book, the lines of words that carried the burden of his dreams, would similarly ripple through and be absorbed into the fabric of society, taken up as an algorithm to revolutionise the way medicine is practised in Australia, in Israel, and indeed, around the world.

His occupational health client, Cockatoo Dockyard Management, had agreed to let him launch his book in their grounds and was ferrying guests across from the mainland in fifteen minute intervals. Sam Fiszman, Mia's father, had organised for the Deputy Premier and Minister for Health in NSW, the Hon. R J Mulock, to launch the book Is Medicine Really Necessary? Eddie believed that the book, written about patient anecdotes taken from his experiences as a GP and a health administrator, might be a vehicle to rally health reformers to his cause. He proposed to change the way General Practitioners, and the health system as a whole, treated patients and illness and to look at what he claimed was the most proven form of treatment that doctors were ignoring – Prevention.

In his book Eddie stated that the current medical system was out of date. He suggested that rather than being absorbed with extending someone's life, a more humane system would focus on quality of life and a patient's overall well-being. He called for a revolutionary change of direction. Redefine health as a sense of physical, psychological and social well-being and having the ability to function without undue pain or anxiety and with confidence that comfort would be available in times of distress for a natural life-span. He also outlined his concerns that nothing was being measured. He suggested that by using modern management techniques the health system could be accurately assessed as to its ability to improve a patient's quality of life. The three management functions he outlined were:

- Planning and setting the objectives - of which he found four different types of health outcomes.

- Organising - What processes were needed in order to meet the health objectives or the goals of a health service?

- Controlling - How were the processes measured?

Eddie pointed out that the current measurements were "faulty criteria" and that true measurements could only be obtained through a quantified questionnaire that measured a patient's health status, now called a Patient's Reported Outcome Measurements (PROMs). Once the questionnaire was completed a patient was given a score on all four components of their health that made up a patient's Comprehensive Health Index (CHI).

The most radical thing about Eddie's book and ideas was the central question he was asking - Was Medicine Really Necessary? He suggested that the current (1985) process of treating the sick was THE major error in the health system. He proposed a rather revolutionary approach, to apply what he saw as the most proven form of health care – to prevent ailments in the first place. He proposed that this would radically improve the health of nations and would save governments and health insurers billions of dollars. He claimed that health promotion and preventive health services were essentially provided by government health departments and provided generally to groups of patients. He felt this approach was flawed and suggested these services ought to be provided by individual doctors and providers to individuals and groups of patients. He felt that preventing illness, not by using early detection methods like mammograms and colonoscopies which did play a role, but by changing people's behavioural habits, environments and diets – called Lifestyle Scripts, was when the system would have the most impact. In 1985 this was only happening, at the most, in 2% of health care services when it should be 20%. According to Eddie, the wrong organisations were providing the right services to the wrong groups. He claimed that the use of health outcomes (PROMs) would be the catalyst to achieve this breakthrough or change. He likened himself to the boy in the Emperor's New Clothes who was the only one to point out that the Emperor was indeed naked. Was he the only one who could see that the medical system was not a HEALTH and CARE system but a disease system? He wanted to offer what he considered "a new set of clothes" - health reform – for real healthcare. The paradigm by which Eddie claimed the health system was currently, and in his eyes wrongly, based was on the biomedical model. It is essentially treating the human body like a car where if anything mechanical breaks then the doctor repairs it, but if it's anything out of the physical realm, if it becomes metaphysical, then it is no longer a concern of the medical practitioner. He wanted the new paradigm to be a holistic approach.

The evening of July 30 1985 was a resounding

success....for the book launch event manager and the PR company. There were multiple articles in the press and many radio interviews. Eddie was particularly pleased to be featured in The Sunday Herald "Quotes of the week" in the same column as Bob Dylan.

Eddie's statement was, *"Some good work is being done in teaching medical skills and prevention at medical school. Unfortunately, all the good work is undone when the students go to teaching hospitals and see how things are in the real world."*

Bob Dylan was quoted, *"I'm someone who's never worked for a living."*

Eddie mused that he rather felt the same as Dylan as he thoroughly enjoyed his work as well.

Dr Lyn Barrow's stated that, *"Dr Price writes with a kind of humility which makes the reader want more of him. I'm certain that we haven't heard the last of Eddie Price."*

He was interviewed on all the major radio stations including Norman Swan at the ABC and Alan Jones at 2UE. The only one of those that interviewed him and who seemed to have read the book from beginning to end and understood it, was surprisingly, Alan Jones. The real success for Eddie would come with the impact of the book to change or to reform healthcare....but this was underwhelming to say the least. He felt that his ideas could, should and would change the health systems of the world to the extent that he was slightly surprised when his invitation to an esteemed event in Stockholm never arrived. Despite no Nobel Prize, the ever passionate Eddie persevered.

Now he'd returned to Australia he no longer wished to work in a system that wasn't addressing what he saw as the basic medical needs of the community. He wanted to work in prevention. Occupational Medicine was an area where he knew companies would invest in to avoid payouts of worker's compensation. He bought an Occupational Medical Practice. Here he had great job satisfaction and a real sense of impacting the health of many when his guidance led to multiple health gains. Of personal pride to Eddie was his involvement in pointing out, to a number of his clients, that the use of asbestos in some of their products was no longer acceptable. He explained that not only should they refrain for ethical reasons but that it could cost them greatly in the long run through health claims. A change to healthier materials was a costly shift for some of the company's processes and they needed a great deal of convincing. He was satisfied when one of several companies, Transfield, ceased using asbestos products based on his advice. He was also pleased to be out on site at the Transfield factory in western Sydney when Pope John Paul came to bless the workers in 1986. The company belonged to two Italian Catholic immigrant partners, Carlo Salteri and Franco Belgiornio-Nettis, dynamic and ebullient characters. Eddie was not only honoured to be together with the other workers, blessed by the Pope, but the Pope was wearing a hard hat as an example to the workers on Eddie's advice.

He muttered to himself, *"Not bad! I never thought I'd be responsible for putting a hat on the Pope!"*

However not all his prevention campaigns gained traction. In one consultation with the union representative for one of his clients, The Cockatoo Dockyards, Eddie tried to push a particular prevention strategy, *"You know we would really do a lot better if we could run a non-smoking campaign and get all your workers involved because, when it comes to cancer, smoking is worse than asbestos in numbers,"* implored

Eddie.

"Doc, if smoking gets you that's suicide, but if asbestos gets you, that's murder," responded the union rep.

Now ensconced in his new and thriving business and acknowledging that Dr Adrian Jones was doing the majority of the work in the Redfern GP practice, Eddie decided to let go of his share in the business he had owned or co-owned for ten years. He was letting go of one asset but he still had his extensive property portfolio and interest rates were skyrocketing. Eddie was enchanted by the lure of Swiss Franc Loan advertisements that boasted of only 6% or 5% interest rates. The opportunity seemed like an obvious investment. His accountant advised otherwise. Eddie ignored this advice and took out a Swiss Franc loan to cover all the mortgages on all the houses in his portfolio. No sooner had he taken out the loans then the Australian dollar started to plummet and he was losing vast amounts of money fast. He had to keep topping up the loans. The only way to fund the loans was to sell one house after another. He watched as, bit by bit, he lost almost everything he'd worked so hard to establish. Their comfortable lifestyle in Israel had given the family finances a dent but this lack of financial understanding on Eddie's behalf brought him to the brink of financial ruin.

So he threw himself back into his work to try and re-establish his family's financial security. He also needed to address some niggling health concerns of his own. He had increasingly more aches and pains particularly in the left shoulder girdle region. His occupational health work made him, a left-hander, consider that this probably came from lugging the twelve-kilogram video camera and battery around Israel while writing his manuscript by hand and carrying around tubby television sets from clinic to clinic. He figured he had some form of strain from overuse. He looked for alternative treatment techniques and took a course on the Alexander Method. This was an Australian-born concept of healing the body through releasing tension and learning to move mindfully. He followed this with a weekend of intensive exercises using the Israeli-born Feldenkrais technique of reorganising connections between the brain and body to improve movement and one's psychological state. During this weekend Eddie had several of what he calls "*aha*" moments! He could improve the range of movement of his arm, neck, shoulders and wrists, within two minutes by a significant amount. It also seemed to relax his muscles and relieve his pain. Not surprisingly Eddie was desperate to understand how things around him worked and he threw himself into researching Feldenkrais. The technique worked in undoing patterns of movement that had been programmed into the brain and these little exercises tricked the brain to not follow its routine patterns and thereby increase movement and flexibility. With such gain in his movement pattern on the motor side of his brain in a weekend, he wondered whether this could be achieved in overcoming psychological patterns on the sensory side of the brain. He decided to attend a weekend seminar on Erhard Seminar Training (or EST), later known as the Landmark Forum. He was fascinated by the proposal that significant psychological breakthroughs could be made via large group processes in a short weekend. He wondered whether this would apply to other areas of health care when he came across a book by Dr John Harrison, Love Your Disease: It's Keeping You Healthy. Dr Harrison espoused that all illnesses had a significant psychological component or origin. It was a book which

Eddie read and re-read. Dr Harrison had a talkback show on the ABC and was a Sydney local so Eddie went to see him as a patient to learn some of his methodologies. This led to a professional friendship. Eddie was learning that the body was so different to what he had been taught in medical school. His research led him to The Dancing Wu Li Masters by Gary Zukov and The Tao of Physics by Fritjof Capra. He concluded that Western medicine had not kept up with Western physics and that the findings of Systems Theory and Quantum Mechanics were not included in the Western Medicine that he had been taught. Some of the health philosophies of the East had some reasonable scientific grounding based on the latest discoveries in physics.

Building finances to support his family and promoting PROMs, whilst extremely time-consuming, were not Eddie's entire life. His family and growing boys brought much happiness to both him and Mia. For Josh and Tull their father, though not always hands-on, was a constant in their lives. He never missed a sporting match or an evening meal with his family. His knowledge of medicine gave comfort to the boys and an immense sense of pride when observing their dad in action. On one occasion he rushed to the aid of an injured child who'd been thrown from a horse in Centennial Park. Their 'Ed' was also an enigma. At times he was barely able to pull himself away from his books. The next moment he was displaying surprising competency on a horse and bolting through a field on a family horse riding camp. As husband he was a provider and a profoundly decent man for Mia to share her life with. In 1986, his friend Bernie Kresner bumped into Mia and Eddie entering the Different Drummer restaurant in Darlinghurst. They were holding hands.

Bernie exclaimed, *"That's amazing. When you guys got married I didn't give you a chance to last but it seems you're doing okay."*

"Perhaps the counselling was having an effect," Eddie thought. Eddie realised that entering a marriage with a caveat had taken it's toll. He had decided that was over. He was now fully committed to the marriage. He was turning forty. His 40th was going to be celebrated with a group of friends and their families at Palm Cove in Cairns. It was a pleasant week. Many philosophical discussions and debates were held in the tropical sunshine by the water in Far North Queensland. The family holiday was to be supplemented with a celebration for his father-in-law Sam Fiszman's 60th. It was a 100th birthday party held in Mia and Eddie's backyard.

In any family celebration Eddie goes above and beyond to make the day particularly special. On this occasion he had organised for Sam's Polish origins to be highlighted with a Mel Brooks song 'Sweet Georgia Brown' to be sung in Polish. All the family and guests participated and it was warmly received by a delighted Sam.

> *"Jaja Dobisch Yosha Dobisch*
> *Sweet Georgie Brown*
> *Jascha Mosa Polish Kutza*
> *Sweet Georgie Brown*
> *Jascha Chebya Bene Yebna*
> *Sweet Georgie Brown"*

The speeches were entertaining and everyone felt the atmosphere, music and catering were in good taste. Sam was a great supporter of the Labor Party. This was based on his communist indoctrination in Russia after the plunders of Hitler and the war. He met Eddie and Mia's friend, Gary

Weiss, at the gathering. Gary was beginning to make waves in the business world. They discussed business and political issues and out of that meeting a strong business/social conscience-oriented bond, and later, partnership, evolved. Sam, who chaired the Major Events Committee in NSW, invited Gary to the Board. Amongst several other endeavours they brought the Gay Olympic Games to Sydney.

In late 1986 Eddie was approached with a business proposition by a friend from his Betar Youth Movement. Morry Stang, with his brother Bernie, was running a business called Regional Medical Supplies. Morry was always interested in innovations and had been offered a new machine that was administering small electric currents to help overcome pain. Morry wanted to trial it for use in Repetitive Strain Injury (RSI). Eddie was keen to grow his practice and saw this technology as innovative and interesting and was willing to trial it for his own ailments. He saw a partnership as an opportunity to practise his preaching and to establish a small rehabilitation centre away from the traditional medical model allowing him to be more proactive and holistic in his approach. As part of their healthcare approach they teamed up with Dr John Harrison to conduct seminars that were focused on prevention and were psychological in their nature. They presented seminars such as "Love Your Disease", "Healthy Parenting" and "Love Your Asthma". They also recruited a leading physiotherapist Feldenkrais practitioner to their multidisciplinary team. The timing of Eddie's collaboration was optimal. The government had closed some of the loopholes in the workers' compensations payments system that reduced payouts to injured workers by instead offered improved occupational health and safety and rehabilitation.

There was also a new emphasis and legal obligation for companies to provide rehabilitation services. Many of the large workers' compensation or general insurance companies also looked to add rehabilitation to their insurance offering. The solicitor for one of the workers' compensation insurers had seen Eddie as an expert witness in a worker's compensation court case and suggested to this insurer that they contact him. Norwich Insurers was interested in investing and Morry negotiated that they would take up 25% of the combined company and practice but they would be responsible for 100% of the finances. Eddie saw huge potential for expansion and was happy to throw his occupational health practice into this combined entity. In late 1987 the deal was done and they were re-named RPS, Rehabilitation and Preventive Services.

Just as RPS had been formed, the largest NSW occupational rehabilitation provider HCA Medicorp was put on the market by their parent company, Hospital Corporation of Australia (HCA). HCA Medicorp was haemorrhaging cash through four of its five centres: Bankstown, Parramatta, North Sydney and Wollongong but in Newcastle, they had access to a large rehabilitation centre with its own hydrotherapy pool, close to Lingard Hospital. Eddie was excited by the opportunity to purchase HCA Medicorp and expand rapidly. Morry and Eddie were really only interested in the workers' compensation business in the Newcastle centre. A great deal was negotiated by Morry, however they picked up a lot of unproductive staff and leases in the other centres. Unfortunately, Eddie's misfortune in business was again soon to present itself. As soon as the deal was closed, HCA challenged a section of the agreement and excluded the lucrative Newcastle arrangement which left Eddie and Morry with the four other unproductive centres that all needed major restructuring and large injections of funds. Consulting with their Norwich backers, an injunction was immediately taken out on HCA that stopped them from breaking the arrangement in Newcastle. They were heading to court and into significant legal costs. Morry had other businesses to run and saw that RPS Medicorp would take a long time before it became profitable. He offered his shares for sale to Norwich at considerable profit for himself. Eddie was left to work with Norwich to help turn around the business and to champion any legal defence that may be necessary. Norwich brought in management experts to help Eddie at the failing four centres but, as legal costs began to escalate, Norwich insisted that if they were to fund the court case alone then they should acquire Eddie's shares at no cost. Eddie obliged.

It was 1987. Eddie was floundering under the weight of the legal battle against HCA and was desperate to turn around the fortunes of RPS and secure the future of his family's finances. Rather than crumpling under the huge stress of the situation he found himself in, he was elated. His delight was his reaction to an announcement from the Federal Health Minister that proposed the "National Health Targets and an Implementation Committee" together with all the States' Health Departments. The Minister explained that there was to be an emphasis on prevention and health promotion. He acknowledged that the difficult task was to achieve action and that it would be critical to get the medical profession, especially the GPs, involved. Finally, Eddie felt there was movement in the right direction and there was a chance his grand designs for the state of the nation's health could be accepted under such a regime. Eddie saw "Targets" could easily be translated to "Objectives" and thus his

Management by Objectives he saw would be a perfect fit. He immediately wrote to the Minister to give his approval of the initiative and this was passed onto the Chairman of the Health Targets and Implementation Committee. He wrote again once the Committee was up and running in November 1987. Eddie set out his suggestions, pointing out that the ideas were based on management principles, knowledge of behavioural science, as well as his background in preventive health using multidisciplinary teams to achieve such goals. He went on to say that this "sociological approach" to preventive health was extremely cost-effective and it ought to achieve rapid results. It was an investment that was essentially one of training and then installing the preventive health care system. When the implementation part of the committee was set up with different programs Eddie wrote to all of them. There was a Cervical Cancer Prevention Program, a National Aboriginal Health Strategy Program, a Motor Vehicle Accident Death Program and a Blood Pressure Control Program. He went to State Ministers as well and the State Authorities such as the Road and Traffic Authority. He wrote to the Minister of Police. He wrote to the Minister for Health, the Hon. Neal Blewett and eventually, through the connections of his father-in-law, Sam Fiszman, had a conference with the Minister. It was February 1989. Despite over thirty submissions and suggestions of how this sociologically-based program would work, little occurred. He concluded that because of the "invisibility" of his concepts people had difficulty seeing the value in such programs. They were not a material thing or something definitive like an advertising program for cancer prevention, or road accident reduction. Deflated, but not defeated, Eddie was still convinced his idea of entirely revolutionising the health system would work and would save thousands and would be more humane. He just needed to keep on thinking of a way to sell his ideas. Why weren't they being embraced by the community? How could he translate the intangible to a tangible society?

Eddie, however, needed to turn his attention back to RPS Medicorp. Senior managers left. Staff salaries (including Eddie's) were cut. The Bankstown office was closed and the Parramatta office downsized. He brought Sam in to become Chairman of the RPS Medicorp Board and to liaise with the Norwich senior executives. It took these managers little time to warm to Sam and his innovative and lateral manner of running the Board. Eddie was forced to direct his doctors to do more work in the more lucrative but, in his opinion, less-effective medico-legal assessments. Norwich Workers Compensation was then themselves taken over by another insurer, CIC Insurance.

One of the more promising legacies of taking over the HCA Medicorp business for Eddie was an Executive Health Program that they had developed. The initiative looked at risk assessments and gave individuals a breakdown of their major health risks with a quantified score. For the next year the executives were being given figures on the chances of them having heart attack, stroke or cancer. Eddie could see many parallels to PROMs and was dismayed that it was only provided to a minority of people within the company. What excited him was the possibility of morphing this program with what he had learned about motivational behavioural change – creating "psycho dramas", setting the scene of what would happen in ten years from now if they did not improve their scores. Mr Jim Jones was an executive who had a high risk of physical breakdown. Eddie painted a mental picture

171

for him of his likely pathway in ten to fifteen years' time.

"Jim, your seven and eight-year old son and daughter will be seventeen and eighteen and I see them sitting by your hospital bedside. You have multiple tubes coming out of you."

Eddie reassured Jim that the kids would encourage him, *"We know you are a tough and resilient person. You will get rid of the tubes dad."* He went on, *"Jim, you're fortunate – you'll be helped out by the coronary artery bypass procedures or the various anticoagulant therapies to maintain a good functional health status."* He also gave Jim an alternative, *"Jim, this hospital admission does not have to be your pathway."*

He advised Jim to enter into his management reports each month a further line in the budget, "Jim Jones' Health". In this he was to enter any amount of physical activities he carried out in the month. This should be a minimum of thirteen hours, "the budget". Similarly, he was to enter the number of fish meals he ate or his attendance at alcohol abstinence programs or quit smoking programs. Jim and many executives came back year after year with improved scores. Eddie wished that all GPs could carry out these lifestyle prescriptions for each of their patients. What an impact on the nation's health it could have!

Chapter 10

Love is in the air

"*I love this family.*" It was the closing line of a slow but loving speech made by Eddie's close friend Edju at Tull's bar mitzvah on the 1st of April 1989. Edju had been serenaded to the stage by the Kooka Bros who sang "*I love to have a vodka with Edju*". This was in reference to his love of vodka and the recent uptake of the song "I love to have a beer with Duncan" at the Seoul Olympics in celebration of the successes of Olympic swimmer and gold medallist, Duncan Armstrong. Edju's long and cherished relationship with the Price family was expressed in his speech and well received. Eddie's heart was full. Despite his disappointment in not being able to forge a life for his family near Edju in Israel, he felt that in Australia they had reached a suitable level of contentment as a family.

He was more involved in his sons' lives than ever before. He was determined to not be the intimidating father that he himself had had. His love of his sons and his love of cricket formed the perfect union for a dedicated and successful coach. Both Tull and Josh played with Tull displaying quite a talent with the bat. Eddie coached both boys' teams over many years as part of the Waverley District Cricket Association. According to some of the former players he was an exceptionally good coach. For most years Eddie's team would begin the season at the bottom of the pool but by the end he would have them winning most games and more often than not, winning the season outright. He had a clear methodological approach to coaching that he broke down into three sections; mastering the basic fundamentals of the game, good strategies gathered from years of playing and watching the game and meaningful ways to strengthen and encourage the weakest links in the team. Eddie recognised that if support and security were given to those that lacked these fundaments in their home environment and you got them to practise, then they responded. His holistic view of the game – not just looking at skills but taking into account the culture of the sport, the social experience of the players and how it interweaves into society - had, whether by design or by default, illuminated the idea that we need to look at systems as part of a whole organism and not just an assembly of parts. It was a theory he would elaborate on in his future publications. He became a role model and father figure to many of the young men he was coaching as well as to many of his sons' friends. The Price family house became their sanctuary and, for some, their home. Amongst the intensely intellectual conversations Eddie would share with his sons and their friends, there was always the underlying quirky and slightly eccentric humour.

"Eddie what are you doing?" enquired a bemused friend of Josh's, Matt Bowman.

"The City to Surf is on. I'm going to run it with them from home," explained Eddie as he jogged on the spot in front of the televised event.

"Bullshit Ed," replied Matt who then sat down and watched on in amusement.

Mia rolled her eyes as over the next two hours Eddie completed laps of their home, pool and repeatedly scaled the stairs whilst the runners were attacking Heartbreak Hill.

In 1992, as Eddie swirled Mia around the dance floor to Love is in the Air at Josh's "Strictly" bar mitzvah' party, he reflected that the song certainly encapsulated his family life during that time. Mia and Eddie were both exceedingly proud of the young men their children were becoming. With one part of his life a success, his unrelenting drive to succeed both financially and in terms of making a contribution to the world still needed addressing. He gazed across the bar mitzvah dance floor at the jovial former Prime Minister and close friend of Sam's, Bob Hawke, and lamented that perhaps he'd missed his opportunity to utilise close family connection to have his theories accepted and widely implemented. For now, he would have to let that unfinished business be. His bigger problem for the moment lay with RPS Medicorp and, the still unresolved, court case.

In late May of 1992 Eddie finally had a court date and welcomed the opportunity to fight the injustice he felt had been done. Despite years of preparation leading up to this moment the high-ranking barristers due to represent RPS Medicorp were, at the last minute, called to work on a major financial court case. The unprepared barrister who took over was, in his eyes, losing them their case. When Eddie stepped into the witness box he knew it was up to him to salvage their cause or face defeat and a huge financial loss. His own barrister's questioning was slow and rambling. He lacked understanding of their argument.

Eddie could hold back no longer. *"I am a believer in justice and this is what we seek in the courts. I am angry, almost as angry as those now rioting in Los Angeles where there is looting and burning going on because of an injustice done to the blacks in the Compton area after Rodney King was beaten by the police."*

For fifteen minutes Eddie continued his impassioned lecture and step-by-step explained their case. He recalls the judge's almost grateful response, *"I should not have allowed*

Dr Price to go on, but for time's sake it was in the interests of the court. I believe him an emotional, but honest, witness. We will take a short break so Dr Price can settle himself emotionally before he is cross-examined."

Eddie received a letter from the Head of CIC, now full owners of RPS Medicorp, Michael Maher, thanking him for his help and acknowledging that his evidence had swung the court case in their favour and RPS Medicorp had won on liability. However, the damages had been separated out and the biggest damage, $2 million for the large rehabilitation centre they were being evicted from in Newcastle, was suddenly dismissed by the other side. RPS Medicorp's solicitors had been out-manoeuvred by those for the defendants. Regardless, damages were awarded to the extent of approximately $400,000 and they could continue to occupy the rehabilitation centre in Newcastle.

"You've won me over. I understand."

Eddie was ecstatic. He had just spent several hours carefully explaining his ideas for the health system to the newly appointed Minister for Health, Senator Graham Richardson, and he understood! *"But I cannot do it alone and you will need to convince the bureaucrats in the Commonwealth Health Department as well. As far as I'm concerned, I will facilitate the introductions via my Head of Department,"* concluded Senator Richardson.

Eddie couldn't believe his good fortune when the Senator, a confidant of his father-in-law Sam, had been appointed to this new role. He had previously explained his theory on health outcomes to Graham at a Doctors Reform Society function and received a positive response. He took advantage of his connections. Now that Graham held this position surely Eddie's ideas would find traction and action would be taken. He was afforded an audience with many different sections of the Commonwealth Health Department – Primary Care, Health Policy, Health Performance Division, and Population Health. He made progress with the Australian Institute of Health and Welfare who were not only willing to carry out surveys using PROMs and assessing risk factors via their population service monitor but they were also aware of a newfound PROM that had been developed by the Rand Corporation in the United States that was accurate at the individual level. They explained it was a generic PROM and that it was applicable to all disease categories and to all ages. This was called the SF-36. Eddie was delighted and immediately made contact with Dr John Ware in Boston, the principal scientist and psychometrician behind the development of the SF-36. Eddie assured Mia, "*Things will happen now!*" And they did. An Australian Health Indicators Committee was set up, chaired by a Commonwealth Health Bureaucrat, with Eddie as a guide member. They used the population survey monitor to assess the SF-36 and worked this together with a risk factors questionnaire that looked at things like weight, smoking and physical exercise.

September 14 1993 and Eddie was three months into his project as Consultant on Health Outcomes to the Minister for Health when there was even more "love in the air". Prime Minister Rabin of Israel shook hands with President Arafat of the PLO in the presence of President Clinton on the White House lawn. They had agreed on a peace deal between Israel and the Palestinian Authority - the Oslo-Accords. Eddie rejoiced in the idea of peace finally coming to Israel. Later that evening he had an appointment with the Health Minister and Alan Bansemer, Deputy Secretary of the Commonwealth Health Department, to monitor progress of his consultancy.

Eddie was so happy with the peace deal in the Middle East that he brought roses for everyone. Everything was going well. Then suddenly Graham Richardson, for his own reasons, resigned from the Ministry after only one year. He told Eddie he would hand the project over to Carmen Lawrence. Minister Lawrence briefly looked at the project and immediately canned it. Eddie was devastated.

He may have faced another disappointment but he had also tasted magic. In the SF-36 he had seen real potential and was determined to explore its possibilities further. He took the SF-36 to one of his clients, Transfield, and trialled it on one hundred of their employees. The questionnaire scored eight parameters such as physical functioning, social functioning and mental health, each out of one hundred. He noted that two employees scored low on physical functioning. Eddie reasoned that if it was a valid instrument then both must have some physical health problem and went to interview them in more detail. One of the employees was a sixty-year-old boilermaker with quite severe arthritis who was able to work on despite his significant discomfort. The other employee was a forty-year-old administrative assistant who was more of an enigma. When Eddie questioned her further she denied having any physical ailments. He asked her more questions as to why she hardly went out and had limited social interactions.

Eventually, after a fifteen to twenty-minute consultation, she elaborated, "*I have trouble controlling my bowels. I'm embarrassed by this. I sit one metre from the toilet as at any moment I might need to go. I cannot go out at night and I am very careful on the bus going home. I always go to the toilet immediately before I leave and immediately after I come home.*"

Eddie suggested that she may have Irritable Bowel Syndrome. She admitted that she was so embarrassed that she had not discussed this in any detail with her own GP. Eddie encouraged her to seek treatment. He thought about this lady for the next couple of days and realised what he had just done. This generic PROM measure, the SF-36, in conjunction with a follow-up consultation, was able to reach a new diagnosis. This was a "eureka" moment for Eddie. He had just discovered a new class of diagnostic tests. When he delved further he found other users of the SF-36 quoted similar experiences and therefore it was possible to view these functional health status instruments as a new suite or set of diagnostic tests. These should be much more widely adopted by physicians in their general practice, not only as performance measures, but more particularly and regularly, as a new form of cheap, non-invasive diagnostic tests. He concluded this would not only change health care, it would also change medicine.

Eddie was now a member of the Medical Outcomes Trustee international organisation that focussed on PROM development and he had already established a personal relationship with the Chairman, Dr Al Tarlov, and the main advocate, Dr John Ware, the author of the SF-36. Dr Ware informed Eddie that he was using SF-36 measures in partnership with Dr Jim Dewey in a company called Response Technology, out of the States. Eddie immediately contacted Jim Dewey who was not only using the SF-36 but a host of approximately thirty other PROMs, to speak with him about his theory that PROMs could be used as diagnostic tools. Unfortunately, Dewey did not "get" what he was trying to explain. Eddie decided he had to start writing a second book to fully expose what he believed he had discovered as it heralded "a new form of medicine." PROMs, and in particular the SF-36, would not only facilitate a radical improvement in healthcare, it would change medical practice, not only in Australia but in the whole of the OECD.

Chapter 11

Outcomes and WorkCover

"I was treating a patient with diagnosed Borderline Personality Illness from my home medical centre when she suddenly heard my 2 year old son cry out and ran at him screaming abuse. I had to physically restrain her and hold her down and I told her she was never to attend my practice again as a patient. She told me, 'I'll get you'."

It was his distraught friend and colleague Dr John Harrison on the phone. Eddie was shocked to hear that he was in serious trouble with the NSW Medical Tribunal who wished to deregister him for alleged sexual misconduct. Dr Harrison's full story has since been told in a book Death of a Doctor published by Allen & Unwin in July 2005. It describes how the medico-legal system backed the allegations made by an allegedly mentally-ill woman to disbar Dr John Harrison for life. John, as set out in his book, used some unorthodox techniques which included touch therapy and other techniques of relating to his patients. *"Eddie would you be prepared to be a character witness in my favour at the tribunal,"* asked John.

"Sure," agreed Eddie.

When he was in the witness box at the tribunal in Macquarie Street Eddie was surprised to be given a handwritten letter addressed to Dr Harrison from one of his patients and was asked to read it by the cross-examining barrister.

"I like you John as a doctor but I won't be attending you anymore if you send me again to this particular masseur. He wouldn't know how to wank himself in the dark."

The barrister then drew attention to a drawing of a stick figure sitting on a chair with the light on what could be interpreted as a person masturbating.

"What do you think of this stick picture Dr Price when I tell you this was drawn by Dr Harrison and sent with the letter back to the patient? Is that very professional?"

Eddie thought, *"I have to think quickly."* He then stated that although he thought it was neither professional nor usual, Dr Harrison's techniques were a combination of Eastern and Western medicine and were his way of trying to empathise with the patient. He explained, *"This is an example of patterning where the therapist patterns the work or the words of the patient and is a well-known part of Professor Milton Erickson's patterning as part of his hypnosis technique. It is like a salesperson who finds out his potential customer plays golf and so discusses golf in order to set up a bond. This was Dr Harrison's methodology, unusual that it may appear to be, of identifying and forming a bond with his patient."* Dr Harrison, after he was struck off, advised Eddie that his medical evidence had been dismissed.

There was quite a deal of publicity surrounding the case and Eddie was seen on television in the company of Dr John Harrison. Two weeks after Michael Maher, Head of CIC, advised him that one of his senior managers thought that the arrangement between Eddie and CIC should change from one of employee to one of subcontractor. He thought back to John Fitzgerald Kennedy's book Profiles in Courage, where President Kennedy had lauded those who stood up for what they thought was right, independent of the consequences to themselves.

Despite his frustrations and disappointment with the

Federal Health Department axing of his plans, the new Director General of NSW Health, Mr John Wyn Owen, who had arrived from Wales to drive change, had put out a paper called "Getting It Right: Health Outcomes". Eddie immediately wrote, on the 13th July 1994, to the Director General affirming his now twenty-year interest in Health Outcomes and enclosed a copy of his book Is Medicine Really Necessary? The Director General didn't respond himself but an administrative assistant thanked Eddie for his contribution and advised there would be a seminar in Sydney on the 12th and 13th of August on Health Outcomes and that he ought to attend. He was down to his last copies of Is Medicine Really Necessary? so he decided to re-publish his book with a more appropriate title and have them available for sale at the seminar. The book was re-published with the title Health Outcomes: A New Way of Defining and Managing Health. Although Eddie participated actively from the floor during the debate at the Outcomes conference, and, despite selling books to approximately 40% of the audience, there was no further initiative from the NSW Health Department. He would have to find other ways in which to exact change. One way soon presented itself.

The newly-elected Labor Party in 1995 was revamping the NSW WorkCover Board which traditionally had a representative from the medical profession. Eddie felt that if he could obtain a position he could then introduce management by Health and Safety Outcomes at the board level. Sam Fiszman and Graham Richardson served as his referees and in September 1995, Eddie became the doctor representative and a Director on the NSW WorkCover Board. The former Premier of NSW, Barrie Unsworth, was to be the Chairman. Eddie was optimistic of what potential opportunities this offered. After the first Board meeting he decided that in order to help break down barriers between the new Directors, and also to say thanks to his father-in-law for his efforts in acting as a referee for him, he would invite the whole Board and their partners to a dinner at his home. Guests included Barry and Pauline Unsworth, Michael Costa and his wife, Anne Keating and her partner, a senior executive at United Airlines, Jenny Neary and partner Belinda, a senior executive at Telecom and Sam and Esther Fiszman. He was pleasantly surprised that the conversation flowed freely. Mia seemed to have more leftist views than Michael Costa, Secretary of the Labor Party, whose conversation reflected a high intelligence but also a tough demeanour. This character trait would be reflected in the future Board meetings when senior WorkCover staff made submissions to the Board. The employers' representative, Doug Wright, showed empathy for the staff member whilst Michael Costa grilled them over and over again to obtain the understanding he required.

Eddie was a voracious reader. He always wanted to understand his world and how others viewed it, particularly in the fields of medicine, management, psychology, business and motivational theory. He discovered the book Re-Engineering the Corporation by Professor Michael Hammer (listed by Time Magazine as one of the 25 most influential people in the world at the time) and James Champy. It was described as a "manifesto for business revolution". The book was making waves in the business world and Eddie felt the underlying theory fitted in perfectly with his theories of the reform needed in health care and how this would be enabled by the role of the new computer age. Feelings about this new theory were further enhanced when he read the

book Re-Engineering Management by James Champy. These
books defined re-engineering as "the fundamental re-
thinking and radical redesign of business processes to
achieve dramatic improvements in critical contemporary
measures of performance, such as costs, quality, service and
speed". The basic question that was highlighted by the word
"fundamental" in the definition was "Why do we do what we
do?" The answer to this, in all cases, was to "add customer
value" for these corporations. That was exactly what Eddie
felt PROMs measured. They measured changes in the patient
or the customer themselves. They measured the customer's
improvement in the value, i.e. in the quality they achieved.
The book that he had started to write could be considered as
a re-engineering of medicine, more than just a corporation.
He wanted to change an entire industry and the essential
enabler to do this he devised would be computers.

While he was busy writing his manuscript, preparing for
WorkCover and doing extensive research, he was still
holding down a full time job running his rehabilitation and
occupational medical practice that had now been renamed Dr
Eddie Price and Associates. Another take-over of the parent
company (CIC) again meant major changes for him. HIH,
another insurance company, had purchased CIC and they
already had their own rehabilitation provider (IRS) and did
not consider that the occupational medical practice was part
of their core business. HIH approached Eddie and asked if he
would take over the lease and equipment and at least one
member of staff at the North Sydney occupational practice
rooms in return for an agreement of a certain amount of work
over the next two years. They came to an arrangement where
Eddie was again able to establish Computerised Medical
Systems and they would trade under the business name of Dr

E Price & Associates. He was his own boss again and free of partners for the first time since 1987. It felt good. He could, and would, concentrate on furthering health outcomes (PROMs) with this time focussing on harnessing the advances in computer technology. *"IT FEELS GOOD!"* Eddie yelled out from his office in Blue Street, North Sydney. At home he and Mia were also working on good vibes. *"Bagels? What have bagels got to do with the boys?"* queried Eddie.

"I think if we make a regular habit of sharing Sunday brunch together, it means we are kept in the loop as to their weekend activities. They might open up to us more. They may even bring friends with them. It's just another way of being a part of their lives," explained Mia. *"Alright,"* said Eddie and the institution of "Sunday Bagels at the Prices" was born. It would become a family tradition to gather together, invite the boys' friends, girlfriends and eventually children and foster a strong bond and open-home policy that both parents felt was so important for their family.

While fostering unity at home, it was a united force he was fighting against professionally. Eddie felt the main stumbling block for PROMs was peer pressure. Currently doctors were operating under one system. It would be very difficult, from a social psychological perspective, to convince some to accept a move to his radically new system of managing health. Doctors needed to belong and to be accepted by their peers. Eddie felt the irony. PROMs, the very thing they were sceptical of, was the tool by which they could measure and prove their achievements to their colleagues. In order for the current establishment to break ranks and adopt his PROMs system, there needed to be incentives in place. He reflected on his management training and Maslow's 5 Levels of Needs and the management theory of motivation that suggests there are multiple drivers of behavioural change, with money being the most important driver when it is viewed as an achievement. Eddie figured out he needed to harness these drivers in order to facilitate a radical change in the medical paradigm. He needed to have doctors being paid for prevention, not cures. So he was elated when an opportunity, through his position on the WorkCover board, arose to test out his motivation theory. WorkCover received regular submissions from doctors regarding their fee requirements particularly orthopaedic surgeons who were the biggest specialist group performing operations on injured workers. When the time came for negotiations with the orthopaedic surgeons, the Chair of Work Cover Barrie Unsworth, deferred the task to Eddie. *"Eddie, why don't you meet and negotiate with the Orthopaedic Surgeons Association as a fellow medico?"*

He eagerly accepted the opportunity but only if he could use it as an opportunity to push his own agenda. *"I would be pleased to do so but part of my negotiation would be to encourage them to use PROMs such as the SF-36 and more body-part-specific PROMs for different body parts."* Barrie was in a hurry and only half-listening. Eddie continued, *"The reason injured workers have these operations, most of which are back operations, is to improve their level of functioning, that is, their quality of life. These PROMs measure parameters such as their physical function (scored 0-100). Their physical role is very important because a return to their work role could radically improve physical score (0-100). One can measure these functions before an operation and after an operation. These would show if the operation was successful. I, and many others, believe that if these were measured then more than 30% of back operations would be proven to not increase their patients' functioning after the operation and similarly with many expensive back injection procedures."*

Barrie was out of the door and away on other business. He didn't really listen.

Eddie met with the orthopaedic surgeon representatives and put his case. *"There are these new measures for functioning, or health-related, quality of life that measure eight health parameters and score them. A patient's physical functioning can be scored out of 100, for a patient's pain level (0-100), as well as their 'role physical' before and after operations. There are also specific measures for different body parts like the hip, the knee or the upper arm."* The orthopaedic surgeons did not have any objections to Eddie's PROMs and put forward the amount of the fee increase they wanted.

He continued, *"I will send you an example of the SF-36 questionnaire and the resultant graphic scores in examples before and after operation."*

He sent graphs to the Executive Officer explaining that these had been used for many years in research and big Pharma to test the effects of drugs, particularly cancer drugs on a patient's quality of life. The Executive Officer replied there was no problem. The orthopaedic surgeons were happy to use PROMs in order to receive their fee increase. Eddie recalled Aneurin Bevan, the UK Minister for Health in 1948, when he introduced the now-famous UK National Health Service (the NHS), saying how when he came up against opposition from the doctors he did manage to introduce his ideas because he "stuffed their mouths with gold". At the next WorkCover board meeting, Eddie again explained how these PROMs measured a person's functioning before and after operation. How, by using these, it would be proved that many operations were unnecessary along with many invasive procedures because they would show little gain. He also claimed that particularly bad outcomes were known to be more frequent in those patients under workers' compensation. When Barrie Unsworth heard the amount of the fee increase that Eddie had negotiated in order to accept the PROMs, he turned to Michael Costa and the other Directors, and said, *"Michael I think we will have to re-negotiate this with the orthopaedic surgeons. Please advise them."*

The fee levels and the requirement to use PROMs were dropped. Eddie saw this as a huge opportunity lost and wondered, *"Was it how I presented this to the Board? Perhaps there was some arrogance in my presentation that came through."*

He further lamented, *"This would have saved NSW WorkCover much more money than the increase in fees."*

Nevertheless, there were other opportunities and he was relentless in his attempts to have his concepts understood. He was Chairman of the Prevention Sub-Committee and an active member of the Rehabilitation Sub-Committee of NSW WorkCover. He met with senior executives of WorkCover on this Committee and explained his theory on safety management by health objectives and on NSW-wide Health Outcomes. *"There is a basic management reporting format. It is used in every major corporation in the world. It is the basis for general accounting management. It is often called a 'budget'. Every nation has one and it is divided into sub-budgets for each ministry. It is really the best example of 'management by objectives' – the objective is to ensure one does not spend more than the target. It works. People work* *to achieve the budget."* He went on, *"It is really much more than a reporting format. To me, it is an object of beauty because underlying it; this reporting format has '16 drivers' that drive human behaviours. If you wish to reduce the work injuries in NSW, you have to implement change through a hierarchy. You need to start at the top. Change needs to happen in each of the five main insurer groups like Licensed Insurers, Specialised Insurers, Self Insurers, Treasury Managed Funds and Run Off Insurers which then implement change through their subsystems. For example, in the case of Licensed Insurers, this would be broken down into twelve companies, from AMP through to Zurich. Each insurer then divides their organisation into, let's say, twelve sections and each section manages between five and three hundred employers depending on size, and then each employer sets each manager their own targets using a management reporting format. The closer to the worksite you get, the more direct control the managers have in avoiding work injuries. (*See Appendix for further explanation) Now, with computers, everything can be measured. This reporting format can work for accident reduction management in the same way it is used for money or budget management."*

He presented a paper to the members of the sub-committee who, after many debates, accepted his thesis that this would ensure a 20% reduction in lost time accident claims in the next three years. The committee endorsed his presentation to the Board. Eddie approached Barrie Unsworth about making the presentation. He was told to wait until there was an opening in the agenda items and to work through the CEO, Ian Ramsay, to find out when he could make his presentation. Finally, he was granted a time slot and made his pitch.

He recalls their reaction, *"So you're telling us that by setting a target and then having monthly meetings, you're going to reduce accidents across NSW?"* queried Barrie Unsworth at the conclusion of his talk.

"Well, essentially yes," replied Eddie.

"Mate, you're off with the fairies," chorused the board.

The reception of his ideas was not as warm nor understanding as Eddie would have liked.

He was about to reach fifty, a score he never managed to achieve in his long cricket career. A party was to be organised. Looking for a more personal invitation, Mia found an old Father's Day card by a six-year-old Josh that read, *"He likes having baths and staying in bed. That's my dad, Ed."*

This was used as an invitation for the party. Eddie paid little attention to clothes and usually deferred to Mia when going out, *"Mia! What am I wearing?"* For this big occasion, Tull announced, *"Ed, I will dress you for your party."*

He took his father to Marc's clothing store where Eddie was dressed wearing a new pair of jeans, a grey jacket and a green shirt. The party was held in a marquee in their backyard, as with most of their family celebrations, with Tim Booth playing guitar. There was dancing, a fun sing-along in Hebrew about the prophet Ezekiel (Yehezkel) who was a bit of a hippie prophet and, as always, there were speeches. Josh's speech reflected both the atmosphere of the night and Eddie's life to date.

> *"It's only fair on this occasion and at this time*
> *That I address my father, Edward Daniel Price in rhyme,*
> *For one thing I have definitely inherited*

Is an ability to, as Tony Frumar once said,
To write poetry that travels from the heart to
The hand, bypassing the head.
Eddie's half century took some time to reach,
It comes long after those of two cricketers he helped to teach.
He is father, coach and author too,
Hails from Lebanon, via Wollongong, but remains a Jew,
'Is Medicine Really Necessary', a question he raised,
Yet now he wonders, 'Why hasn't Health Outcomes been praised?'
In days gone by Eddie would both recite and quote
Woody Allen, Murray Banks and other comedians of note,
Today quantum healers and marketing men
Provide wisdom and writing which have displaced comedians.
Not forgetting the prophet Yehezkel (Ezekiel)
A name with which few words rhyme,
As you can probably tell
My mother is often forced to defend
Claims she treats her pet better than her husband,
But Mia insists she is not at fault
She has only noted this tendency to malt.
On a more serious note
I feel that everyone here can openly gloat
That their husband, father, relative or mate
Is one that is, in simple terms, great.
He likes having baths and lying in bed
That's our dad, Ed".

Eddie's smile was genuine. Despite his professional frustrations, he had a family who loved him. He'd just been appointed chief medical officer for the Harness Racing Authority (the Trotters) and at work things were moving ahead and he was rebuilding his family's finances. With what money he'd been able to accumulate, he turned to his friend Dr Gary Weiss to ask for some investment advice. Gary suggested two or three unrelated companies that he felt may be a good bet and advised Eddie that he would ring him when he felt it was time to sell. Just before the end of the year, Gary rang and told Eddie to sell. He'd gained $10,000 in two months. He immediately invited Gary and his wife to dinner as a thank you. Gary's wife volunteered at the dinner that, "*Many people approach Gary nowadays for advice from which they benefit, but you and Mia are the first to invite us out as a thank-you.*" They laughed a lot that evening over Woody Allen and Bob Dylan yarns and life was good. They discussed Eddie's PROM questionnaire to reform the health system and Gary's comment illuminated the main stumbling block, "*Questionnaires are really subjective measures. Doctors will rightly demand 'objective' measures and not just opinions*".

Chapter 12

Supramedicine

"Morning Tull," greeted Eddie as his eldest son emerged from his upstairs room.

"Hi guys. I assume you're expecting me to have a 21st which is coming up soon. I don't want to have a party. What I would prefer instead is a trip to the UK and the USA. You see," Tull continued, *"kids are not doing up their laces and I have designed a sneaker without laces that could be a slip-on. I want to see whether other people in the world have done the same. My friend, Rodney Adler, is interested and he has marketing abilities and as a business partner, the two of us would like to do this trip together."*

Eddie was only slightly taken aback by Tull's plan but not surprised. When Tull had been told some years earlier that he had to work to supplement any university or gap year he may be considering, it was this entrepreneurial son, a mould of his Grandfather Sam, who replied, *"I would rather create some groovy bags. I will set up a business name called 'Naked'."*

Tull had then designed a leather bag and had "Naked" T-shirts designed and took them around to various shops. Eddie was surprised when he made some sales. Tull was reluctantly going to university studying economics but Fashion was his passion and main business interest. So Tull and his marketing mate Rodney set off. In both London and in the US they made contact with some hip-hop artists and they returned via South Korea. Home again; Tull impressed his father with his drive and ambition.

"Ed, this is a prototype sneaker we had made up in Korea.

They don't exist anywhere in the world and we want to go into production."

Eddie naively replied, *"There is a great place to launch them at Bondi Junction - at General Pants or a similar store."*

Tull was adamant, *"No, the launch has got to be out of London."*

"Bondi Junction sounds good to me! What's happening with the investor? I thought Rodney's grandfather was going to invest."

Tull explained, *"That's not going to happen by the looks of it. He was unwell, but he seems to have recovered."*

"So, how are you going to make up the initial run of shoes?"

"Well," said Tull, *"The company in Korea wants a line of credit of $200,000."*

"So where are you going to get that money now?"

"I'm not sure," said Tull, *"But we need it straightaway to start production."*

Eddie turned to see Mia who had a look on her face that suggested they should mortgage their home to invest.

"Are you crazy?" cried Eddie. *"This is a 20-year old kid with minimal experience in business and you want me to mortgage our home?"*

Mia replied, *"If you don't do it he will go to Sam and you know what he's like. He will front up with the money."*

Eddie replied, defeated, *"I need time to think about it."*

A week later he spoke to Tull. *"Only because of your mother's insistence, and against my better judgement, am I giving you the line of credit or guarantee. This involves us putting a mortgage on our house SO this is on the basis that you find another investor before the 30th of June."*

A delighted Tull reassured him all would be well, *"Yeah, I've got some friends whose fathers are in business and are relatively well-to-do. I've started to speak to a couple of them."*

Weeks passed and Eddie checked in with progress, *"Tull, how are you going with the money that's required from another investor?"*

"I'm talking to the father of a couple of our friends and one is reasonably interested," said Tull but Eddie was concerned, *"I will need something written from him because the line of credit is converting to cash shortly and I need to know that I can get cash out."*

Tull sighed, *"Give me another month."*

"That would be halfway through May and things will be getting tight!"

Leaving his financial fears at home, Eddie himself was off to Israel and then San Francisco for the State-of-the-Art Health Outcomes Conference convened by the Medical Outcomes Trust (Boston). It was held at the opulent New Palace Hotel and was centred on Patient-Reported Outcomes Measures (PROMs) and how these were the best way to evaluate health services and quality of care and how there was increasing interest in their use within the pharmaceutical industry. He was excited. He re-ignited his personal relationship with the President of the Medical Outcomes Trust, Dr Al Tarlov, and also met up with Dr John Ware, the author of the SF-36 PROM, and a leading psychometrician.

"John, do you mind if I use the SF-36 and some of your graphs as the centrepiece of my new book?" asked Eddie.

John was delighted, *"No, the more you write about it the better it is. You go ahead. You have my permission to include it. The more the better."*

His book could now proceed. In it he would discuss a recently devised shorter form of the SF-36, known as the SF-12 (because it comprised only 12 questions). This more concise PROM was not only considered extremely accurate at the individual patient level but it was much easier to understand.

On his return to Australia he was eager to capture the energy of the conference and resume work on his book but there was the matter of Tull's loan to sort out.

"Well Tull?" said Eddie, *"Where's the written agreement from the investor?"*

Tull replied, *"I've been speaking to this fellow, Barry, around the subject matter for quite a while...."*

"I want something written! What's this 'talking around' the subject all about? Give it to me in writing." He was incredulous.

"No problems Ed," said Tull. *"When I was speaking about it in conversation with Barry he suggested that we needed a written agreement. Now that he has suggested it, I can start to prepare the agreement and I will get that to you in one week."*

He was amazed at Tull's natural understanding of human behaviour. He would never have thought to "talk around" a subject. He was impressed and relieved when the agreement arrived within the week. By the 28th of June there was a delivery of shoes and Tull was off to London again and the exact amount of money, over a couple of hundred thousand dollars, was placed into Eddie's bank account by the investor. Soon after Royal Elastics was launched in London by the hip-hop artist Goldie. An office was set up in Eddie and Mia's home and sales were happening. There was a hive of activity upstairs.

Business was also going well in his own practice. To help with workers' compensation clients and to aid in managing his constant efforts to educate medical departments and practices as to the importance of using PROMs, Eddie employed a customer relationship manager. Jillian was a dynamic and outgoing lady who had worked in a medical records department. Together they pitched to the newly-formed Divisions of General Practice (later to become Primary Health Networks) that they should consider using PROMs. Eddie saw the divisions as an integral vehicle for his ideas as they were a Federal government-supported peer group that discussed new concepts and innovations. If he could get them on board then word would spread. He also wrote to the Medical Educator at the Royal Australian College of General Practitioners suggesting they use the SF-36 to enhance general practice work. Then he discovered another organisation in Australia, the Australian Health Outcomes Collaboration. They were planning to have a conference in Canberra in November. He saw a willing market for his new book, found a small publisher, Murray David, and began writing furiously.

Supramedicine was the title of his new book. He was exploring the concept of an entirely new medical paradigm brought about through Systems Theory and the implementation of the SF-36 PROM. Eddie claimed that current medicine was preoccupied only with the body's structures and functions in the body's subsystems such as the cardiovascular and neurological systems. He was proposing that there were systems above the individual (Supra-systems) including the patient's family, the living environment, the patient's habits and diets and activities. All of these had an impact on one's overall health and ought to be measured to understand the true wellness state of an individual. Eddie was suggesting a holistic approach was necessary for mainstream medicine and that PROMs were the means of getting there. PROMs, when used as diagnostic tests, would open up a whole new area of medicine called Supramedicine. He was aiming to validate his PROMs measurements of health with the sceptical medical community by demonstrating that health promotion is scientific, based on diagnosis and treatment, as shown through "new physics". It was the first time someone had amalgamated the advances in management theory, systems theory, organisational theory, learning theory, quantum theory, relativity theory, psychometrics, and information technology and applied them to the task of Health Management.

The book publisher, Murray David, worked tirelessly to have the book ready so the first two hundred copies could be available for sale at the first Health Outcomes Conference. Over two hundred like-minded people were meeting in Canberra and Eddie thought he may sell all two hundred of his books. He sold twenty but enthused that he now had a whole series of potential new contacts and supporters for his Health Outcomes or PROMs ideas by the time the conference finished on the 1st of November 1997.

Never one to shy away from an excuse to celebrate, he soon organised a book launch. Sam managed to enlist the Premier of NSW, Bob Carr, to do the honours and helped acquire the large reception room over the IMAX Theatre for the event with an exquisite view overlooking Darling Harbour. Eddie arranged for computer scannable PROMs questionnaires to be available on the night to any interested guests. He also provided a doctor familiar with PROMs to be on standby to counsel people if they received unexpected results. Over two hundred attended on the 28th of January 1998. Murray Child, the editor, serenaded the crowd on his saxophone while they completed their SF-36s. At least two of the two hundred guests needed their results explained with care and caution by the attending GP.

In his speech he claimed, *"Supramedicine is not an airport book – no sex. Jackie Mason states the authors of airport books claim they don't put sex in their books to sell more books, it's in there because that's life. Everybody does it. It reflects life. He reckons that everybody eats soup and, in fact, he thinks more people eat soup than have sex. They should put soup in their books."* He continued, *"Supramedicine, despite its name, doesn't have soup in it either – but it is a recipe book. It is a recipe book for solutions to the health system crisis."*

He was well received that evening and over the following week. He spoke on multiple radio shows and was asked, *"With the Premier launching your book, does this mean these changes are going to happen?"*

He hoped this would happen and to his delight Bob Carr made contact and said he wanted to discuss issues further with Eddie on one of his walks. At 8:00pm, on the 19th of February, the two met outside the Pavilion in Coogee and Eddie launched into his passionate spiel. After nearly an hour of in-depth explanation as they pounded the footpath they were suddenly approached. *"Phone call for you Premier,"* said the man, handing Bob Carr a phone.

"Where did you come from?" said the now dismissed Eddie.

The man explained, *"I'm Bob's bodyguard. I've been walking a distance behind you the whole time. The funny thing is Eddie, you would have been mistaken for the bodyguard had anyone had any ill-intent.*"

"*Thanks!*" said Eddie.

The walk was completed but he was disappointed that he had not been able to win over the Premier and give him the understanding of just how revolutionary and progressive his ideas really were. In a vain attempt to follow up on their conversation, he prepared papers for Bob Carr and created a comprehensive NSW Health Index using Management by Objectives (target figures) together with PROMs. Again, there was little response. The book did not make any records in sales but he was buoyed to some extent at least by one review in an article by Ron Lord that appeared in the magazine Health Cover. Ron had read the book in detail and had understood the message. The article was entitled "The SF-36 and IT: Building Blocks for a Re-Engineered System?"

Despite twenty-five years having passed with Eddie trying to sell his ideas to governments, health departments, ministers and health managers with little success, he was encouraged by the popularity of the computer scannable PROMs at the book launch. It was proof that an interest in PROMs was there and computers and the internet were the future. *"At some point someone will make money from this. It may as well be me,"* thought Eddie. He decided to go into business as Computerised Medical Systems (CMS) offering a computer-scannable system of PROMs to GPs, hospitals and device manufacturers. He purchased a database system along with quite a few PROMs from a company called HCIA located outside of Boston. He appointed a part-time manager to look after the promotion and implementation of PROMs. Kathy Lawson was a warm, extremely competent and caring lady. A grant was sought from the government's Innovation

R&D Grants. They made their submission to a bureaucrat at the AusIndustry organisation who had great difficulty in understanding their innovative research project. No grant was given. Regardless, Computerised Medical Systems started their research projects with injury insurers, a medical device company, Vax-D, and one hospital. As they were collecting their early research data using PROMs Kathy found a website called QualityMetrics and the president of the company was none other than Dr John Ware. One of the other directors was Jim Dewey, the founder of HCIA. Eddie commented to Kathy, *"Looks like we're behind the eight ball but many doctors will be like me, not particularly computer literate, and be happy to use or have their assistant staff use, computer-scannable formats. Nevertheless, we should start to move into the internet age and have a website for our PROMs".*

What excited Eddie was that he believed PROMs were diagnostic tests and having them computerised created a digital medical laboratory. He saw it being similar to a pathology laboratory. Rather than handling blood tests, they were handling a patient's "Functional Health Status", their "Cared-For Status" and their "Preventive Health Status" scores. He decided to change his business trading name to eMedilab. He set up a website and he and Kathy approached Divisions of General Practice with their concept. Disappointingly the feedback was that these were subjective measures and medicine was based on objective measures. There was less enthusiasm amongst the doctors than Eddie had anticipated. He lamented to Kathy, *"It's not bad science is it Kathy? This is what health care is all about."*

"Yes. Improving one's quality of life is the main reason people go to a doctor. Don't be discouraged."

In 1999 the Prime Minister, John Howard, announced new Medicare Items for GPs in what was going to be called "Enhanced Primary Care". The supporting documentation claimed that these changes were to promote education of mobility and function and were "preventive in their nature". There was also an acknowledgment of the need to address risk factors and the determinants that contribute to ill-health. Eddie was delighted with the proposal and saw it as an exciting development. He could see the valuable contribution that PROMs could play in implementing the government's proposal particularly when they led to lifestyle "preventive prescriptions". The potential product for eMedilab was "Care Plans" in which the PROMs could be hidden and Eddie planned to sell this to GP practices.

"Kathy, THESE people will get the importance of this!"

His assurance to Kathy conveyed his eternal hope that the two hundred plus delegates streaming in through the Intercontinental Hotel doors in Sydney for the 1999 Royal Australian College of Medical Administrators Conference would finally listen, understand, accept and implement his ideas for a healthier health system. Many delegates did attend their stand and completed the SF-36 and, to his surprise, he had to counsel two doctor delegates, only one of which was aware he was suffering from depression.

"Kathy, that shows you that these can be used as diagnostic tests. I have just diagnosed depression in someone who was unaware they had it." Their attendance at the conference was just part of his continued assault on the health system. He threw everything he had, professionally, emotionally, intellectually and financially, at instigating his revolution. Eddie looked for a financial backer to assist in his cause. Tin Shed, a venture capitalist organisation, advised Eddie he

would need to upgrade his "product" before they would consider investing. An idea was not enough.

After Jillian left, Eddie employed another dynamic client relationship manager, Mitchell Hunter, who assured him that he could "sell coal to Newcastle". Mitch had meetings with potential clients over beer after work and asked Eddie to fund these outings that became bigger and bigger. He rapidly increased business but Eddie was concerned his style wasn't conducive to the professional image of an occupational medical practice. Kathy did her best to keep Mitchell in line and was appointed overall practice manager. A comprehensive package of training and guidelines was drawn up. These instructed GP practices on how to carry out Senior Health Assessments and Chronic Disease Care Plans, leading to preventive or lifestyle prescriptions. In mid-2000 a practice nurse, Rebecca Miller, a forward-thinking young nurse from New Zealand, was employed to help with training, selling the system and carrying out the Care Plan or Health Assessment. Their ex-employer and now referring company, HIH, had grown through taking over another insurance company.

They said to Eddie, *"We want to refer more work your way but you have to have bigger premises, particularly in Parramatta, to handle the up and coming workload."*

A former Chinese restaurant on the ground floor of their building at 127 Argyle Street, Parramatta was available and Eddie took over this large space and Head Office was moved from North Sydney to Parramatta. The move coincided with Mitchell's leaving for the Sunshine Coast much to Eddie and Kathy's relief. The practice had grown but in Eddie's eyes its reputation was slightly tarnished. At the opening party for the expanded premises at Parramatta a lot of alcohol was consumed or disappeared and Eddie was reasonably confident that some of it was on its way to the Sunshine Coast. He said to Kathy, *"A small price to pay."* He would let Kathy interview and select the next client relationship manager.

He was off to Israel again in April 2000 as he had discovered research on the SF-36 at Tel Aviv University. Ever wanting to maintain ties with Israel and encouraging the use of Health Outcomes practices in the country, he employed a nurse to set up a further company called eMedilab Israel. Like its Australian counterpart eMedilab Israel provided doctors with a system of computer-scannable Care Plans that lead to Prevention Lifestyle Prescriptions. Eddie's good friend Edju was at the time building malls in Poland. Eddie sent him a Polish version of the SF-36 and Edju emailed back, *"I found the questionnaire very interesting indeed."* As Eddie wandered his beloved Israeli streets he pondered again on the capacity of reach for these management tools. What could they achieve across various disciplines if value could already be seen in such different fields as medicine and, following discussion with Edju, construction? There was a reduced number of soldiers on the streets of Tel Aviv and the feeling of hope in Israel that peace was around the corner. The Israeli Prime Minister, Barak, and President Arafat were due to meet in two months' time with President Bill Clinton at Camp David in the USA. All indications were that an agreement had been reached. For a solider at the frontline that Eddie spoke with it was a time to be cautious. *"It will be crazy to be killed now for we will have peace in three months."*

The atmosphere of hope seeped into Eddie, believing that eMedilab could revolutionise healthcare in Israel and it would hopefully give him an excuse to travel back and forth more regularly to this cherished country. One day he received a call from his brother Michael back in Australia.

"Eddie, Penny doesn't want to continue with the marriage, it's all over. I've purchased her share in the software business but now my major client, CALTEX, is refusing to pay for all the GST compliance alterations that I have to make to the financial accounting systems. The workload is huge. I'm really stressed and I'm struggling."

Eddie raced back to Australia to his brother's side to help sort out the financial and emotional mess. Eventually CALTEX wanted out of their arrangement with Michael's company but they wanted to purchase his software code. They'd caught him at his most vulnerable and acquired it at a bargain-basement price. However, for Michael the financial pressure was off and he could concentrate on healing his emotional wounds. He refers to Eddie as a saviour in this most traumatic time of his life.

Tull's Royal Elastic Shoes had expanded at such a rate that they now had an office in Manhattan, New York, and they had partnered with the Australian distributors for Reebok. Tull was flitting around the world attending to business. His shoes featured in a shoe magazine under the title "The shoe that changed the World" and Tull was invited to speak at an international shoe conference in The States.

Eddie was impressed, *"That's a great honour. When are you going?"*

Tull replied, *"Eddie, it's a shoe. It's only a shoe. I'm not going."*

The business continued to expand and there was interest from a large tennis shoe company in The States, K-Swiss. Accordingly, they moved their offices out of the home and

Eddie turned the former Royal Elastics Office into the research and development office of eMedilab.

He felt eMedilab's new computer-scannable Care Plan that led to preventative or lifestyle prescriptions was now the product that the venture capitalist organisation had claimed he was previously lacking. He now felt confident they had a product that would be suitable to the GP market so he took the system to the Australian General Practice Conference and Exhibition in May of 2000. For three days he stood and preached to one GP after another about the many reasons to use eMedilab's health assessments. *"You will improve your patients' health status and have evidence to prove it. You will increase your practice income. For each patient you will obtain quantified results. You will receive scores on nutrition status, body mass index, physical function, mental function and the probability of repeated hospital admissions. You would also have a list of all their risk factors,"* and continued, *"This information would be collected by nurses in your patients' home with no interference to your normal practice."*

To his delight many GP practice names and details were collected but to his dismay over the following weeks and months only a small number of practices signed up and in those the doctors made little time available for training.

Eddie was never one to take sick leave; in fact, his family cannot recall one day that he was not passionately following his endeavours. He did however take a two-week break and closed all his offices in September of 2000. This unprecedented step was not taken due to ill health....but for love....Eddie's love of sport. It was the Sydney Olympics and he wanted to relish the euphoric atmosphere of his home town. Sam managed to obtain tickets to attend the swimming. Mia and Eddie enthusiastically watched Ian Thorpe win the 400 metres. They cheered wildly and Mia cried as the Australians won the Men's 4x100 metre swimming relay. They were also fortunate enough to watch Grant Hackett win the Men's 1500 freestyle over Kieran Perkins. At the athletics they were in the stands watching as Kathy Freeman won the Women's 400 metre race. Eddie's sport-induced happy delirium overcame any feelings of despondency at the lack of importance given to his ideas. He constantly questioned why doctors didn't really understand what he was offering for their patients, for their practices and for the world. Sport, as it often does, had had its galvanising effect. He returned to work inspired and energised and resolved to do everything in his power to bring true healthcare to the world.

As 2000 slid into 2001 the euphoria took a plunge once again. There were rumours that HIH, the company that had been feeding his practice work for years, was in financial distress. It proceeded to dissolve into one of Australia's largest corporate collapses. Eddie's business was well enough established that, despite minor cash flow problems, they managed to survive. Again he attended the annual Australian General Practice Conference and Exhibition and obtained many practice names for follow-up but the numbers were underwhelming.

"How is it when I worked for the Family Medicine Program, not a business of my own, I managed to sell extremely well. Yet when it is my own business, my enthusiasm is less?" Perhaps it was Eddie's father's inculcation against benefitting financially through business, *"We are not celebrating Mother's and Father's day. They've only been developed by business to make more money!"*

Henry Price would claim. Eddie felt that when he viewed his own business as profit seeking, rather than a public good, he was a diminished sales person. During a Health Outcomes Conference in Canberra put on by the Australian Health Outcomes Collaboration, in front of two hundred delegates Eddie raised, *"These PROMs measurements are, in my opinion, a new set of diagnostic tests."* Following his comments, Eddie was perplexed by the merciless attack that he received from senior executives of the collaboration and wondered, *"Was it the way I made my comment? Do I display arrogance? Perhaps it is the fact that I don't have a university attached to my name."*

Chapter 13

Model Discount

"He has septicaemia. I don't think we can rescue him from this situation," confirmed Sam's good friend and cardiologist Dr Paul Roy after examining Mia's father. Following numerous bouts of illness and hospitalisations he was too weak to fight any more. Sam Fiszman's life support was turned off and he passed away on the 23rd of March 2002.

A gaping void opened up in the lives of all those who knew and called Sam family or friend. This man who had survived so much as a teen in war-torn Poland and who had achieved so much in post-war Sydney, had become a pillar of strength, advice and love for all those around him, none more so than his daughter. Mia was distraught. Eddie was devastated. He had lost a confidante....someone he respected and relied upon.

Death brings a sense of one's own mortality. For Eddie, at fifty-five, he felt that his time to shine, his ambition to sell his ideas to the masses, was more pressing than ever. He needed more traction and international recognition for his ideas and his book. He resolved to travel to Boston to attempt to meet up with a Dr Michael Hammer. Dr Hammer was an engineer by training and a professor at MIT. He was known as one of the founders of the management theory of business process re-engineering and admired by Eddie. He wanted an opportunity to speak with Dr Hammer about his own philosophies on re-engineering healthcare as outlined in his book Supramedicine. Hammer was a Jew and a child of holocaust survivors so Eddie decided to take advantage of their common ground. He asked his Jewish friend, Dr Mark

Moscovitz in Boston, if he would be able to arrange a meeting. Moscovitz happily agreed to make the introductions and Eddie prepared for his trip.

On the morning of his departure he received a fax from Dr Moscovitz, *"My mother-in-law has just passed away so according to the Jewish religion, we are now in seven days of mourning (sitting Shiva) and I will be unable to meet with you."* Eddie was deflated. What should he do? He figured that Mark would be mourning in a synagogue and possibly the same one as Hammer would attend. He decided he would try and find the synagogue and spot Professor Michael Hammer. On arrival in Boston Eddie went directly to the Council of Synagogues.

"Can I help you?" came a greeting.

"Yes. I'm a friend of Dr Mark Moscovitz and I believe his mother-in-law just passed away."

"Oh, you mean Mrs Keller. Did you know her?" the greeter queried.

He explained, *"I'm from Australia, but I am a colleague of Dr Moscovitz. Would you know which synagogue he attends?"*

Without any hesitation he was given the name and address. That night he walked to the synagogue and as he entered, draped his Jewish prayer shawl, the Tallis, across his back. There was a tap on his shoulder. *"We don't wear the prayer shawl on Friday night."* After his apology and hasty removal of the Tallis, Eddie spotted Mark Moscovitz but could see no sign of Michael Hammer. After the service he approached Mark and expressed his condolences in the Australian Jewish way, *"I wish you long life."*

Mark replied, *"That's not what we say here but some South Africans have said something similar."* He apologised with an awkward smile for the second time that evening. *"I didn't see Michael Hammer at the service. You told me he was a Board member."*

"Eddie, you're quite correct. We had an argument on the Board of the Synagogue and half the Board left. See that house across the road. They have taken out a lease on that house, got their own rabbi and half the congregation now goes there. If you go there tomorrow morning for the Saturday service you will definitely see Michael Hammer," explained Mark. *"Eddie, although we are sitting Shiva, the tradition is that the rest of the community makes meals for us at this time and we have plenty of food. Why don't you walk home and eat with us?"*

After eating well with Mark the previous night, Eddie woke early with excitement at the prospect of meeting one of his philosophical mentors. He arrived early at the new meeting hall and was greeted by a young rabbi excited to see someone new.

"Are you a new congregant?" said the rabbi.

"Oh no," replied Eddie, *"but I would like to meet one of your congregation, Professor Michael Hammer."*

"No problem. I will introduce you to him after the service but we've got a long service today. We've got a call up for an incoming wedding. We have a bar mitzvah and we often have a guest speaker giving the sermon from the various luminaries at Harvard and other universities. One is on today. Before the service, however, we are having a lesson on Jewish beliefs and we're starting now. We'd love you to attend," enthusiastically replied the young rabbi.

Eddie had little choice. It was a long morning and halfway through the service he recognised Professor Michael Hammer arriving. At the end of the service, the rabbi approached Hammer and made the introductions. *"Michael, this is Dr Eddie Price from Australia. He's a friend of Dr Moscovitz's."*

Eddie smiled, *"Nice to meet you Michael."*

"It's Saturday," said Professor Hammer. *"I can't talk now but get Mark to ring me after he finishes the Shiva which I think is in a day or two at the most and we will organise it from there."*

Two days later, after speaking with Dr Moscovitz, Professor Hammer invited Eddie to his home. Eddie gave Hammer an understanding of his theories and the contents of his book Supramedicine. The Professor then spent the following hour quizzing Eddie about the book and the role it played and why Eddie believed it was a "re-engineering" of healthcare. Despite the thorough examination, Professor Hammer explained to Eddie that he would no longer be persisting with a health focus in his company (Hammer and Co.) and therefore there would be no requirement for his book. He left disappointed. He rang Mia. *"Eddie, what do you expect stalking him in the synagogue!"* she reasoned.

"I am sure he is as passionate about his ideas as I am about mine. He is just no longer interested in healthcare."

From Boston he limped to Rhode Island to the head office of QualityMetrics who work with the world's largest healthcare companies to measure and better understand health outcomes. They were the current international promoters of PROMs and Eddie was there to speak with them about "Australianising" some of the language in their PROM questionnaires. He was afforded an audience with QualityMetric co-founder Jim Dewey and other members of staff. He advised them that what they had with their various PROMs were, in his opinion, really diagnostic tests and would be much more effective if used daily in clinical medicine. It seemed to him that nobody was really listening and the only thing to come out of the meeting was a friendship with Jim Dewey. Jim would later confide in Eddie that his training was as a scientist and he was struggling with running QualityMetrics from the management and administrative point of view. *"But I'll be over your way soon Eddie,"* Jim declared. *"My daughter is studying for a year at the University of Sydney and I'm headed over for a visit."*

"Well you're invited to come to our home and our office when you are there Jim," said Eddie.

He moved on to LA where Tull was living. Royal Elastics had grown and through his arrangements with K-Swiss, Tull had been given a US visa for four years under a special achievement arrangement. A number of acquaintances of Eddie's, from various times in his life, all chanced to have converged on LA at the same time. There was Eddie's intern friend from Israel, Dr Mario Rosenberg, who was now a practising gastroenterologist in LA as well as Sam and Esther's family friend from Israel, Mike Burstyn, who was doing some acting and shows in LA, and finally, Mia's cousin Roslyn happened to be visiting LA from Tucson, Arizona. The unlikely group met for dinner near Tull's home at an elegant Italian restaurant in Venice Beach. Gazing around the table and joining the peals of laughter, he was pleased these friends from such diverse parts of his life were intermingling so well. It was a memorable evening.

Despite being buoyed by the camaraderie of his family and friends in LA overall it was a somewhat disappointing trip professionally. He hadn't even been able to sell his ideas to the converted at either QualityMetrics or to Dr Hammer. How then would he ever be able to overcome the doctors' objection to PROMs? He had already tried to hide PROMs in Care Plans to overcome their "too subjective for science" objections but most GPs still did not see the immense value that Dr Eddie Price, and a few doctors associated with the Medical Outcomes Trust and the Australian Health Outcomes Collaboration, saw. Just when he was at his most despondent, a phone call elevated his spirits and re-ignited his seemingly endless hope.

"Eddie, one of my patients has completed your SF-36 forms on a couple of occasions. This is exactly what we need here in orthopaedics. Can you come over and discuss? I am in the St George region."

It was Dr Ian Harris, Associate Professor of Orthopaedics at Liverpool Hospital on the other end of the phone. Eddie could hardly believe what he was hearing. It was early 2003 and finally there was some interest, from a practising clinician, in PROMs. He continued, *"Eddie, I want to do some research and I think that the SF-36 would be most helpful."*

Eddie enthusiastically agreed, *"It would help Doctor, and what would be really beneficial to your work, is having the entire process online. We are hoping to move the SF-36s to an internet format. I'm in discussions currently with QualityMetrics to progress this technology."* It was a small win. After so many general practitioners reporting that "subjective measures were not good science" at least Eddie had one orthopaedic surgeon, and an academic to boot, who felt the opposite.

"Eddie, our new apartment is too small for you to stay with us, so I've booked you into The Tribeca Grand Hotel. There is a fashion parade going on at the moment and I get a 'Model Discount' so it's all sorted." Gemma Hamilton was

Tull's model girlfriend. She and Tull had just moved to NY from LA. Eddie was on his way to Israel to check up on his business there and had dropped into visit Tull and Gemma on his way through. It was April 2003 but rather than thawing into spring, the Big Apple was being battered by late season snow storms. He braced himself for the brutal weather, determined to comply with the extensive shopping list Mia had supplied of purchases from Banana Republic and Gap. He savoured his time browsing through the cosy back rows of glossy books at the Barnes & Noble bookstore in Union Square and poured over the latest science, management, self-help and psychology books whilst sipping a warm hot chocolate at the in-store lounge. On his return from each trip to the US, his bags would be laden with books from their collections. Tull took him to his favourite restaurant, Bar Pitti, on the corner of 6th Ave and Houston and later to his local gym. When Eddie tumbled back to the Tribeca Grand after his busy day he tried to enter his room, only to realise that his room key and its cardboard folder with hotel name and room number on it, were missing. He advised the hotel staff that he had lost his key. They said, "*Not a problem sir,*" and gave him a new one.

At 3am Eddie was awoken by his door going "*beep, beep, beep*" and opening.

"*Who's there? Get out of here!*" he demanded. The door closed. He flicked on the lights and looked straight at his bedside table where he'd left his TAG watch, a gift from Mia's parents for his 50th birthday. The watch was gone. Eddie called reception, "*I've been robbed!*"

"*One minute,*" they said. "*We will send up security.*"

Security arrived, "*Yes Ms Hamilton. What can we do for you Ms Hamilton?*"

"*I'm not Ms Hamilton. I'm Dr Price. Someone just came into my room and my TAG watch is gone!*" Security scoured the room and balcony but could find nothing. They suggested he call the NYPD. "*We will despatch a squad shortly,*" said the operator. Twenty minutes later, four burly NYPD officers, all over six foot and broadly set, entered the room. They overturned the mattress, every cupboard, and every bag was examined. "*So Dr Price, it seems strange that your room is actually booked for a Ms Gemma Hamilton. What are you doing here?*" the police queried.

"*Gemma is my son's girlfriend. She booked the room for me. She's a model you see.*" he explained uncomfortably. How was he suddenly under suspicion? It was his watch that had been stolen and was seemingly the least concern to these officers.

"*Was your watch insured?*" the NYPD officers enquired.

"*I only have normal travel insurance,*" replied a deflated Eddie.

After half an hour of intimidation they left. Eddie was frustrated. His watch would be long gone by now. He took two Valium.

The next morning, as he walked the busy streets of Manhattan, Eddie slipped in the icy snow only barely avoiding a nasty fall. At Newark Airport later that day he watched a TV news bulletin that reported the death in NY that morning of Dr Atkins, famous for the Atkins Low Carbohydrate Diet. He'd slipped on the icy snow and hit his head on the pavement.

"*That could easily have been a report of the deaths of two doctors, Dr Atkins and Dr Price, in the same way!*" he thought.

Eddie had arrived early for his El Al flight to Israel. He

knew the drill of the usual questions. They were always more strenuous when they noticed that Eddie was born in Lebanon but he'd never had this line of questioning before.

"*This is very nice,*" said the security officer, motioning to his new T-shirt. "*Would it happen to be new?*"

"*Yes,*" said Eddie. "*I just purchased it earlier today.*"

The security guard replied, "*I know. It's got three labels on it, on your chest and abdomen. I suggest you might like to remove them.*"

He grimaced with embarrassment while the next security officer asked for his surname.

"*Price,*" he said.

The security officer queried, "*Is that Edward Price or Dagan Price?*"

"*What?*" said Eddie, "*I'm Edward but Dagan is my cousin. Is he on this plane as well?*"

"*I can't say anything,*" said the security officer realising her faux pas.

He looked at the assembled passengers as they were arriving. One after the other looked like they all came out of Crown Heights with the Hassidic Jewish look. He realised Passover was coming and they were all heading back to Jerusalem for this festivity. Eventually, he spotted a young man with a blonde girlfriend and approached them.

"*Dagan?*" Eddie asked.

"*Yes, how did you know?*"

"*I'm Eddie Price. We have met once before. Do you recall? I think you were producing a show on an Israeli director who was suffering from HIV.*"

"*Yes,*" said Dagan. The two reconnected, but Dagan pointed out, "*I'm pretty ill myself today. I've got a high temperature and I'm not looking forward to this flight.*"

They arranged to catch up when they were both settled in Israel.

Back in Israel he stayed with their close friends Betty and Edju. He also enjoyed visiting his cousin Gershon Price on kibbutz Ein Dor and his son, Eliav, who had moved to kibbutz Hazorea outside Haifa. The kibbutz visits brought back fond memories of his time working at Kibbutz Yiftach and he enjoyed observing the kibbutz cottage industries. In town he re-connected with his colleagues from Clalit and his very competent executive assistant Raquel. Eddie was incredibly impressed, but not surprised, by the trajectory of this dynamic young woman. A Russian doctor had noted Raquel's competence and had asked her to take on a role managing a nursing home outside of Petah Tikva. Raquel had apparently replied, *"Dr Dubrov, I would be happy to do so but I would also like a share of the nursing home."* According to Raquel, after some tough negotiations, this was agreed to and she had a reasonable percentage in a nursing home that was taking in its first residents.

"How exciting," Eddie effused. *"You're a better businessman than I!"*

Chapter 14

A fractal between the squares

During 2003, Eddie's term as a Director of WorkCover NSW came to an end.

He reflected to Kathy, *"I didn't and wasn't able to get my ideas across. I am disappointed. Is it my manner? Are the ideas too new? Are they difficult to explain?"*

Kathy tried to placate him by reminding him, *"We do have more general practitioners using the computer-scannable system of PROMs now Eddie."*

"Yes, but more training is needed and there is a lack of general understanding!"

He was still able to serve the people of NSW when appointed as a Director of the NSW Sports Injury Prevention Committee. He held this position for nine years until it was abandoned by the new Liberal government and incorporated into their much-reduced State Insurance Regulatory Authority (SIRA), which had also incorporated WorkCover and the Motor Accidents Authority.

He was still looking for ways to engage with Ministers for Health or the Shadow Ministers to whom he could spruik his ideas for the health system. He heard there was a small meeting arranged with some Shadow Ministers at the Aria Restaurant in Sydney and managed an invitation to the gathering. The Shadow Ministers attending were Julia Gillard, Shadow Minister for Health, and Wayne Swan, the Shadow Treasurer. For 15 minutes Eddie spoke with Julia Gillard and tried to explain the potential power of the SF-36. She asked that he forward the information to her office. After sending through all the relevant information, he received the following letter:

"I strongly agree that our primary health care system must be focused on preventive health and disease management, and General Practitioners are likely to respond well to incentives that reward them for achieved better health outcomes at the patient and community levels.

Just how we go about doing that is the major question. I find your proposal to use the SF-36 survey through e-Medilab interesting, but I am not sure this is the right approach for Australian doctors and their patients.

However, I do appreciate your efforts in this area and the opportunity to consider them.

Yours sincerely

Julia Gillard, MP

Shadow Minister for Health"

Another rejection and another opportunity lost. If Julia Gillard did indeed agree that what he was proposing needed to happen, then Eddie couldn't understand why she couldn't see that PROMs were the way in which to achieve those goals. Again he questioned his ability to effectively communicate his ideas. He was convinced that his Patient-Reported Outcome Measures (PROMs) were good science and felt the repeated objection of doctors, that they were just subjective, did not stand up.

It was the 26th of January, Australia Day, time for the "famous picnic" now being held at Clarkes Point. *"Hi Tom, before I forget, here is Bill Bryson's book you lent me, A Short History of Nearly Everything, about Physics and Science",* said Jan Kingsbury who had previously hosted ABC's television show, Extra Dimension. *"I really liked it."*

Tom Atkinson said, *"It was great but I want you to give it straight to Eddie who is really into the New Physics"*.

"Thanks Tom," said Eddie, who was lamenting to his long-time friend, James Benjamin, his frustrations. *"I'm continually criticised and rejected by my peers. They claim my work lacks objectivity. It's not real science for them. I need to find a way to prove my ideas scientifically."*

Both men had at various family gatherings over many years shared ideas and talked philosophy and science. It was their conversation on this occasion that would have a dramatic impact on the way in which Eddie viewed his constant rejections as well as opening up a whole other intellectual world for him.

James stated, *"I am currently reading up on Complexity Science and that is really interesting. It is a modern way of describing systems that are dynamic, unpredictable and multi-dimensional. It is a science that debunks the traditional cause and effect thinking. I think this science can be applied across many different disciplines in life. You should look into it Eddie."*

Eddie was jubilant. He had just found his answer as to why his ideas were not acceptable – they were being judged by "old" science - they needed to be viewed through a new paradigm... a complex paradigm. He could also see how this actually confirmed his own theories of our bodies as more complex / supra-systems.

James' brother Tim joined their conversation, *"I find this stuff fascinating. I'm actually thinking of making a movie about Schroedinger's Cat. You know the thought experiment that presents the proposition that a cat may be simultaneously both alive and dead, in a state of quantum superposition."*

Harry Smith chimed in, *"You guys should read The Scientific American. I have a regular subscription and I love reading them."*

All of a sudden there were five or six members of the famous picnic group who all showed a curiosity and an interest in new science or new physics. Eddie was fascinated to hear more about Complexity Science and suggested that if they were all interested in this subject matter then maybe they should form a discussion/brainstorming group. He had just read about the Santa Fe Institute in New Mexico - a group of scientists who had broken away from Los Alamos, where the atomic bomb was researched and developed. The Institute would discuss and research the commonalities between social sciences, economics and the physical sciences - believing there must be an underlying commonality. Eddie was excited, *"Our group can be called the Sydney Chapter of Santa Fe."* Within three months they gathered for their first meeting of the Sydney Chapter of Santa Fe, concentrating around the topic of Complexity Science that combined Chaos and Order theories. They met periodically throughout the year - for many years – pursuing the application of complexity and where complexity science could lead. They discussed topics such as Quantum Mechanics and Einstein's theory of relativity and Eddie organised international experts to attend and give presentations. All meetings were held at his home and were followed by Mia's baguettes.

Eddie enthusiastically threw himself into the study of Complexity Science. He and James both completed an on-line course run by the Santa Fe Institute and he read voraciously. He delved into Wolfram's, A New Kind of Science, and was impressed with Fritjof Capra's book, The

Web of Life. He enjoyed the work of Feigenbaum and Liebhaber. He read many books on Systems Theory and the New Physics and read, and thoroughly enjoyed the book on Chaos by Glick. In particular, he found the stories and research of Benoit Mandelbrot of great interest.

He commented to Mia, *"Can you believe there is a famous scientist by the name of Mandelbrot (which in Yiddish is the name for almond bread)?"* Benoit Mandelbrot had coined the term "fractal" – an abstract object used to describe and simulate naturally occurring objects. Eddie was fascinated and explained to anyone who would listen that there are various dimensions in the world and a straight line is one dimension, a plane is two dimensions, a cube is three dimensions, but Mandelbrot had discovered the formula for in-between dimensions. Mandelbrot would ask, *"How long is the coastline of Britain?"* He would then answer in terms of dimensions that it was 1.54 dimensions, that is, between 1 and 2 that explained the jagged edges. A crumpled piece of paper bag may end up being in between a plane and a cube and it would be 2.45 dimensions.

Perhaps Eddie's fascination with fractals was more than a pure intellectual appreciation for personally he had been something of an "in-between" his whole life, never fitting the mould. He was a fractal between the squares. Did his social, cultural and intellectual outsider status give him a unique insight into the energy, the magic, that can be found in the space "between", that which we cannot see, or is not always obvious, clouded by our physical and socially constructed "bits"? Eddie had found the spark, the beauty, the fractal of life - that which will give us all what we seek most of all....quality of life. If only we'd listen.

The Santa Fe group's study of quantum mechanics brought

further clarity to Eddie on why his ideas and his concepts to change the way medicine could be practiced around the world for the improvement of health and for cost savings were constantly being dismissed by the medical and health establishments....the benefits seemingly invisible to their understanding. Quantum mechanics illustrated that items can both be particles (things) or waves (invisible flows of energy like radio waves or Wi-Fi). The latter was more difficult to conceptualise in our physical world. Eddie realised PROMs were thus. They weren't concrete enough for those stuck in the "old science". They were of a different realm and intangible in a tangible world. Eddie found this idea was also affirmed by Heisenberg's Uncertainty Principle – that the more definitively you see the particle, the more uncertain the wave becomes and hence almost impossible to see. Putting these findings to work in the health system paradigm shows that what people really go to doctors for most of the time is to improve their functional state. If they have cataracts they go to improve their eyesight which will improve their overall functioning and their quality of life. However, quality of life is not something physical like a liver or a knee joint, it is a sense of well-being. Quantifying life's quality seemed impossible to those locked into seeing only the physical. Eddie was proposing that PROMs were the way to achieve the impossible by accurately measuring this invisible energetic wave. Now he had the science that would support this.

Ever the eccentric, he didn't disappoint his friends and colleagues when his scientific and fractal fascination turned into a celebration. Eddie decided he'd had enough "round" birthdays celebrated, such as 40 and 50, and that the in-between birthdays were discriminated against. So, in a bid to educate his friends and family on the existence of fractals, he threw what he called a Fractal (58th) birthday. He plastered signs around the house on fractals and the theory behind them and invited absolutely everybody he knew. All his staff attended along with the famous picnic group friends. His former Betar friend with whom he'd had little contact with over the years and all the Bondi walkers were there. The group of above-middle aged men who walked most mornings at 6:00am from Bondi to Bronte. The food was good, but Eddie's speech was a disaster. As he tried to explain fractals to an uninterested large raucous audience he was hauled off stage with the majority of his message indecipherable to those gathered. Bernie Kresner described discussions with Eddie as similar to a journey through the white pages of a Berlin telephone directory as he sprouted his latest theories and quoted his latest idol... Heisenberg... Einstein... Feigenbaum... Libchaber... Feldenkrais... Mandelbrot.

Undaunted by the lack of enthusiasm for fractals by his family and friends, he looked further at the proposition that a combination of theories, that of Chaos Theory (Disorder), together with Order, created a new science - Complexity Science. What he was now interested in was whether he could stretch the idea into Complexity Medicine and use this to justify his "subjective" medicine.

Rejuvenated by the possibilities of injecting "real science" into PROMs and his eMedilab Care Planning system, Eddie acknowledged that his computer scannable technology was out of date and in drastic need of an overhaul. Michael advised Eddie that the Care Planning system could be adapted to the internet and he would be happy to help. Michael was commissioned to oversee the development of the program. Eddie reflected that this was a further measure to again hide the PROMs from view of the sceptical doctors who questioned his "subjective methods". The product was named ADEPT for Advanced Dynamic Enhanced Primary Care Prescription Technology.

At the same time, he became aware of a QualityMetrics trusted partner agreement where they would allow their internet-based computer adaptive tests to be done through eMedilab's website. However, this was an expensive purchase and programming had to be done at the eMedilab end. This would turn eMedilab into an electronic laboratory for doctors to measure patients' Functional Health Measures in a similar way as they would send tests to a pathology lab. Eddie employed Tull's good friend, Ronny Endrey-Walder, a computer IT expert and web designer, to create their end of the trusted partner link with QualityMetrics. Eddie had gone from no internet presence to suddenly having two eHealth products under development.

While many parts of his professional life were seemingly coming together, it was his family life that came apart. In early 2005 after many debates with Mia about her ability to be incredibly charming and outgoing with all except Eddie's family, he could no longer put up with the reoccurring rift. Mia had her own take on the situation and they decided to separate. Eddie moved upstairs and Mia lived downstairs. The situation was devastating. He had always envisaged his family as being together. They were paramount to him and the situation he now found himself in was demoralising. A pre-arranged trip to India with their Israeli friends Edju and Betty and Myrna and Eric was already booked and paid for but Mia declined to participate. Before leaving on this trip he attended his GP, Dr Gillian Deakin, and stated he wanted some blood tests before going overseas. Gillian asked how he was coping with the recent separation. Eddie said he was almost suicidal. Dr Deakin replied, *"Well you'd be the first person who is thinking of suicide who wants to have blood tests to make sure they are well!"* He took her point and moved on to India.

Despite his distress over what was going to happen in his marriage he was glad to join his friends and enjoyed a wonderful trip touring Rajasthan in a large van and frequenting the majestic Taj Hotels as they went. Although he was not always in the most positive frame of mind he kept his sense of humour....hiding the shoes of their driver and challenging young locals to games of street cricket with his friend Eric. The eighteen-year-old Indians took great pleasure in bowling at immense speeds at the now beyond middle-aged men. The group fell in love with naan and Eric insisted on green tea ice cream everywhere they went. Eddie, ever eager to seize an opportunity, thought there was no reason why his PROMs system wouldn't work in India. They were staying at the Jodhpur Palace Hotel which was partially converted to a hotel but was still the Maharajah's residence.

He thought to himself, *"You could request an appointment with the Maharajah if you wished!"*

To Eddie's surprise and delight an audience was granted and he presented his ideas on reforming health systems using PROMs and how they could be used as preventive measures in India. The Maharajah was interested and asked him to come back for another meeting the next day. That very evening the son of the Maharajah, the Prince, was thrown from his horse during a polo match, rendered unconscious and hospitalised with severe head injuries. The meeting was cancelled. Again acceptance had been within Eddie's grasp, only to be whisked, frustratingly away.

The group continued with their tour of India and Eddie was able to reignite his love of horse riding at the Great Lakes Palace Hotel in Udaipur. One morning he was venting his emotions, flying across the countryside, when the horse he was riding came across a group of wild brumbies. The horse took off and was galloping at a great rate. In its excitement it was headed straight towards the front of the hotel. At this time each day a grand parade was held with elephants, camels and marching bands and they began the procession in front of the hotel. He imagined the carnage if he didn't get his horse under control. Somehow, at the last minute, he managed to pull on the left rein and avoid one of the 14 elephants in the line-up. He casually alighted, parted company with the horse and happily watched the parade from the front entrance of the hotel. After such an eventful ride, he retired to his room and picked up a book his cousin Dinah, a counsellor, had suggested he read to better understand his situation with Mia. The book was called Reinventing Your Life by Jeffrey Young and Janet Klosko. He devoured this book that was based on what is known as Schema Therapy or life scripts. It claimed that people having relationship problems all have life scripts where they re-enact the worst part of their childhood. Eddie concluded that he had three life scripts including unrelenting standards, emotional deprivation and subjugation – the ramifications of his authoritarian father. He saw this Schema therapy as a productive way in which he could work on himself to help restore his relationship with Mia. That is, if Mia was also willing to do so. He would discuss these with her when he returned and he would commence counselling with a counsellor who used these techniques.

"Has Eddie lost the plot?" thought Kathy. He certainly had lost a lot of weight and he was asking her to make posters for a polo fundraiser that would send money and a Health Outcomes program to a hospital in Jodhpur, India. Eddie had been in discussions with the offsider of the Maharaja of Jodhpur after the tragic accident where the Prince had been left in a coma. Eddie had arranged for money from the fundraiser to be sent to the local hospital under the provision that it be used for work with the Health Outcomes program. The donation was made in the name of Will Ashton, part of the famous Australian Ashton polo family and a boy Eddie had coached as part of the Waverley Cricket Team. Will's mother was also a sometime participant of his Sydney Chapter Santa Fe meetings. Will had been killed in a motor vehicle accident coming back from a polo match and Eddie suggested this donation, made in Will's name, would be a fitting memorial. Mrs Ashton expressed her gratitude with an invitation for him and Kathy to attend the Windsor Polo Test between Australia and New Zealand as guests of the President of Polo Australia.

Kathy worked through Eddie's idiosyncrasies. She counselled him about how she thought they should move forward in the business suggesting, *"We need to concentrate on developing the ADEPT system as well as the Trusted Partner agreement with QualityMetrics. It may be slow but it is progressing. I think we need to focus on these things and not get distracted by all this science."* He acknowledged that she may have a point. Many of those who heard his speech at his fractal birthday party also thought he was a little crazy. Although he agreed to remain on topic with ADEPT and his agreement with QualityMetrics, he kept his private research into Complexity Science bubbling along with the prospect of writing another book looking at Complexity Medicine.

On the 18th of May 2005, he again attended the Post Health Budget Breakfast Meeting, this time with Tony Abbott, Minister for Health. Eddie was surprised to get two minutes of his time and Abbott suggested he make a submission and get a further appointment. He eagerly complied; however once again, after the submission was made and he had spent a couple of hours speaking with an advisor of Minister Abbott's, there was little understanding of his ideas. Following Kathy's edict to focus on pushing ADEPT, he decided that they needed to train nurses in the ADEPT program (that incorporated the SF-36) if they wanted the system to be a success. Training rooms were booked at Westmead Hospital and they had enough nurses eager to train with them. It seemed ADEPT had become more acceptable to those in that profession. Even the Federal government, hoping that eHealth would save them money, showed an interest in Electronic Care Planning. Michael, who was looking after the computerised systems of ADEPT was invited to demonstrate the program to the Adelaide Urban Divisions Alliance of GPs. The organiser was Dr Peter Del Fante. Michael impressed those attending with the speed at which referrals to Allied Health Professionals were executed in front of them. The ADEPT program was systematically set out. Two weeks later Eddie received a call from the South Australian Health Department who were running a research pilot program on Electronic Care Planning. They'd heard about Michael's demonstration and asked eMedilab to submit a proposal. Eddie was beyond elated. Finally, his ideas were being accepted by the mainstream and by a government department no less. All his time and investment would finally pay-off for him and the impact on the health of the nation would be significant. However, he was concerned that his intellectual property might disappear and asked whether they would be happy to sign a non-disclosure agreement.

"No problem," replied Andrew McAlindon, Head of the Project. *"Just send it through."*

Eddie who was not a person of detail had just signed an agreement with QualityMetrics in America for the Trusted Partner arrangement and so he instructed Kathy to just change the name and the details of the people and use that non-disclosure agreement. Kathy did just that and nobody looked at the details of the contract. His phone rang.

"Hello. Look, it's Andrew McAlindon here. The non-disclosure agreement you sent us threatens to sue us if something goes wrong with penalties and so forth."

He apologised and stated it was an amended agreement from the States and obviously they are much more litigation-aware.

Andrew replied, *"You don't need to submit your ADEPT system further if this is reflective of your attitude."*

The ADEPT system incorporating PROMs was dropped, another system was chosen and a lot of money invested. Putting aside his own loss, Eddie lamented for healthcare. The other system did not even consider "functioning" which was, in his opinion, the underlying reason for doing Care Plans. A simple administration error had abruptly ended a very promising lead.

"Give me another word for a thesaurus. My mobile phone voice message says: *I'm home right now, please ring again when I'm out...."* Mia and Eddie crumpled together in peals of laughter in their seats at the Enmore Theatre listening to the one-liners coming from comic Steven Wright. *"I'm*

writing an unauthorised autobiography."

To Eddie's delight the evening out together was a success. He and Mia were laughing at the same jokes and Mia had agreed to counselling. His desire was to re-establish his family. After many months of counselling and eight months apart he moved back downstairs.

The ADEPT system, although not implemented by the South Australian Health Department, was now functional and Michael and Eddie had organised training for GP nurses at the Royal Melbourne Hospital. The now internet-based system was showcased at the yearly Australian General Practice Conference and Exhibition in Melbourne and more interest was shown. All this development and training had again cost Eddie a good deal of money and his budget was being stretched. He was interested in applying for a grant program called Commercial Ready from the Australian Innovation Department, Austrade. A weighty document of two hundred pages was prepared and submitted on 23 April 2006 for this project seeking $750,000. They made other grant submissions at the same time including an Application Service Provider Grant under the Broadband for Health Program, which was an Australian Government contribution to Health Connect. The submission suggested that they would pilot the ADEPT program, and for that to happen, funding was needed. None of the submissions were successful. However, the Federal Government now had other projects to encourage electronic healthcare planning and there was a research project for one million dollars. Peter Del Fante rang Michael, *"Michael, you should submit to this. However, your company is a little small. I think you should partner with another company. We would recommend DAN Computer Systems with Dan Smith."* In such an arrangement,

Dan Smith would be the lead organisation, but with a consortium of partners. Dr Del Fante thought that on what he had seen of ADEPT, especially with eMedilab's already proven inter-operability, that they were a chance to win the contract. Eddie was reticent to partner with DAN but acknowledged it may be his only option financially.

All their attention until now had been on promoting ADEPT in GP clinics. Now he also saw there was a role for PROMs within the hospital system, particularly when dealing with adverse events and avoidable mishaps that had been in the media increasingly of late. These cases were being overseen by the Australian Commission of Safety and Quality in Healthcare and they were holding a seminar in Adelaide. The brothers decided to attend. Eddie wrote a submission paper entitled "An Unsolicited Proposal for Improving Quality in Hospitals and Thereby Avoiding Adverse Events". His suggestion was again a management system across the hospital that used PROMs as health targets. The beauty of this system was that surrounding the reporting methodology there were at least sixteen underlying behavioural change drivers that would motivate the doctors and hospital managers and place peer pressure on them to ensure better outcomes. Despite the lengthy submission, and one that Eddie felt held great opportunity and benefits for hospitals, he again had little response.

The rejections were frustrating for them but what came next for ADEPT and Eddie was financially crippling. The Federal government decided to revamp the Enhanced Primary Care Items and added seven new health assessments. This may have been deemed as a minor change in the health system but meant major changes to the ADEPT system. Eddie had reached his budget limit and decided they could no longer market or promote their product and their best bet for survival would be to work with DAN Computer Systems, as part of the Dan Smith consortium, to win the Federal government grant worth one million dollars. If they were successful, then 50% of the grant would mean ADEPT could be turned into an excellent inter-operable program. Health Connect wanted an eHealthcare Planning system that would give healthcare providers a web-based Care Plan for patients with chronic conditions. This is exactly what the ADEPT program was capable of doing, designed to do and was already doing in two practices. Surely they would be successful with such a presentation. He begrudgingly joined the group. When the presentations were made by Dan Smith in Adelaide in 2007 he was shocked that they did not present any of the ADEPT program. Despite this omission, the consortium went on to win the tender and a more formalised subcontractor agreement was presented to eMedilab. Whilst the agreement was signed with the consortium and the Federal government in early 2008, almost all the money was spent on developing DAN Computers Primary Care Interface, rather than developing the ADEPT electronic Care Planning System. Almost no money was earned for eMedilab out of the project. A following evaluation of the Health Connect project reported that the development and testing of a shared electronic health summary and communications solution was not completed within the project period. The Primary Care Interface was acknowledged to have had some benefits.

They went on, *"As the EHCPS was not fully developed and implemented, the HCSA Project was not able to achieve its objective."*

Eddie was confused. If Dan Smith had implemented

ADEPT as planned they would have fulfilled the government's brief, and possibly, been considered for further government funds. Their greed of taking the full grant and dismissing his ADEPT program, Eddie saw as very short-sighted. He was disappointed in what might have been and again questioned his business acumen. How was he once again blindsided in his business ventures? When would he get his break? When would the world acknowledge his ideas and reward him with accolades and the financial gains he felt entitled to! And if it were to happen, would it happen in his lifetime? Financially he had almost run out of options for the ADEPT Care Planning Program. Adding to his woes, the Trusted Partner Agreement with QualityMetrics had also failed to work. He questioned his life's work. Was this the end of his championing of PROMs? Would the world never benefit from his idea of taking on the current "disease" system and creating a true HEALTH system? He resolved that whether or not they were, he was determined to keep professing their virtues till the day he departed this earth. He picked up his pen and began to write. This time his book would discuss Complexity Science and how his way of looking at the world, he believed, could lead to new medicine – Complexity Medicine. He acknowledged that perhaps his ideas were not being accepted because communication and writing weren't his forte. He figured that maybe if he took his ideas to a great writer they would have more success in the interpretation. In Eddie's eyes, that great writer should be Bill Bryson. After receiving no response from his first letter, he heard that Bryson was touring Sydney to launch his book The Thunderbolt Kid.

"Mia, these ideas are important," said Eddie. *"I really must get someone capable, like Bill Bryson, to write the book. I'm*

going to go to his book launch and prepare a summary of my book for him." Mia shook her head. At the first book launch at the Stanton Library in North Sydney he approached Bill Bryson to purchase his book and have it signed. He exchanged it for a pre-written request for cooperation in writing his book. That evening, there was an additional book launch at Mosman Art Gallery and Eddie again approached Bryson.

Mia whispered, *"Eddie! You are disgraceful stalking someone in this way."*

Ignoring Mia's comments, he asked Bill Bryson if he had read the letter and said he would be happy to just have a response. Bryson assured him he would respond to the letter. About three months later he received a response from Bryson's London address stating that although he understood the importance of the concepts that Eddie felt were necessary, he was busy writing a book on Shakespeare and was unable to help. In the interim, Eddie had found a writer with experience in the scientific field, Barbara Cameron-Smith, and commissioned her to help edit and write the book.

Immortalising his ideas in a book was becoming more pertinent for Eddie, as was the importance of spending time with life-long friends. He was now in his early 60's and many of his friends from Betar days were facing ill health or had had serious operations. Geoff Williamson, having been diagnosed with Hodgkin's disease, decided it was time for the Betar boys to re-connect on a regular basis and thus began a series of social evenings at Abdul's Restaurant in Redfern. Zvi Berkovic, Bernie Kresner, Eddie Adamak, George Berkowitz, Peter Keeda and Geoff Williamson - six friends, and Eddie, all in their sixties with their behaviour degenerating into that of sixteen year olds. The hilarity that ensued was medicine for the soul and very much a morale booster for all the men involved.

Chapter 15

So you think Medicine is modern?

"AUSTRALIAN TOURIST LOST ON ITALIAN LAKE!" It was the news headline Eddie envisaged as he drudged with the heavy boat back to shore. His efforts were hampered by the slippery mud and the fits of giggles he kept collapsing into. He and Mia, along with friends Edju, Betty, Myrna, Eric and Iris were on a trip through the Lombardy region of Italy. The first outing as a group had been to venture onto Lake Garda on small boats. Eddie and Iris had fatefully chosen one that broke down mid-lake. The rest of their journey was somewhat less eventful. The friends all piled into a van and reminisced of their days in Israel in the "Magic Yellow Van". They stayed in picturesque private villas in the middle of olive groves or in beautiful towns like Bellagio with the gently spinning watermill lulling them to sleep at night. The posse travelled all the way across to Venice, up to Lake Como and Eddie insisted they cross into Switzerland for his favourite hot chocolate. Sitting in the coffee lounge he and Edju debated as to why the dogs were allowed inside.

Edju observed, *"The dogs that are well-behaved are obviously Swiss."*

"The more hyperactive ones must be Italian," laughed Eddie.

Their friendship had always been one of friendly banter, liberally peppered with cheeky comedy, and it had not waned with the passing of time. In Verona, Eddie, Edju and Eric (the three E's) became the three tenors and performed a wonderful rendition of O Sole Mio. They re-enacted Romeo and Juliet at the Casa Di Giulietta. If Eddie was ever running late, Mia would roll her eyes and comment, *"We have to wait for the comedian."* The entire adventure was a success with all the old friends bonding as if no time had passed since their fun-filled days together in the early 80's.

Eddie and Mia then went to visit Tull in New York. Four years had passed since he'd resigned from K-Swiss and he had since opened his own company, Feit, which catered for luxury footwear. His brother Josh managed Feit logistics and ran the Sydney store. Tull was also in the process of developing a shoe division for an up and coming fashion label Rag and Bone. Being on US soil Eddie also took the opportunity to catch up with his half-brother Peter Schrag before heading home to Sydney.

2008 began with a frantic search. His book was complete. He needed a publisher and someone who could officiate at the launch. The old medical bookshop at Sydney University had gone into publishing and agreed to take on Eddie's book. He just needed a speaker. As the details of the book release were worked through he made another bid to the Federal Health department for them to embrace his ideology. Mia's brother, Robert, had maintained the close ties with the Labor Party that his father Sam Fiszman had established over many years, particularly in NSW. Through his good favour, Eddie made an arrangement with the Federal Minister for Health at the time, Nicola Roxon, to meet with her Chief of Staff, Mick Reid, and discuss his ideas. Eddie flew to Canberra, at his own expense. On arrival at Parliament House he was greeted by a junior doctor who claimed Michael Reid was no longer available. Eddie was furious, *"I've taken a day off work and flown myself down here as I was advised I had an appointment with the CEO!"*

"Dr Price this is the offer. You can meet myself, or no one," came the reply.

"Please give me a couple of minutes to settle down."

His large portfolio of documents, explanations and graphs on how his ideas could work, was a refinement of the submission he had given to Tony Abbott's Advisor, a Dr Pham, in 2005. The difference now was that it included an underlying scientific explanation as to why this sociological management approach, plus PROMs methodology, would work and save the government a good deal of money via Medicare and reduce hospitalisations for people with chronic diseases. Although the discussion went on for one hour, it appeared to be falling on deaf ears. He flew home in a rage.

Remarkably he again composed himself, rallied his inner fortitude, and prepared to launch So You Think Medicine is Modern? - his third book. It discussed the connection between complexity science and functional health and suggested that a human's capacity to adapt to an ever-changing environment was the basis for maintaining health. He proposed that there were now two models of the human body; the current biomedical or standard medical model, constructed by Descartes and Newtonian ideologies and which was correct in 50% of cases. The second model aligned more with what the Eastern philosophies had to offer which was based around complexity science - what he saw as an energy or "Einsteinian" model. He claimed that using a combination of both models would be the medical practice of the future. He also proposed that PROMs were the major agents to bridge the models. PROMs were practical, simple to implement and would facilitate change and lead to better health outcomes. The book also introduced the concept of a new vaccine, a new drug - the Non-Pharmaceutical

Pharmaceutical - a behavioural vaccine. While he saw pharmaceutical drugs as specialised formulas of chemical energy, he argued that giving a patient a lifestyle script was a form of physical energy. The source was the patient's own potential energy of movement combined with the doctor's prescription of quantity, frequency and duration.

The book also discussed his revelations and realisations regarding "origin of life" and how his findings supported some of the underlying philosophies of Complementary Medicine. His scientific knowledge, all self-taught, had expanded to such an extent that he had hypothesised a few theories on the body's cellular coding system that he claimed predated DNA. His research and theoretical intuition had led him to conclude that within a simple vesicle, but also within each cell of the human body, there was a movement pattern in between solid and fluid that followed a chaotic pathway. He named this movement pattern a 'SOPHTID', which stood for the mnemonic **S**econd **O**rder **Ph**ase **T**ransition **Id**entities. The same concept was later to be called "Extended Criticality" by Longo and Montevil in their book Perspectives on Organism. Eddie hypothesised that this "movement pattern" was very important. When stabilised by combining with an external environmental substance that entered the cell through its porous cell membrane, it would form a fractal shape and could "barcode" the external environmental substance. As no fractal form is the same, this "barcode" forms a unique "fingerprint" and has the capacity to inform the rest of the protocell of the recorded information it has on the environmental substance. He concluded that this was a fractal coding system that took into account people's life experiences and as such recorded these experiences. He claimed it was less stable than DNA but would compete and cooperate with DNA within every cell of the human body. This information processing is sometimes called "cognition" and Eddie believed that it occurred in every cell, and that every cell thereby could cognate without the need of a brain or a spinal cord. His hypothesis was based on Complexity Science and supported the complementary medicine approach that we are dissipative structures. We are very much interdependent on our environment and thoughts and social situations. An individual's lifestyle, diet, risk factor habits and social interactions were important determinants of a person's health and physicality. A passage from his book explains this connection further.

"The Butterfly effect, I maintain, has direct relevance to the practice of evolved or complexity medicine and complementary therapies. Take the example of structurally coupled information that has triggered emotional tension via the body's self-reinforcing feedback mechanisms. The resulting muscle tension, in the back for example, may be a physical embodiment of that rigidity or blockage. Here is where a complementary or holistic therapy such as acupuncture or massage may equate to the butterfly effect that initiates a significant outcome elsewhere in the system. The loosening of a muscle block via appropriate massage, via a multitude of self-reinforcing feedback loops, may precipitate a change for the better that helps to loosen a blockage via the butterfly effect therapy, and so contribute to overcoming the individual's condition."

The butterflies in Eddie's stomach were certainly having an effect on his constitution in the days leading up to the book launch. The event was to be held in the grand old buildings of the Sydney University Medical School and its courtyard.

Reba Meagher, NSW Health Minister, had agreed to launch the event, thanks to the Robert's connections. September 25th, 2008 was only a few days away when Eddie received a call from Robert, *"Eddie, I've just heard that the Health Minister has resigned!"*

It wasn't long before the Premier himself also resigned. Eddie needed to find an alternative speaker for his launch, and fast. Fortunately, Professor Geoff Gallop, previous Premier of Western Australia and now of Sydney University was on the Australian Hospital and Health Commission, a Federal Labor Government initiative and had responded that he was keen to attend the book launch. Eddie immediately enlightened Geoff to his predicament. Geoff gallantly agreed to launch the book and the evening was a fantastic success. He had only ordered a small run of his books, as they were extremely academic, but to his delight, they ran out. With the second print run only a few books were sold and, to Eddie's eternal bewilderment, there was no significant impact on health reform or on the general public.

Then he found a friendly audience in AIMA, the Australian Integrated Medical Association, and one of his articles was accepted for their journal JAIMA entitled "Complexity Medicine Scientifically Based Theory for Understanding Holistic Healthcare" and discussed how Eddie's science backed up some aspects of "Integrative Medicine". Disappointingly for him he had little response to the article. His findings did however resonate with an organisation known as the Society for Chaos Theory in Psychology and Life Sciences and the group welcomed Eddie to present his findings at their 18th Annual International Conference in Richmond, Virginia.

"What do you think I should do? I've carted my best shirt,

tie and suit all the way here from Australia, all through New York and LA!" Eddie appealed to a fellow delegate on his realisation that almost all other attendees were dressed in sandals and t-shirts and had long hair. His formal apparel may not be entirely appropriate.

"Go half way. It's fashion now to wear a t-shirt with a suit."

Eddie embraced the idea and thought "how fitting" because in Complexity you have order, as represented by his suit, together with disorder or chaos, as represented by his T-shirt. However, his outfit choice was the least of his concerns. He realised that most of the scientists in attendance were more occupied with the underlying maths of Chaos Theory and Complexity Science, and interest in his theoretical approach to healthcare was minimal.

Eddie continued his search for other avenues in which to find supporters of his theories. He felt he had found an ally when he came across a book by Professor Michael Porter and Dr Teisberg, entitled Redefining Healthcare. Professor Michael Porter was a world-renowned Harvard Business School Professor who had turned his eye to helping to solve "the healthcare problem" and was the first academic writer to point out the importance of improving Functional Health Status. Professor Porter spoke of "value-based healthcare", but the important issue for Eddie was that he saw "value" as improvement in the patient's PROMs score (what he called the "*health that mattered to patients*") divided by the cost. At the same time, Eddie came across the latest edition of the American Medical Association's Guidelines to Permanent Impairment. This book was used as guidelines for the various injury management systems and health systems to pay additional outgoings for permanent impairments that injured workers or motor vehicle occupants may have suffered in accidents. This guide had taken a paradigm shift – the new assessment of disablement was called the International Classification of Functioning, Disability and Health (ICF). For the first time this involved a "functional" component and in each subsection of the human body they had recommended the use of certain PROMs. Finally, a breakthrough; at least a small part of the world was acknowledging what he'd been trying to establish for decades. In Australia the various motor accidents authorities and the NSW Workers Compensation Authority were still using earlier AMA Permanent Impairment Guides. When the ICF appeared all of the doctors, insurers and even the workers' compensation authorities ran the other way. This did not make sense. They ought to be using the latest edition but because they all felt functioning could not be exactly measured they wished to rely on the earlier versions. Eddie gave an example as to why this was erroneous. If a patient who was injured at work required a total hip replacement and had that operation then they would receive the same permanent impairment assessment before, as after, the operation in terms of dollars awarded. He argued the reason they had had the operation was to improve function. A total hip replacement was a very good operation and it was shown in the research using the PROMs that it improved functioning by one and a half standard deviations in most patients, an excellent result. This would mean that the patient had less permanent impairment than before the operation. To him it seemed unscientific that they should go with the old assessments and he argued with the various authorities that they should adopt the new guidelines. Some States in the US had legislation encouraging the latest guidelines and those who did use them (as published in early 2012) found a 20%

reduction in payouts.

His business and advocacy of PROMs was hit by another blow. Kathy, his practice manager was leaving to pursue a life in hospitality with her husband. He was extremely disappointed, telling Kathy how much he relied on her input and that she had made work a pleasure every day. She had been a forward thinker in terms of the Health Outcomes program for ten years and an excellent teacher in the training programs they rendered. She would be sorely missed. Theresa Stanton who was competently running the administration department was asked to take over as practice manager. She expressed her desire to only work part-time, but would accept the role, at least initially.

For Eddie the constant roller-coaster of elation at finding individuals or organisations interested in his ideas....but then the disappointment when little or nothing came of his endeavours continued. In 2009 he made contact with Professor Garry Egger, Professor of Health and Human Sciences at Southern Cross University and an Advisor to the World Health Organisation. He is viewed as one of the pioneers of Lifestyle Medicine and was one of the initiators of the Australian Lifestyle Medicine Association (ALMA). Eddie explained to Professor Egger that the use of PROMs would lead to Lifestyle Prescriptions by doctors as it was now based on science. In 2010 he presented a paper to the Australian Lifestyle Medicine Conference at the Manly Pacific Hotel. At that time, Norman Doidge's book The Brain That Changes Itself, based on neuroplasticity, was a bestseller. For Eddie this plasticity applied to the whole body and not just the brain. He suggested that the PROMs scores were a way of measuring this plasticity and that higher PROMs scores were indicative of adaptability which were equivalent to "fitness" or "health". If you wanted to increase the score, doctors needed to prescribe healthier lifestyles and the patients needed to implement them. Later he would call these Lifestyle Prescriptions "ePROMs treatments". Only two delegates understood the importance of Eddie's presentation, the rest once again only saw a mad professor trying to buck the system.

Chapter 16

A year of pain

"Ed, I've got a bit of a problem. I purchased a small apartment in downtown New York and I had a mortgage lined up but the bank has gone bust. I have exchanged contracts and the system here is such that the longer I don't pay; I get hit with penalty interest rates."

It was April 2009, the effects of the Global Financial Crisis were still being felt around the globe, and Tull in New York had just been caught up in the drama. Eddie agreed to send money to help pay off the apartment until a bank mortgage could be re-established. He discussed the loan with one of the Bondi Walkers. He was a businessman who dealt with overseas suppliers all the time. Eddie had already been bitten once with foreign currency dealings and he wanted to make sure that this time he got it right. He was advised to take out a "vanilla option" that was essentially a security against fluctuations in the Australian dollar. Eddie rang one of the big four banks and was told they had something almost identical to a "vanilla option" and suggested that he use that facility. Two years later, when the "option" was due, he found out that things were not as he'd been lead to believe and his finances had again taken a hit. He was furious and a lengthy legal debate took place with the bank eventually agreeing to double the initial compensation they'd offered.

"Eddie, turn on the TV!" said one of Josh's friends.

"Matt, I'm busy. I don't have time to watch TV right now," he replied.

"Eddie, turn it on. There's an interview on Foxtel with your hero!" insisted Matt.

"*Who? Einstein? He's dead!*" Eddie teased.

Matt persisted, "*NO! The other one – the Fractal guy.*"

"*Professor Benoit Mandelbrot? Bye Matt!*"

He raced to the television. After the interview he was inspired by the knowledge that Mandelbrot, at his advanced age, was still actively engaging the public with his ideas. Eddie emailed him about his recent book So You Think Medicine is Modern? In the email he explained that he had his own theories on the origin of life. He hypothesised that a fractal physics-based informatics structure was the precursor to DNA and the initial basis of cognition and that there was a fractal, experience-based, coding system in each human that cooperates and competes with DNA.

Eddie wrote, "*As these hypotheses are based on fractals and your work, I was wondering if these ideas are of interest to you?*"

To his delight, within a day, he received a return email that indeed they may well be of interest and Mandelbrot asked him to send further details. Eddie despatched his book and told Professor Mandelbrot he may be in the States shortly to visit his son Tull. Professor Mandelbrot gave him his phone number and suggested that he ring once he arrived in the USA.

Mandelbrot was one of Eddie's idols. He was a Polish-born, French/American mathematician with broad interests in the practical sciences, especially in what he called "the art of roughness" or "a fractal". But physics wasn't the only area in which Eddie felt a level of camaraderie with Mandelbrot. His Jewish family had emigrated in 1936 from increasingly nazi inspired antisemitism in Warsaw, Poland. The family's move to France as refugees saved their lives but as much of France was occupied by the Nazis at that time their existence was one fraught with danger. Mandelbrot recalls this period, "*Our constant fear was that a sufficiently determined foe might report us to an authority and we would be sent to our deaths.*"

"*Professor Mandelbrot? It's Dr Eddie Price from Australia. I'm in Boston!*" He couldn't believe it. He was speaking with the founder of Fractals!

"*When can you come over?*" asked Mandelbrot.

"*Any time you say we can come over.*"

"*Who is 'we'?*" queried Mandelbrot.

Eddie explained, "*Myself and my wife, Mia, would probably like to join us.*"

Professor Mandelbrot invited them to his home on the following day. Eddie was bubbling with excitement. He and Professor Mandelbrot spoke for an hour and a half.

Professor Mandelbrot concluded, "*Look Eddie, I've heard your theories. I cannot vouch for them one way or the other but I would strongly recommend you complete your theoretical research along those lines. By the way, how did your book sell?*"

"*Not well. I was advised it fell between two schools. It was not academic enough for the academics and it wasn't public enough for the public.*"

"*Two schools?*" responded Professor Mandelbrot. "*Mine fell between nine schools. The economists said it wasn't about economy, the health workers said it wasn't about health matters, the bankers said it wasn't about banking, and the general public said similar things.*"

Eddie left giddy with delight.

Inspired by his discussions with Mandelbrot and hoping to enlist more like-minded operators in the medical industry to his theories, he lined up a few more meetings while in the

US. The first was with Charlie Kenney who had just published a book on Don Berwick and his Institute for Health Improvement called Best Practice: How the New Quality Movement is Transforming Medicine. Eddie thought he may be interested in his book and his own thoughts on transforming medicine. Alas, there was little understanding of what Eddie thought were real measures that would make a difference. He also organised an appointment with Professor Ary Goldberger who had researched fractals and had found that a changing heart rhythm was a predisposition to a heart attack. Professor Goldberger agreed that if PROMs had to do with adaptability, he felt they had something to offer medicine. Finally, Eddie had an appointment with Dr Don Berwick himself, deemed a revolutionary for his system of transforming medicine. Dr Berwick had just been appointed Advisor on Health Matters to President Obama and Eddie was optimistic of the opportunity to convince such an influential man of the potential of PROMs. The meeting began at 8:30am but barely had the conversation gone into any depth when Dr Berwick's phone rang. His daughter was in labour and he needed to go. It was with an all-too-familiar, disappointed resignation that he left the meeting. He trawled through the books on Complexity and Information Theory at Barnes & Noble bookstore before returning home to Sydney.

With no real progress to show for his efforts overseas, he turned his attentions back to his ADEPT program. It was a good electronic care-planning program and he decided to speak to the various companies which already offered clinical IT systems like "Medical Director", "Best Practice" and "Zedmed" to GPs. He had met with these organisations at previous conferences and had spoken to most of the proprietors. Some were willing to go into more of a discussion about their Care Planning systems although none of them mentioned PROMs. He thought that this would be the area where he needed to concentrate. At a conference in May 2009 he met Dr Owen Banks from the Physicians Company who indicated they were interested in buying practices. Eddie thought this may be worth investigating. With the impact of the Global Financial Crisis, he was keen to relinquish at least the medico-legal side of his practice. The Physicians Company expressed a strong interest in purchasing his entire practice and their sales advisors stated they were very keen on the ADEPT program. A deal was brokered and The Physicians Company purchased shares in Eddie's company, Computerised Medical Systems (CMS), paying 50% of the agreed price for the practice upfront, with a five-year ongoing contract for his continued service. If only he had looked up a scam-warning website he would have seen a notice that read, *"If Dr Owen Banks wants to buy your shares - run, run, run!"*

Although the deal was completed late in 2009 Eddie did not hear from the company until July of 2010 when he heard rumours that one or two of their practices had gone into liquidation. He was phoned by Con Street (who also went by the name Con Mikonis), from a company called Laund, who claimed he had purchased Eddie's practice from The Physicians Company. They had gone into liquidation. Con Street moved his people into Eddie's practice in order to take control of the accounts. The attitude and behaviour towards Eddie's staff was such that many began leaving. On the 10th of December he received a phone call from Theresa stating that she too was going to resign. He tried to talk her out of it but her mind was made up. She was leaving. Something was wrong. Eddie asked Con Street as to his personal five-year contract and was advised that Laund had not purchased that from The Physicians Company. So where did that leave Eddie?

He was nervous but somewhat relieved that he had not sold the ePROMs system – neither the website, eMedilab, nor the ADEPT system. He needed to find out more about The Physicians Company. He rang several other practices in The Physicians Company portfolio. One after the other there were examples of unscrupulous practices by the staff of Laund. One practice reported an incident where a patient was ripped off an ECG machine in the middle of a procedure. Others were apparently threatened with "*Buy the practice or we'll shut it down.*" Eddie googled Dr Owen Banks and found a history of similar activities. He then realised what had occurred. The whole scheme was an intentional arrangement of going into liquidation and defaulting on monies owed, in particular to the banks. The banks were pursuing The Physicians Company vigorously. What were his options? How could he protect all that he had worked so hard to establish for so many years? He contacted the AMA (Australian Medical Association) of which he'd been a member of for many years and requested their urgent assistance. He was advised that through the Avant Medical Insurance legal defence policy he would receive $150,000 support in legal fees but he was tied to using their solicitors. He made contact immediately. Unfortunately, it was mid-December and all solicitors were already on leave and would only be able to assist in mid-January. He was desperate and felt he could not afford the time to wait. He needed to move now if he was to salvage his company and his finances. He discovered a Gold Coast General Practice that was one of the only practices that had successfully survived an attempted take-over by The Physicians Company and were independent again. He was advised they had used a solicitor, Anthony Freestone, on the Gold Coast, and his associated liquidator advisor, George McMillan. Eddie rang George on the 17th of December and asked for advice on how to save his practice. He was given a series of instructions. He engaged an ex-administrative employee and bookkeeper at his home to re-create an accounting system and to re-create the practice working out of his home. He then rang approximately fifty specialist consultants, who were working sessionally for him, to advise them of what was happening and to explain that he was going to attempt to save the practice. The practice would be closed until the 8th of January 2011. He also contacted his business advisor, Gary Weiss.

To Eddie's surprise Gary said, *"My son, Ben, took this guy to court. He was a lecturer in Business Ethics at the University and he commissioned two students, Ben and a friend, to ghostwrite a book for him, promising them 15% of the Royalties. The book was published and sold to students, but Ben was not paid. He took him to court and won. The magistrate had many uncomplimentary remarks about Mr Street's evidence."*

Eddie now had a better idea of who he was dealing with. He worked tirelessly over Christmas and spent many thousands of dollars on legal fees.

By the 14th of January, the lawyers from the AMA were back and agreed to take over the matter. He had received no payments for work performed from December up until April of 2011 from Laund and, in fact, would not be repaid for outgoings on his own Visa card. Eddie tried to explain to the new solicitors that they were dealing with professionals in making money out of bankruptcies and then taking over and selling or running practices. His main doctor had been offered a higher percentage of work to stay with Laund but then they double-crossed Eddie's manager, and had a pre-calculated falling out. The manager left and set up the former practice as his own business. In a bid to salvage some of his work he had conversations with his friend from RPS Medicorp, Robert Migliore, who ran his own practice as a rehabilitation provider. They came to an agreement that they would share the residual amount of Eddie's practice and work out of Robert's city office. He figured by this stage that he had only maintained 25% of his previous practice.

Then came the cruellest of blows. Laund found Eddie's password and took down the eMedilab website, and all of Eddie's files on PROMs and Health Outcomes with it. He begged them to return to him his life's work and passion. He knew he was no match for these professionals and by April 2011 he had given up on any court action. Rather than starting a revolution, of even retiring, as many do at 65, he had to re-build his practice, what was left of it, and re-assess his income and the status of his beloved PROMs project.

Echoing Eddie's internal turmoil over his business future, the Australian political arena's future was in disarray. Prime Minister, Kevin Rudd, had fallen victim to a very open coup and had been replaced by Julia Gillard and she had then called an early election for the 21st of August 2010. On the 22nd of August Eddie was listening to the news, waiting for a result in the election when he received a call.

"It's Dion," a friend of the boys and an international rollerblade champion and mini-celebrity in the Bondi area who had spent some months living with Mia and Eddie. *"I'm going to drop Lara at the back door. Please look after her,"* gushed Dion.

He was dating Lara Bingle, the well-known Australian model whose relationship with Australia's cricket captain, Michael Clarke, had only recently dissolved. The press were trying to photograph Lara and Dion together and the paparazzi were tracking them. Lara came into the house whilst Dion was trying to lose the paparazzi. Eddie relished the opportunity to look after the blonde beauty and took the opportunity to explain to her the situation in the election, the balance of power and how it was up to each party to obtain a majority of 76 seats. It looked likely that they would have to win over Independents. Lara listened quite intently for a few minutes and Eddie was surprised at her knowledge and interest. Several hours of hiding out passed and he had run out of election banter. He then enquired as to whether she, from her cricket-boyfriend days, understood the difference between "around the wicket" and "over the wicket" bowling when Dion's friend, Milo, rang, *"Take Lara out the front, I'm picking her up."*

Eddie was reminded of Hugh Grant's flatmate in the movie Notting Hill and thought he may look similar to the paparazzi. Milo collected Lara to take her to Caves Beach. Dion reported that he eventually got to Caves Beach but that he was followed by the paparazzi all the way to Swansea. He knew Swansea well and parked at the back of an arcade. Lara was well-ensconced in the Caves Beach holiday home when Milo drove to the front of the arcade and collected Dion who abandoned his car with the paparazzi parked next to it. According to Milo, when he went to collect Dion's car at 5am the next morning, the paparazzi were still in their car nearby, sound asleep.

It was now early April 2011 and Robert Migliore and Eddie had set up a new organisation, OMLC (Occupational and

Medico-Legal Consultants). They were working out of Robert's Actevate office in the city but maintained peripheral offices at other practices in Newcastle and Parramatta. The work involved a lot of re-marketing and talking to clients to reassure them. The business was solid and starting to grow. However, there were more financial and business woes to come. Mia's brother Robert, indicated that the Fiszman family company, established by Mia's late father Sam, could no longer pay its debts and was being placed in the hands of an administrator. Eddie did all he could to ensure minimal damage. He attended the creditors meeting and did his best at advising Robert. A friend and solicitor, Zoe Hillman, was recruited and helped out enormously. Eddie was so impressed by her capacity that she was established as the Fiszman family's new solicitor. Tull and Josh became heavily involved with Tull taking over as the principal business advisor to help rescue what he could of the family assets. Sadly, much would be lost in the liquidation, including a flat that Mia loved overlooking the southern end of Bondi Beach, as well as the large warehouse that Sam had owned in Danks Street, Waterloo.

"Ed! Mia's hurt!" It was Josh on the line. *"She was trying to retrieve a Bali couch that she had stored away at the upper level in the Danks Street warehouse. She climbed a five-metre ladder and the ladder slipped and she's fallen onto the concrete floor! She's in the ambulance on her way to the hospital now."*

He raced to the hospital. Mia had fractured her left elbow and had a nasty blow to the head. The elbow had to be replaced and he sat by her bedside for a week as she recuperated. The head injury unfortunately wasn't so quick to heal. When her head hit the concrete it caused a contralateral side bruise and black eye, but there was long term damage done as she would go on to gradually develop trigeminal neuralgia that Eddie believes was caused by the fall. The excruciating condition is known as "the suicide disease" as many people cannot put up with the pain.

2011 was a year that had brought much pain to the family, in so many ways, but in late December they were given a wonderful and uplifting gift.

Eddie and Mia had a call from Tull. "*Natasha is pregnant!*"

Eddie queried, "*Are we happy about that?*"

Tull replied, "*Well I certainly am!*"

"*Okay, that's good news. We're very pleased. We will certainly come to be with you in New York for the birth,*" said Eddie and Mia.

The prospect of new life injected a sense of hope and happiness into their home.

Eddie however, wasn't happy. He was downtrodden and deflated. After decades of research, writing, advocating and working, working, working, what did he have to show in either financial terms or in terms of change and making an impact on the world? Very little. Now he found himself working like crazy to rebuild a practice that he had thought sold. He had wanted to distance himself from that to concentrate on his work in Health Outcomes and to really achieve something in this area before he was too old. He wanted out. He spoke to other larger occupational and medico-legal companies and offered to bring over the 25% of his practice he had saved. He approached both MLO (Medico Legal Opinions), who with Recovre owned an occupational health arm, and Sonic Healthcare who also were developing an occupational health practice. Both were interested. Robert and Actevate spoke at length to Eddie hoping he would not leave after only one year together but Eddie didn't want to work to just rebuild the practice to where it had previously been. He decided to join MLO in March 2012 and was employed as a subcontractor. He had his independence and his freedom back.

Tull and Natasha's baby was due in early August 2012, but Eddie and Mia decided to head to New York a little ahead of the due date and rented a pensione near Tull and Natasha's apartment. He used the time waiting for the arrival of his first grandchild to put his stalking skills to good use. He'd recently read a business book called Black Swan, a best seller by Nassim Taleb. Taleb had moved from being a hedge fund financier to being a Professor at the NY University and he had dedicated his book to Mandelbrot. To his delight, he found, after some research, that Nassim worked only ten minutes away from Tull's apartment. He also discovered that his associate, Charles Tapiero, had also done some maths on Complexity Science. Eddie didn't like his chances of obtaining an audience with the now celebrity of Nassim Taleb so he decided to first approach Charles Tapiero. Charles was happy to converse with him on a number of occasions and was very hospitable. He quickly understood that Eddie was in stalking mode and his main Professor of interest was Taleb. By default or by Tapiero's design, during his second visit to Professor Tapiero, he was in the lift with who he thought was a very young student in a T-shirt.

Eddie said to him, *"Wow, you really look like Nassim Taleb,"* to which the student replied, *"Many people tell me that,"* and they both got out of the lift together.

Eddie smiled and said, *"Ah, you are Nassim Taleb. I gotta tell you I was also born in Lebanon."* Taleb was very proud of his Greek-Lebanese origin and this shared background opened a conversation between the two. They spoke for three minutes at the end of which, Eddie presented Taleb with his book So You Think Medicine is Modern? and departed with, *"The book is based on the same Complexity Theory that you write of. I hope you have time to read it."*

On the 18th of August 2012, Sam Isaac Price was born, named after Tull's beloved grandfather. Eddie and Mia were elated at the arrival of the beautiful addition to their family and proudly called all their family and friends to spread the happy news and invite as many as possible to attend the naming ceremony and circumcision on the 26th of August. Despite the fact that they were in New York a wonderful assembly of friends and family gathered; Mario Rosenberg, Eddie's half-brother Peter Schrag and wife Jeanette, their friend Myrna and from Eddie's mother's family, Peter Simon. Music by a former jazz musician, Sam Price, was chosen for obvious reasons. It created a wonderful atmosphere in which to welcome this new life to the world and to the family. Tull's speech paid tribute to baby Sam's namesake, espousing the virtues of the incredible man who had gone before him....from surviving war in the Polish underground from age thirteen to building an incredible business and life through his connections and street smarts. Mia often recited her father's adage that, *"Money does not protect you. Knowing people of influence does."*

Eddie acknowledged that it had been Sam's connections that had opened so many doors and opportunities for him professionally. Sam had given him opportunities time and time again with health ministers, shadow health ministers, state health executives, even state Premiers....but he had failed.

His concepts were too difficult to understand, or at least, too difficult for Eddie to explain in simple terms.

Chapter 17

Melting icebergs

"Louis. I'm here in Ho Chi Minh City and looking forward to catching up with you," cried Eddie on the phone.

Louis replied, *"Wonderful Eddie. But I'm in Hanoi!"*

Robert Stevenson, nicknamed "Louis" by the Bondi Walkers, had been a long-time benefactor for many young Vietnamese with medical problems and had often organised to fly them to Australia for operations. Louis was currently working in Vietnam and Eddie and Mia were in town. Off the back of such a successful Italian trip some years earlier, they had joined their friends Betty, Edju, Eric and Myrna for another adventure. This time it was in Vietnam and they were also joined by Betty's sister Janet and her husband.

Louis said, *"I may have a function in Ho Chi Minh City, of some graduating students, in the next couple of days. I'll let you know."*

While waiting for Louis' call the friends fell into the hilarity of travelling together and sharing fun times. On the bustling streets the group managed to avoid being run over by the twenty-deep river of motorbikes and scooters that wound its way through the city. The men resumed their clowning ways with Eric showing Eddie a new stretching exercise that was apparently required every two hundred and fifty meters. They were a strange sight as they slowly stretched their way around town. They loved the Vietnamese people and enjoyed the food. They stayed three days in tropical Hoi An, enjoying the quaint streets dripping with plant life, and took their first lessons in Tai Chi on the white sandy beach. Back in Ho Chi Minh City Eddie was off to attend the graduation ceremony of some of Louis' Vietnamese students. He found his way to The Miraculous and Famous Wedding and Events Venue. He managed to attend three weddings on the lower floors before finally locating the correct venue on the fifth floor. When he walked into the gathering of two hundred and fifty people Louis introduced him to the students and their families that he supported - advising them to take everything that Eddie said with "a grain of salt". He enthused as to the good work Louis was doing and later recalled that Robert "Louis" Stevenson always said his hero was Mother Theresa – how fitting.

On returning to Australia, Eddie was determined to re-establish some of his work with PROMs that was destroyed during his practice take-over. He decided to get the eMedilab website back up and running only to find that the purchasers of his practice had taken over the name. Eddie decided to take on a broader title, eHealthier. The eHealthier website would provide doctors, health providers, health insurers and hospitals with a platform to which they refer their patients who could complete PROMs or ePROMs and then provide ePROMs treatment or lifestyle prescriptions. At this stage in his career he saw it as his last attempt to show the world that through continued measuring of functioning and promotion of preventive lifestyles one could promote greater health and health outcomes. One set of clients was a group of executives for whom he produced medical profiles. Each executive received a "physical health score" and a "mental health score", both of which had "normal" scores of fifty. Eddie advised the executives that if they could maintain a score of sixty for both categories then they would have a behavioural vaccine against heart attack. He only wished he could be giving such lifestyle prescriptions to a much wider audience.

Privately he and the family were going through their own medical crisis. Mia's mother Esther was diagnosed with an aggressive B-cell lymphoma and was admitted into hospital for chemotherapy. It brought back painful memories for Eddie of his own mother's long and painful cancer battle. What astounded him was the dramatic difference some fifty-five years of medical advances had made. After four rounds of fortnightly chemotherapy Esther's haematologist stated there was no further evidence of the cancer and she was in remission. There was much rejoicing.

The family celebrations continued with a trip to New York for grandson Sam's first birthday. Mia had a rule. At least one grandparent should be in attendance for the celebration of his life. Eddie, whilst taking young Sam on a walk through the countryside in upstate New York nearly put an end to that life.

A driver pulled over next to Sam's stroller. *"Look, there's a bear over there that's just walked down the road behind your house."*

Eddie excitedly replied, *"Oh wow! Where can I go to see it?"*

The driver looked at him incredulously, *"Ah...No! I'm telling you to warn you not to go near it. I think it's a mother with cubs and you would be in great danger!"*

Eddie took the advice and did not approach the bear.

His fearless approach to bears was echoed in his dogged pursuit to have his theories recognised and implemented around the world. He'd recently come across an American organisation call ICHOM – the International Collaboration on Health Outcomes Measures. It was a not-for-profit organisation, established by Professor Michael Porter of Harvard Business School who had earlier written the book Redefining Healthcare that advocated PROMs use, with partners from the Boston Consulting Group and the Karolinska Institute (one of the leading hospitals and university institutes in Sweden). ICHOM had been established to ensure that the specific PROMs measurements used around the world were all standardised by establishing "50 Standard Sets of Measurements" for different diseases. Eddie was delighted that such a group of like-minded professionals existed and he immediately contacted Professor Porter's office, dispatched his three books on Health Outcomes and requested an audience. When Dr Caleb Stowell, Professor Porter's CEO and general manager of ICHOM agreed to meet, Eddie decided it was so important to him and for PROMs that he needed to return to the US again and have a face-to-face meeting.

He was buzzing with anticipation when he arrived at the ICHOM office for his meeting with Dr Caleb Stowell.

Stowell greeted him in a small coffee lounge, *"Eddie, you've been rather prescient in your books."* *"Have you had a chance to look at them Caleb?"* enquired Eddie.

"No, I haven't as yet, but how would you advise we go forward with ICHOM?"

He took a deep, disappointed breath and continued to present his ideas. Despite having express-posted his books and written other notes and observations on Health Outcomes to Stowell, nothing had even been read and there was little feedback on Eddie's ideas. Dr Stowell had his own agenda. There was no interest in enlarging the scope of PROMs but only seeking ideas on how to ensure the best functioning of ICHOM internationally. Eddie left their one-hour meeting desperately disappointed. Refusing to be brushed off so easily he went to Harvard Business School in search of Professor Porter himself. Porter's office was in a small white house on the expansive Harvard Business School campus that was affectionately referred to as "The White House". Professor Porter was unavailable so Eddie left his three books for him. He also noted that the next ICHOM conference was to be scheduled later that year, November 2014, in Boston. Eddie would be returning.

Back in New York he was advised that Nassim Taleb was speaking on the importance of Complexity Science and Chaos Theory at the "Zurich Meets New York Conference" and there were tickets available. *"A small consolation,"* thought Eddie.

He made sure to connect with Taleb once more. *"Hello, Professor Price!"* recalled Taleb.

Eddie was inspired by Taleb's words and by the very existence of ICHOM. The world was catching up with his ideas. Health systems seemed to be organically evolving towards what he had been preaching about for decades. The thought was some consolation for his personal frustrations. At least things were heading in the right direction. If only they'd listened to him earlier and if only they'd listen now to the many more intricate details he had to offer! There was indeed a movement towards underlying Complexity Science in the business world (thanks to Nassim Taleb). The mere existence of ICHOM was encouraging for PROMs and there were further advances in their use. The NHS in the UK had been using PROMs since 2009 for hip and knee replacements, varicose veins and hernia operations and results on health gains were categorised by surgeon, hospital, region, as well as across England. This reporting hierarchy was very similar to what he had set out in his 1987 book Supramedicine.

He resolved to further upgrade his website and re-invigorate it towards PROMs. His major stumbling block now was how to do it? The online world was certainly not his forte. Mia suggested their friend James Benjamin. He had a background in the financial markets, plus a strong understanding of Complexity Science and was a major contributor in their Complexity Science group. He would be an ideal candidate to assist in getting the PROMs website and concepts up and running again. James happily came on board and the sales pitch for PROMs became as passionate as ever. On the 9th of October 2014 Eddie presented a paper to his College, The Royal Australian College of Medical Administrators NSW Division, on the "Relationship Between Complexity Science and PROMs" and how this led to "Complexity Medicine". Despite his enthusiasm other attendees didn't see the great potential that Eddie espoused.

"Please just shave Eddie. You look like you've stepped back to the sixties!" Mia pleaded.

"Sorry Mia, it's for an important cause - Movember! Did you know that Movember is one of ICHOM's biggest sponsors? It's wonderful to see a successful Australian charity acknowledging that PROMs are a valid and valuable form of treatment and as such see ICHOM as a worthy recipient of their funds. I can't very well turn up to the November ICHOM conference WITHOUT a moustache!"

Ever the outsider, to his knowledge he was one of the very few at the conference who had specifically grown a moustache for the event. He welcomed the extra warmth his addition brought to his face at such a cold time in Boston. His heart was also warmed by the more than two hundred and fifty attendees and by the very theatrical and impressive presentation by Professor Porter who proved to be an excellent presenter. Eddie fondly recalls Porter finishing the conference by claiming, *"Organisations (i.e. Health organisations), who do not measure using PROMs, will be the last icebergs to melt. Objections to Patient Reported Outcomes Measures no longer stand up."*

Chapter 18

An unmarked grave

The phone was running hot in January 2015.

"Natasha is pregnant again," said Tull from New York.

"Mazel Tov."

"Emmy is due to be married in September this year. You are coming!" said Betty from Israel. *"Mazel Tov."* It would be a year on planes.

Exciting times also seemed to be ahead for Eddie professionally. The big private health insurers, Medibank, put out an article on its new quality program and he rang one of the medical directors, a Fellow of the College of Medical Administrators, and advised that they should include PROMs in their program.

Dr David Rankin was interested, *"Eddie, can you put forward a paper for us? I need you to outline how PROMs will help achieve the quality we desire."*

He was happy to oblige, *"Not a problem."*

"What are you going to charge?"

Eddie eagerly replied, *"I've been endeavouring to have interest in this area for years. I'm happy to do it at no cost."*

"Ha, ha! Yes Eddie, I'm sure, but of course I'll pay you for your work! I need the completed report by May. I will then review and make changes and thereafter pay the fee in full," ensured David. Eddie and James enthusiastically put together a report entitled "A Rationale for a private health insurer to utilise ePROMs". Eddie was excited. It was the first time he was getting paid as a consultant for his knowledge in the PROMs area. Emboldened by the interest from such a large and influential Australian organisation, Eddie and James

acknowledged that their website was in drastic need of an overhaul.

Tull suggested they go further, "*Eddie you can't start a revolution from the top down. Give up on the doctors. Give power back to the masses. A revolution by design needs to come from below. Start an app and market to the individual.*"

Eddie was inspired by the idea on an app but there were problems in going to the general public. The validated PROMs questionnaires belonged to others who, in general, gave permission to use them for free for health research but would expect payment if one went to the general public. Others such as QualityMetrics had made questionnaires available to the general public for years with little uptake. Most importantly, the general public private health insurers who had tried this represented in Eddie's theories of the 80/20 Rule, the 80% of influencers who at the most would have 20% of the effect and that would not change the health system. He pointed out to Tull that there are many joggers, gym attendees, vegetarians....but they were not changing the health system. He wanted to change the health system and medicine. He was determined to implement PROMs as "diagnostic tests", and Lifestyle Scripts and ePROMs treatments, initiated by doctors, to motivate patients to change their behaviours in order to have a real impact on overall health. PROMs themselves were all about giving power back to the patient but within the medical paradigm. He believed he could create the non-pharmaceutical pharmaceutical....an illness-prevention app that would heal the world. There were thousands of apps on the market place to lose weight and to stop smoking so there was no reason why doctors couldn't prescribe this preventative app instead of a drug.

His mind was far from thoughts of his app as he gazed at the beautiful sunset over Tel Aviv beach from the rooftop of The Fitzroy Restaurant. The sense of calm, of joy and of belonging that washed over him whenever on Israeli shores had again swaddled him with its intoxicating magic. Surrounded by so many lifelong friends, his beautiful wife and his beloved land, Eddie was at peace....much like the country itself. They were in Israel to join the much anticipated reunion of old Betar friends. The three-monthly dinners with his Sydney friends from the Betar Youth Movement had continued. They had given themselves the name "The Survivors Group" as most had overcome major health issues. It had been mooted that a reunion dinner should be held with their other friends who were now in Israel (Leo, Bish, Ros, Flapper and Ilana and others) and that a dinner should be held over there. All parties agreed and a date was set for April 2015. Leo had gone to Israel with Mia as part of the Australian Jewish youth assistance group during the Six-Day War and had stayed for good. He had only recently retired from his "government" job and his wife, Celia, was a cooking advisor to restaurants in Israel. Celia had selected their choice of dining and the food hadn't disappointed. Bish announced to the jovial crowd the details of a tour he had arranged for them, *"We're headed into the Upper Galilee and on to the eastern slopes of Mount Kna'an to the quaint little village of Rosh Pinna. It is one of the oldest Zionist settlements in Israel. We'll stay in an old stone hotel, wander the cobbled streets, and visit an ancient synagogue and Baron Rothschild's gardens. From Rosh Pinna, we'll be on a bus with a guide to tour the Golan Heights."*

Before embarking on the group trip, Mia and Eddie were

treated to their own private tour with Leo who knew the area and history well and was in love with every rocky outpost of Israeli land. They visited towns and villages jutting in and out of the West Bank. The rugged and varied landscapes where people existed threw light on why it was such a difficult task to resolve the disputes of such tightly interwoven histories of both Israel and Palestine.

After their time with the Betar group, Mia, Eddie, his brother Michael (who had also been a part of the reunion) and his partner Lyn spent some time catching up with Israeli relatives. Schlomo Rosenberg put on a dinner for his Australian cousins and they also met Yehuda Price and family at Kibbutz Nahshon.

Yehuda had some interesting family history for Eddie and Michael, *"This is your grandfather, Dr Edward Price."* Yehuda proffered a weathered old photograph. *"He was working in Katowice, now Poland, at the time. I've also got these minutes from a board meeting of the local synagogue. It lists Edward Price as a Director."* The cool arm of the past reached out from the blurred black and white image Eddie held in his hand and curled up inside his chest. There was the longing, the call for an understanding of who he was and where he'd come from. Was this why he could never be at ease with what he'd become? Always striving for more, to be more, to achieve more....because he didn't really know where he'd even started. Men like this; his namesake - who was staring out at him through the passage of time - had to put up with so much more than he and yet had achieved so much. Another much loved and worn family image was placed in his hand when they met up with Nitzan Price in Jerusalem. This time the man in the photo was their great-grandfather, Marcus Price, a face that neither Michael nor Eddie had ever seen before. Prior to heading home, they visited Eliav Price in Kibbutz Hazorea north of Haifa and his mother and brother in Kibbutz Ein Dor.

Refreshed and rejuvenated from the journey through Israel, Eddie was further delighted by the news that Dr Stowell from ICHOM had been invited to come to Australia by an offshoot of the NSW Health Department to hold a seminar for those interested in PROMs. In May of 2015, Eddie enthusiastically attended the seminar with James, only to be incensed by the way Dr Stowell began his presentation. Stowell put up a photograph of Dr Ernst Codman and said Dr Codman was his hero because he thought differently. He was illuminating the fact that the idea of "Outcomes Medicine" had been around for a long time and that it can take many years for even great ideas to be acknowledged. He told the story of Dr Ernst Codman of Boston, the surgeon at Massachusetts General Hospital, who in 1912 stated that the surgeons did not measure what really mattered and that they should follow their patients for a year to see the "end results" or the "outcomes" of their surgery. The other doctors did not take his advice and, accordingly, he resigned from Massachusetts General Hospital and then applied for the job as Surgeon in Chief on the grounds that his results were better than those of other surgeons and he had the evidence to prove it. Codman was summarily dismissed but set up his own hospital called End Results Hospital. He was excommunicated from the mainstream of healthcare but continued to work and monitor his outcomes. When he was dying, it is claimed that he said, *"I go to an unmarked grave. Honours except those I have thrust upon myself are conspicuously absent on my chart but I am able to enjoy the hypothesis that I may receive some from a more receptive generation."*

One hundred years after his resignation, in 2013, the American Association of Surgeons attended his grave and placed a plaque in honour of his work on health outcomes and vindicated his stance. To Eddie, this story could have been his own, and Stowell had been one of those to show little interest in his ideas no less. It was like a red flag to a bull.

After the seminar Eddie confronted Dr Stowell, *"Caleb, I will let you know how Dr Codman's colleagues felt about him. I express-posted three books to you about Health Outcomes and my work in this field. You didn't read them. I came to Boston specially to meet with you and I was given one hour. How do you know that the stuff in my books is not important and doesn't have something different in it to what ICHOM is doing! Why the fuck don't you read my books!"*

"Eddie, Eddie!" James tried to diffuse the situation with other questions, silently ruing Eddie's outburst, *"You're burning our bridges Eddie! Look at his body language. You're offending him."*

Eddie cooled down and sent an email to Dr Stowell apologising for his rant. James also sent through an email with a couple of questions for Dr Stowell. Only James received an answer.

Despite being incensed by Stowell's worshipping of Dr Codman, Eddie was intrigued by the previously unknown Dr Codman who seemingly had had a parallel trajectory to himself. He found that Codman also had many similar philosophies to his own, *"The 'End Result' is an idea which is merely the common-sense notion that every hospital should follow every patient it treats long enough to determine whether or not the treatment has been successful, and then to determine 'if not, why not?' We had found that this routine tracing of every case, interesting and uninteresting, had brought to our notice many things in which our knowledge, our technique, our organisation, our own skill or wisdom, and perhaps even our care and our consciences, needed attention."*

Codman was a maverick of his time. His ideas and his passions were not accepted at the time by the medical establishment. He died a pauper with an unmarked grave. And here was Dr Eddie Price, some sixty years later seeking to not only promote similar concepts to Codman, but expand on them and give them a process by which modern medicine could facilitate them....and yet was he too headed for the same fate....an unmarked grave?

On the 10th of June Mia and Eddie flew to New York for the birth of their second grandchild. They were at a wedding reception lunch for Tull's good friends, Geha and Katcha, whose wedding Tull had to miss, when he rang to say that Natasha was in labour. Eddie and Mia took a yellow taxi up the west side of Manhattan but due to traffic it took its time to get to the hospital. By the time they had arrived so had Ezra Price. There would be a second circumcision and naming ceremony.

While there, Eddie decided to touch base with a venture capitalist, Tom Higley, who he'd met at the 2014 ICHOM conference. He was hoping that Tom might be interested in investing in Eddie's app. Tom was happy to meet but he was in Denver.

Eddie rang Super Cheap Fares to ask about flights to Denver and back to New York, *"Certainly Dr Price. We can get you to Denver but there will be a three-hour stopover in Charlotte, and a four-hour stopover in Cleveland on the way back,*" advised the sales clerk.

"*No problem,*" said Eddie, "*I have family and friends in both towns. Am I able to leave the plane and re-connect?*"

"*That is no problem,*" said the airline, "*however, the fares change radically with two proper stopovers.*" The Super Cheap fares had become super expensive fares but they gave Eddie the opportunity to reconnect with his mother's relatives. In Charlotte he spent a night with Lyn Edelstein, her husband Paul and their four children and families that were all in town for Father's Day. When Eddie arrived in Denver he found Tom Higley's office in a converted warehouse that was being shared by various businesses. Colorado was a state that had legalised cannabis sales and the company next to Tom's had a name that made Eddie laugh; Great Shit Pty Ltd. Tom listened patiently and asked many questions over two hours. He advised that Eddie's app and the company were not far enough advanced for him to invest but he made helpful suggestions as to how Eddie needed to advance his ideas, his app and eHealthier in order for them to be more enticing to venture capitalists. It was one of the most productive and positive rejections he had ever received. On the way back to New York he met with Professor Richard Martin, who was Professor of Neonatology at Cleveland Children's Hospital and his wife, Patricia, a psychiatrist – both colleagues of Eddie's from medical school. He always enjoyed his time with Richard and Pat, even relishing the opportunity to answer Richard's concerns about the usefulness of PREMs.

"*They ask questions about whether the food in the hospital is hot enough and so forth. Do you really think that's a high priority of medical care?*" Richard queried.

"*Look Richard there are significant difficulties in that area and that is why I've come up with the concept of a person's Cared-For Status as a measure of their confidence in the healthcare system, together with their social support. These would replace PREMs."*

Spurred on by the advice of Tom Higley Eddie returned to Australia and approached other venture capitalists for funding for his app. Again he was advised, *"You must further develop the app. In its current form it's not fit for funding."*

In August of that year, the Federal Government stated that they wanted "Healthier Medicare" and called for submissions on how to go about doing this. Eddie and James put in at least five submissions about how this could be achieved using PROMs. Eddie spoke to the Head of the Review, Professor Bruce Robinson, to explain how PROMs could save the government two billion dollars a year by avoiding preventable hospital admissions. He claimed that this was simply possible with GPs advocating and prescribing Lifestyle Prescriptions. Health Minister, Sussan Ley, sent the submission to the Health Department and again Eddie flew at his own expense to Canberra and met with four members of the Commonwealth Health Department. Little interest was shown and there was no significant response. Again he was faced with the ongoing frustration that the world either found his ideas too simplistic, or indeed, as his research into Quantum Mechanics had shown, they were incapable of seeing their true potential, "the wave" aspect of this new scientific theory.

Back in Israel for Betty and Edju's son's wedding, Eddie made PROMs presentations to Professor Ron Balicer who was now in the job that Dr Aviva Ron had done in 1980 to 1983 when Eddie worked in the Clalit Health Insurer. He also presented to the second largest health maintenance organisation, Maccabi Health Insurance Providers. Maccabi wasn't interested but Professor Balicer thought there was some real value in working together and offered Eddie sabbatical work in his department. Eddie would have to be self-funded. That wasn't going to work. He and his secretary from the 80's, Raquel, also met with a venture capitalist attached to Maccabi Insurance but he did not see the value in PROMs either. Despite all the rejections he was again spirited by the fact that it seemed more and more people around the world were at least coming to some of the realisations he had made forty years earlier. This was highlighted in an ABC Four Corners program, "Wasted", led by Dr Norman Swan, that indicated, amongst other issues in the health system, that there was a 30% wastage in unnecessary operations. This Eddie had espoused in his very first book in the 80's! He felt that any operations that couldn't be shown to increase PROMs scores should no longer be acceptable. Dr Swan also supported the use of Lifestyle Prescriptions, suggesting they would result in better health and a radical reduction in medical costs.

So doctors were now coming forth with the same concerns and ideas that Eddie had had decades ago. Complexity Science was backing up his claims. Insurance companies were using PROMs as they recognised great savings could be made. So why wasn't the medical world prepared to listen to him? It was the great conundrum of his life.

While he was endlessly searching for the professional success he so desperately craved, success had come in other ways. His grown sons were a source of much love and pride. To Mia and Eddie's delight the addition of grandchildren had extended their precious family.

"Eddie and Mia. Listen." said Josh one night over dinner.

"We are, that is, Jess is pregnant."

"Congratulations! Mazel Tov!" cried the emotional Eddie and Mia.

Mia queried, *"How pregnant?"*

Jess and Josh replied, *"Five to six weeks."*

Eddie was surprised, *"That's pretty early to announce it."*

Josh explained, *"We are just telling the family."*

"Great, keep it that way," encouraged Eddie.

The family secret wasn't kept for long. Soon after Josh was a groomsman at his cousin's wedding and he confessed, *"Ed, with Jess not drinking and all the excitement I could not help but tell my mates."* There was a double celebration at the wedding.

Back to business. Eddie and James had established the need for an app and an app that would be able to be integrated into the mainstream medical system. Any app they developed needed to have interoperability with the various systems that were already utilised by practitioners like Health eNet, MyHealth Record and especially GP clinical software systems like Medical Director and Best Practice. That was going to be costly. Developing such an app was not in either of their capabilities so their first step was to employ an app developer. After two months work he was let go as they were not producing the desired product. Further quotes for professional help were prohibitive so Eddie set about trying to up-skill himself by doing research, attending expensive courses and workshops. What he learned from one workshop was the need to determine whether there was a "product market fit". To do this, one should approach potential clients to see what their interest was like. He made a presentation to executives of a private health insurance company in early January of 2016. The executives advised him that, in fact, they were well-connected with ICHOM and had one of their staff members doing Professor Porter's course in Boston at that time. They felt they could do all that Eddie was proposing on their own. He was happy that they were embracing PROMs, but noted the irony that his rejections were now no longer based on lack of understanding, but because they were already doing what Eddie was offering. How times had changed.

Then he decided to reach out to doctors directly with the idea of a PROMs app in the hope that someone would be interested in trialling it in their practice. The Sydney North Primary Health Network had heard of PROMs and gave Eddie a positive reception. They would happily find a tech-savvy GP to test his app once it was up and running. All he needed was a developer to deliver the product....but all quotes were again out of reach.

On the 9th of February 2016, he read in the eHealth electronic magazine "Pulse IT" about a company, Coral Health Systems (CHS), who offered health developmental services in IT software. Their Chairman was Dr Jack Herman. Eddie eventually got through to Dr Herman who advised him to ring Coral's CEO and their Chief Operations Officer, Dr Ronald Gupta.

At more or less the same time he attended a gathering of start-up companies and spoke with Julia Forsyth, "*Eddie, tell me a little be about eHealthier.*"

He eagerly explained, "*Well, it's a concept I formulated back in 1973....it's finally taken off since Harvard Business School and a Professor Porter there saw PROMs as the solution to the healthcare cost crisis. But what I have with eHealthier offers more again. It's beyond what Porter and ICHOM currently offer.*"

"I hate it when Americans take ideas that were initially Australian," said Julia. *"My company would be interested in talking to you Eddie."*

Julia handed him her card. She was from CMCRC, a Federal government funded innovation initiative. Soon after, Ronald Gupta from Coral Health arranged to meet with Eddie. After going through all the specifics of what was required of the app, he was informed by Dr Gupta that Coral (CHS) was not interested in his product....but....Dr Gupta was. He had CHS's permission to work on this product with his own group of developers from India and Singapore. Dr Gupta put together a quote and a program for development. Eddie was elated. The quote was for $70,000 and was just within Eddie's range. He was prepared to stretch himself as Dr Gupta appeared to have an impressive knowledge of the eHealth system in Australia and he was Chief Operating Officer of a company that had been in business for eighteen years. Finally, Eddie saw this as his big break, his time to shine and his life's work to be recognised and integrated into the health systems of the world. He quickly agreed to the original scope of work. It was a three-month project with five milestones. He advised James and Ather (a project manager who had joined eHealthier) as to what he had done and both commented that that was a big investment.

Not forgetting his interactions with Julia Forsyth and her mention of interest from her company CMCRC, he put in some calls and arranged a meeting. Eddie and James walked into the CMCRC offices. They had a glimpse of the many IT personnel sitting at their workstations.

Eddie commented, *"James, can you feel the brain power in this room? I last felt this on the Harvard campus."*

They met with the Chief Operating Officer David Jonas. To

Eddie's delight, David too, had heard of PROMs and was particularly interested in putting the patient in the centre of the healthcare process. They immediately exchanged non-disclosure agreements and Eddie sent them many articles on eHealthier's plans, including a business plan and projects they suggested they would run in Israel.

Chapter 19

An idea whose time has come

"Hi. I'm Juliet, how may I help you today?" came the vibrant voice through the phone.

Eddie had made the free call to the new NSW Government Get Healthy over-the-phone coaching program. *"Hi Juliet, I just want to learn a little about how you operate and what you can offer me."* His reply thinly masked the real reason for his call, to find out if this program would be a good adjunct for ePROMs treatments.

"Ok Eddie. Tell me a little about your current lifestyle and health status," replied Juliet.

Over the next few weeks this charming young voice lured him to exercise more, eat better, look after his levels of stress and sleep. Without consciously requesting it, Eddie had been given his own lifestyle prescription and suddenly he felt motivated to follow her advice and instructions. There was hope that he could perhaps get off his blood pressure tablets. It started to work. He lost five kilograms and was looking and feeling much healthier.

"Yes?" The mobile phone showed a number from Israel.

"Hi Eddie. This is Eran. Do you remember me?" said a voice.

"Of course I remember you. You stayed with us back in 1986 when you were touring as a backpacker. Then you went into the white water rafting business on the Jordan River in Israel. How is Estie?" asked Eddie.

"Oh it's no longer Estie. It's Hila. She's my wife and, in fact, she is the reason why we're here in Melbourne. And, we're coming to Sydney! Hila is making a presentation. She

works for the Tel Aviv Municipality and various cities are exchanging ideas."

Hila and Eran were immediately invited to Mia and Eddie's for a pizza meal when they arrived in Sydney. After catching up on some thirty years since they last saw Eran, Eddie explained about his lifelong pursuit of the implementation of PROMs.

Hila suggested, *"We have in Israel what is known as a Social Impact Bond for preventing Type 2 Diabetes in the Tel Aviv area. That might be of interest to you Eddie. They are essentially* a contract with the public sector where a commitment is made to pay for improved social outcomes that result in public sector savings."* He had never heard of these Bonds and was fascinated by the concept. He looked up Social Impact Bonds and found, to his surprise, that the NSW Government was very active in promoting them as well. After much research Eddie was convinced that the best way for the Government to measure the outcomes of Social Impact Bonds was through using PROMs. It was a true fit.

"Eddie, when you're in Israel for your conference later this year, give me a call. I'll see what I can work out for you with my contacts," offered Hila. It was an offer he had no intention of refusing.

The London ICHOM conference was bustling with more than 800 delegates. Australia was well-represented amongst the speakers with the CEOs of Ramsay Health Care and HCF, both advocating for PROMs. He met with two Israeli doctors from Tel Hashomer hospital where Eddie had done his internship. They were just starting their journey on PROMs. In London the government had passed a law making it mandatory for private hospitals to use PROMs in eleven operations. The PROMs were used by the UK as an invaluable tool to accurately monitor the quality of treatment in the hospitals. Results were available so patients could make informed decisions on their health providers based on price and on quality of service. The whole conference was abuzz with the potential of PROMs to help reform the health system.

Eddie then flew to Israel for the International Health Policy Conference.

"Look at you, Eddie. You look like a street sleeper. Your clothes are too big on you. You've lost weight. I have to take you shopping," Betty exclaimed as she dragged him off to buy two pairs of more elegant jeans and a couple of T-shirts. The sales girl offered him jeans with buttons.

He said, *"At this age, I can't deal with buttons. I'm developing a tremor of my hands. I might not manage in time."*

"Not a problem," said the attendant, *"in what size?"*

"I don't know. I've recently had a baby," he explained.

"Congratulations!"

"Strange things happen nowadays," said Eddie, now suitably decked out with new clothes.

True to her word, Hila had arranged some appointments for him while he was in Tel Aviv. Yaron Neudorfer was the Chief Executive of Social Finance Israel, the implementers of the Social Impact Bonds and Eddie was afforded an audience. They would also cross paths at the upcoming International Conference on Health Policy where Yaron was presenting. Another appointment was made for Eddie with the Deputy Head of Public Health in Israel's Health Department. They too were attending the conference. At the conference in Jerusalem he introduced himself to Dr Eyal Zimlichman, Deputy Director and Chief Quality Officer, of the Sheba (Tel

Hashomer) Medical Centre. He was the leader of PROMs in Israel. Eyal explained how he had worked on PROMs at Partners Health Care and at Harvard in Boston. He reviewed the PowerPoint presentation that Ronald Gupta had set up for Eddie on eHealthier and PROMs and Eddie also outlined his desire to open a branch of eHealthier in Israel. They agreed to keep in touch. He met again with Yaron Neudorfer and with the Heads of the two smaller health maintenance organisations in Israel, Leumit and Meuhedet. They all showed an interest in Eddie's PowerPoint of the potential of PROMs. The most promising discussions for Eddie were held with Professor Ron Balicer, the Director of Health Policy Planning at the Clalit Research Institute. Professor Balicer was interested in possibly doing pilot projects and hoped that these might work in his research and development project. Balicer indicated that he would put together a project plan for implementing something and have it emailed on to Eddie.

Whilst overseas he learned that Ramsay Health in Australia was already implementing PROMs using a Canadian PROM system. On returning home he immediately made appointments with Dr John Horvath, the Head of Quality at Ramsay and a former Chief Medical Officer of Australia. Eddie explained that eHealthier had a Cared-For PROM which was different and in his eyes an important part of the future of true healthcare.

Dr Horvath said, *"Yes, caring is very important. I can tell you out of my personal experience that when I was hospitalised as a young man a nurse sat with me and just talked. I remember her and her name to this day."*

Alas Eddie's app was not yet ready to operate so the Cared-For PROM was not taken up, but Ramsay, to this day, use

287

functional PROMs in all their hospitals and are, in Eddie's opinion, the most forward thinking of all the private hospitals in Australia. The lack of a functional app hampered other willing adaptors like the ACI (The NSW Health Agency for Clinical Innovation). He could only hope that the app would shortly be ready for operation. In August 2016, his developer, Dr Ronald Gupta, told him that he was going to reduce his work with CHS because he was so sold on the prospect of the eHealthier product. Dr Gupta proposed to work two days a week, for a fairly hefty fee, but this, he reassured Eddie would cover all future development costs of the app. Eddie was desperate to move the app into health practices and signed up quickly. Ronald had impressed him with his thorough knowledge of all parts of the health system, despite not yet delivering his product.

On the 14th of July Josh and Jess' son, Zevi Price, was born, the third grandson. A beautiful naming and circumcision ceremony under the auspices of a lady rabbi, Jackie Ninio, was held at 60 Queens Park Road.

He was nearing his 70th year and finally all the pieces of his puzzle were falling into place. He had three grandsons. He was developing an app. In Australia he had a government-supported-organisation and general practitioners interested in implementing this app once it was completed and there were more doors opening to him in Israel. The world was finally embracing PROMs and his ideas. The heavy blanket of weight was lifting from his soul. He was physically, and now, mentally lighter. Rejuvenated and energised by the possibilities of his app, he mused, "*I'm the oldest person in the world with a start-up. I need to buy myself another 20 years.*" So, he did. The invitation to his 70th... eh, sorry, 50th birthday read:

"Ed's Placebo Party! Guess who's turning 50?! Five months ago I awoke to realise it took 42 years to get my healthcare ideas company to be a start-up. I figured the only way it will be a functional business; I would have to work 20 more years. That was only achievable if I could change my year of birth to 1966, which I have mentally achieved. It would help if my social environment reinforced that belief. If you can all be 20 years younger on the 2nd of September, that would keep the Placebo effect alive.
Thanks for your efforts in anticipation.
Eddie."

The festivities began with a Santa Fe meeting before lunch at their home. Discussion was had as to how he could really be fifty rather than seventy. Dr John Harrison commented that he would only achieve this if he had feedback from his environment and from others indicating to him that he was indeed fifty and that he should cease to invest meaning in the notion of age in general. Unfortunately, that was not the feedback Eddie received. Some reminded him that he didn't look fifty; a maths teacher suggested he was still bad at maths and wished him a *"Happy 90th!"* Edju chirped in with, *"And they say that I'm slow!"* The celebrations continued into the afternoon with the remainder of his family and friends in attendance. He was pleased that Mia had organised Tull and Josh to give speeches for he heard sentiments from them, and from Bernie, that he may not have otherwise heard.

Josh concluded his, as per usual, poetic speech with, *"Now we all realised pretty quickly that Ed is not normal, but it took me till later in life to realise that not only is he not normal and not ordinary, he is in fact extraordinary. The great physicist Richard Feynman once suggested that his students should 'stop trying to fill their heads with science – for to fill your hearts with love is enough'. It is not only to my great benefit, but to all of ours that Eddie has chosen to do both.*

So here's to the next 50 years! I love you. Happy Birthday."

Tull's speech was read out by one of Eddie's close friends, Tony Frumar, as Tull was still in the US. His words highlighted the great respect Eddie's sons had for the father he had been, not only to them, but to many young men.

"During the (cricket) season I watched you treat each kid like they were your own, no matter how bad they were, no matter how anti-Semitic their parents were – and there were a few – to you each kid had potential and a skill somewhere within. You would identify that point of potential, bring it out, work on their weakness and then drum in the basics – catching, fielding, bowling – the forward defence. I saw kids thrive as you put some belief into them. For some I think it was the first time anyone had. You were a great cricket coach. How you managed to get some of those kids to be half-decent I'll never know. Whether it was for your love of cricket, or to support and spend time with your son, or a bit of both, I can't be sure, but either way, I believe it's the same and believe it shows the man you are and the man I've been happy to have as a father to this day.

Thanks and Happy 50th!"

Eddie also treasured a gift given by his "third son" Matt Bowman.

"I thought, what am I going to get this bastard? He doesn't need anything or want for anything... oh I know... a

tombstone for that unmarked grave that he's always harping on about!" explained Matt as he presented Eddie with a tombstone inscribed "Edward Daniel Price – The Fractal Between the Squares". Overall it had been a great day. For the unstoppable Eddie it was back to work and to eagerly await the presentation of the app development to date. A month later, in October of 2016, Ronald Gupta delivered.

As the app presentation drew to a close there was a stunned silence. Eddie wasn't sure how to respond. Not wanting to upset the hard working staff in India, he chose his words carefully....but what he saw in front of him, his eagerly awaited app, was a complete disaster. He was desperately disappointed. Despite the grave concerns, Ronald assured him the app would come together and they should be ready to market in the New Year. Josh was made a Director of the company to present a more youthful appearance for marketing purposes. James however was reticent and wary of the quality of work produced by Gupta to date and he felt any marketing was premature. Eddie however, was swept up in the enthusiasm of Ronald who also explained that CHS would be marketing PROMs as part of their combined product. Further encouragement for Eddie was an email from CMCRC stating that they wished to be involved. Their caveat was that they needed to know that the app was up to standard to be associated with their reputation. David Jonas said they would invest in kind offering programmers and members of their staff who would work on ensuring the app was of a decent standard. Eddie was delighted with this opportunity.

For decades he had felt that he was the only one with vision and that the rest of the world was blind to the possibilities that PROMs presented....but now the blindfolds had been torn off. The impact and potential of PROMs were gaining impetus around the globe. On the 18th of January 2017 the OECD's Health Ministers put out a Ministerial Statement. They claimed that "The Next Generation of Health Reforms" would have to do with the publishing and reporting of Patient-Reported Outcomes for international comparison. All thirty-five country members signed a letter of intent to collaborate in the collection of this data with ICHOM. They agreed to promote person-centred care so it would become the new "normal" for health systems. These initiatives were to be put in place through an OECD program called PaRIS (Patient-Reported Indicators Survey). The program was to be run in close collaboration with ICHOM so they could globally standardise the Patient-Reported Outcomes Collection in key disease areas. These results would be published to support patients, clinicians and policymakers. The World Economic Forum (WEF) announced that the costs of healthcare were no longer sustainable and concluded that 30-50% of "the spend" was wasted and that they were looking to PROMs to help solve the problem. They claimed that the only way health systems would survive was if they moved to value-based healthcare and as such set up a program that would look at improvement in PROMs divided by episodic costs. There were also positive developments in Australia. Jacob Lippa, one of the senior executives from ICHOM, visited Australia for ICHOM's first Australasian conference. The conference showed there was a great deal of movement towards "Value-Based Healthcare". The Director of the NSW Health Department, Elizabeth Koff, talked of this type of health system as "An idea whose time has come" and more was to come. Innovation and Science Australia released a report called "Australia's Planned Prosperity

Through Innovation". In it they recommended that Australia should seek to become the healthiest nation in the world. Eddie rang their CEO, Charlie Day, to suggest that the methodology he had been advocating for over forty-five years was based on the most recent and innovative science, Complexity Science. Eddie was confident that this would make Australia the healthiest nation on earth by the year 2030. He was ecstatic that so many individuals and economic organisations were advocating ideas he'd spelled out so many years earlier. Finally, they understood. Now they needed to take the next step. He felt that, despite their rhetoric, they were still radically underestimating the value that PROMs would bring to change, not only in healthcare administration, but to medicine itself. Still, this was the closest Eddie had ever been to his nirvana......if only he could get his app to work cohesively with the developing paradigm.

"Eddie I have great news!" It was Ronald Gupta. *"eHealthier, in combination with CHS has received a 'Request For Quotation' (RFQ) from NSW Health ACI (Agency for Clinical Innovation) to be submitted by CHS, eHealthier and CMCRC as a consortium to quote on Patient-Reported Measures (PRM), software, implementation and support services."*

"Ronald that's fantastic!" enthused Eddie....but then he recalled the close working relationship he'd observed at the London ICHOM conference between ACI and a competitor of eHealthier, Health Outcomes Australia. They had ties with a much larger company Quantium Health Outcomes and didn't like their chances of winning the bid. With little chance of winning the tender it was agreed that a tender should be submitted nonetheless. Shortly thereafter, as

expected, eHealthier were advised by the ACI that their application was unsuccessful. Eddie continued to place his hopes in his developer, the COO of CHS, Ronald Gupta, and followed his lead and advice when addressing an integral part of their app. In order for the app to be acceptable as part of the health system it needed an interoperability known as an API (Application Program Interface) which included interfacing to a multitude of other software programs such as Health eLink, Linked EHR, MyHR, Best Practice, Medical Director, SMS, Health eNet and Health Pathways to mention a few. Doing this was expensive but Eddie was advised that CHS would also be investing in the development.

"I'm excited." Eddie's deadpan voice fell flat against the gathered delegates. The attending eHealthier staff held their collective breath in anticipation of the reception he would receive. Then the tension broke. His wry smile and twinkle in his eye informing his audience that indeed this was a moment to be celebrated; a time when a man who had been fighting his whole life for an idea, a concept that might just change the course of medicine, had his time. Eddie was being acknowledged as someone with something to say, a message for the world. A relieved smattering of chuckles rippled around the room. It was the 18th of May 2017 and CMCRC had convened health industry leaders for their "Emerging Trends in Digital Health Conference". Eddie was presenting the concept of utilising PROMs through his app and highlighting the way in which PROMs were being heralded around the world. Despite the honour of being asked to speak at the conference and the overwhelmingly positive response from all delegates to his presentation, he was staring at the grim reality – the app was not yet developed. On a family holiday with Mia, Tull, Josh and

their growing families in LA, he pondered his situation. He decided that the best way forward would be to design a much simpler app and create what he called an ePROMs Survey. It could be used by Primary Health Networks as a sample survey to assess the change in health needs of their population year to year. Eddie felt it would be a simple program to write and should be ready to market within one or two months.

"I've got some good news and some bad news," announced Juliet, Eddie's over-the-phone health coach.

"Well, what is the bad news?"

"I'm leaving," Juliet replied.

Eddie was disappointed. *"Oh no, you can't let me down this way. I'm struggling to maintain my weight loss and how will I manage without you?"*

"The good news is I will be replaced by Pierre who is most competent."

"Where are you going?" asked Eddie. *"Are you going to take a gap year tour in Europe or Asia?"*

"No. I'm going to Jerusalem," she replied.

He was shocked, *"Jerusalem! Why would you do that?"*

"That's where religious Jews go," explained Juliet.

He was incredulous, *"After I told you that I ate too much at Passover and explained Passover to you, explained the concept of Bar Mitzvahs to you, it turns out you are one of our tribe!"*

Juliet laughed, *"Yes indeed."*

Then Eddie had an idea. *"Well, I'm developing an app and I wouldn't mind having an office in Israel and I admire your work. If you're going to be there, once you settle in, perhaps you could contact me and if the app is more developed than it is today, we could get it going. If you're interested, and wish to read up on my work, there is only one copy of my three books in Israel, located with my friend, Edju. Email me and I will give you Edju's phone number if you're interested in these concepts."*

Juliet said she would and when he received her email he found out her surname for the first time. She had, in fact, played touch football with Josh across from his house in Queens Park. They would open a dialogue regarding the app but Juliet was quick to say that, *"the app does not seem to be developed enough for me to implement it at this stage".* She was right. Eddie had to concur.

"Periodically aluminium comes before 80% of the French-speaking world while 50% of barium comes after." Eddie's long-time friend Bernie had sent through his usual cryptic invitation to their twice-yearly luncheon for the Bondi Walkers group. Eddie had now been a member of the group for many years looking after his own mental and physical wellbeing. These luncheons were not only another chance to socialise but they came together for a good cause. The group of around thirty men would, at an average luncheon, raise between five and ten thousand dollars for a designated charity. Bernie's cryptic passages revealed the location of each lunch and Eddie had struggled to decipher the fourteen prior puzzles.

"I've got it!" Eddie woke Mia with a yell at 10pm one night. *"Periodic aluminium means Al, it comes before 80% of the French-speaking world and the word for 'world' in French is 'monde', and 80% will be monde without the 'e', whilst 50% of barium comes after and that would be 'bar'. The restaurant is the Almond Bar!"* He was extremely excited. *"That's where the Bondi Walkers will lunch,"* he sighed. He would sleep soundly that night.

"Eddie, I've resigned from CHS! This is a great opportunity for me to dedicate myself 100% to eHealthier," Ronald Gupta's animated voice rang through the phone. *"We just need to iron out a few little bits and pieces. They've cut me off from my email and we'll have to change our eHealthier email access code, but all is good, it's a positive step."*

Eddie wasn't quite as enthusiastic. Niggling thoughts of *"Why haven't we yet succeeded to produce this app? What is taking so long?"* began to creep into his thoughts which were further supported by his colleague James' ongoing apprehension to involve Ronald at all. Eddie so desperately needed this developer to succeed that he told himself, *"Perhaps it is because nobody has been dedicated full-time to the app development. With someone working full-time, maybe we will achieve the breakthrough we need. With somebody as dedicated and with the knowledge that Ronald has of the health system, full-time, we can have the ePROMs Survey, as well as the ePROMs platform up and running."* It was agreed that Ronald would come on board with eHealthier under full-time employment.

Eddie turned to his brother Michael with his years of software experience for advice. Michael was extremely sceptical. He not only advised Eddie to pay only on deliverables, but he also developed a requirements document outlining how this ought to be done and most importantly set out a system design for the ePROMs platform. This was a state of the art design document backed up with multiple PowerPoint presentations that would become the basis of eHealther's platform. Michael took over as the product manager. The brother's were working together again.

To keep up with his physical health and mental well-being Eddie was walking during the week with his Bondi walkers and, on weekends, he'd begun walking around Centennial Park with his brother Michael, cousin Dinah and her husband Len. The family troupe was also holding cousins' dinners every two to three months where they were joined by Dinah's sister Sharon. Discussions during these gatherings began to dissect Eddie's attraction to colourful people with whom he had difficulty standing up to and saying NO to. Like Mia, like Ronald Gupta....like his father. The echoes of the past were again haunting his very functioning and he was reminded of his readings into Schema Therapy. They suggested we have life scripts where we re-enact the worst parts of our childhood in current relationships. Was this why he was drawn to people who embodied many similar traits to his late, domineering father? Dinah, who had worked as a psychotherapist for many years, suggested another counsellor who used emotional-focussed therapy and he began attending sessions immediately.

"*Ahh... back again,*" mused Eddie as he settled into his seat at the annual ICHOM conference at the Marriott Hotel in Washington.

Dr Caleb Stowell rose from his chair to open a session of the conference. "*How many of you came to this conference by UBER?*" he queried.

A few people put up their hands.

"*In five years' time at this conference how many of you think you will be coming by self-driven cars?*" he asked.

Several more hands rose.

Stowell continued, "*You believe change happens in a hurry?*" Then he pointed to the picture illuminated on the projector screen. Eddie could hardly believe his eyes. Caleb's very first slide was the cover of Eddie's book Supramedicine. "*This guy talked of change, talked of PROMs, twenty-five years ago and yet it is just happening now!*" proclaimed Stowell.

Finally, ICHOM was acknowledging that he had been trying to tell the world about PROMs, to no avail, for twenty-five years. He raised his hand to acknowledge Caleb and received a smattering of applause. He was delighted to accept even this small token of recognition. After the conference, he wrote to Stowell. "*Caleb, thank you for the honour you have bestowed upon me. I thought I would be going to an unmarked grave!*"

The reference to their mutual hero, Dr Ernst Codman, would not be lost on Stowell. The first official speaker to take the stage following Dr Stowell was Dr Eyal Zimlichman from Israel. Eyal's presentation looked at the work that was taking place in Sheba Hospital that showed a huge advance in their use of PROMs. Eddie thought, "*Well it helps coming from Israel where they are starting to expect advances at the cutting edge.*" He wondered if any of his persistent pushing of PROMs in Israel had been of influence. He was even more amazed by the next speaker, Professor Judith Baumhauer of Orthopaedics Association, who presented a paper that sparked his interest. She demonstrated how by using PROMs scores to measure workers' physical health status and then by introducing a physical strengthening program, they were able to prevent back injuries because they could show an improvement in physical health score. Eddie thought, "*This is how PROMs can be used in a preventive way to increase wellbeing as I have been advocating, not just on workers, but everybody.*" Judith Baumhauer also found that by using PROMs such as the PROMIS-10 she had been able to diagnose in orthopaedic patients, from their mental health scores, the existence of depression. *"FINALLY,"* he thought to himself, *"A further demonstration that these are really diagnostic tests!!!"* In the concluding oration of the conference, Professor Porter spoke about the potential of PROMs being used by GPs rather than concentrating on hospitals, as in all his previous presentations. Eddie was excited that everything was moving ahead in the PROMs world towards what he had envisaged. Ironically, it was now the development of his own app that was slow to move.

"Serendipity: The International Conference on Systems and Complexity for Health Care being held only a few days after the ICHOM Conference....and both in the same city!" He was intrigued and delighted by the work of Aaron Antonovsky and what Eddie considered was an excellent PROM called "The Source of Coherence", a 13-question PROM that accurately reflected a person's capacity to remain healthy. He soaked up any opportunity to expand his knowledge base by combining Complexity Science and Health Care....and PROMs. It was his utopia.

Eddie concluded, *"I'm certainly going to be implementing 'The Source of Coherence' as a PROM in my app... if it would only get going!"*

Elated by the accolades he'd received and buoyed by the international movement of PROMs, he returned to Australia resolved to ensure the success of his app as soon as possible. His euphoria soon came crashing down. At an eHealthier Executive meeting Ronald suddenly no longer wanted to integrate with CHS. Eddie was confused. Part of the huge expense he had incurred with Ronald Gupta was to supposedly take advantage of the interoperability that CHS offered as a means to working within medical practices. Eddie had trouble understanding Ronald's explanations.

Clarity came some weeks later when in mid-January 2018 he learned that CHS had gone into voluntary administration. Eddie called the Chairman of CHS to glean a little more information on his developer Ronald Gupta. Dr Herman said, *"CHS spent a huge amount of money on the programmers in India and we had even sent one of our senior programmers out to train them, but nothing seemed to work."* His worst fears were realised when he heard of a prior company to CHS that had also spent huge amounts of money on programs, supposedly implemented by Ronald Gupta and his development team that had similarly proved ineffective. Eddie re-Googled "Dr Ronald Gupta". From September 2017 when Ronald was supposedly working full-time on Eddie's project, he was allegedly also the COO for another company, ABC Clinical Data, and a co-founder and CIO of a company in Latin America, AB Medical. Eddie had been deceived, once again, and he plunged into the depressive task of attempting to salvage his work....once again. He managed to engage the services of MKM Health to lift and shift the parts of the app that were developed, however he had exhausted any finances his family could spare.

Ambition clouded and destroyed by passion... his fatal flaw.

Chapter 20

Nostradamus

We, in the "western" world, are experiencing the dawning of a new age. There has been a monumental shift in the global community to a greater acceptance of more holistic health that embraces many of the age old practices of "eastern" medicine. Many now see the body as more than just a sum of its parts but as a dynamic and extremely complex energy system. There has also been a broad acceptance and understanding that measuring outcomes is an essential part of running an effective health system. Whether Eddie's life's work has intrinsically been a part of this revolution, or whether change has occurred despite of it, Eddie has perhaps been the Nostradamus of the evolution of modern healthcare.

In his eyes there is still so much that can be done with so many more of his ideas and observations to be understood. In 1980 he claimed that 88% of what doctors did was not measured. In 2018 he sees that figure dropping by only two percent, to 86%. He also believes that doctors still do not prescribe the most proven treatments, and that health care systems in the OECD have not been able to come to terms with Drucker's effective management techniques that reward both prevention and caring. He still believes that there are radical potential improvements in health and significant reductions in costs to occur. He predicts that in the next ten years, as people start to measure these "invisible parameters" through PROMs that the cost of health care will fall by a minimum of 8% in the OECD countries - with or without Dr Price. Eddie claims that the 2% shift has commenced and now it is an unstoppable force. This momentum is mimicked in the admirable passion within Eddie himself. The passionate drive to strive in the pursuit of acceptance, in the face of adversity, that will only be extinguished by death itself.

As Eddie passes the baton of his dreams and desires onto future generations he bestows upon them the challenge to take his beloved PROMs to greater heights....to turn them into "CROMs"- Customer Reported Outcomes Measures. Eddie believes CROMs can measure and improve quality of life in all areas of life: education, the arts, fashion, social status, even religion. He sees them as providing greater understanding of the human condition. They could even be utilised, he claims, as an extension of democracy, giving everyone a voice, and, as a result, could transform "quality of life" across social structures around the globe. Eddie again defers to science and to the "Butterfly effect" explaining, *"Globally we are all interconnected and if we are to make a disturbance here....there will be effects over there."* He may not realise it, or give himself credit for it, but he has found the formula for exacting his boyhood dream, to make a difference in the world. He didn't need to be the Secretary General of the UN....just an Australian Jewish doctor with an idea. Let's hope, unlike many a philosopher who is only fully appreciated after they are long gone, that we don't leave it too late to capitalise on the true potential of this great intellect and send him to an unmarked grave.

A complex life intellectually, physically and emotionally. A life slipping between the norms, between expectations, between countries, between religious and cultural expectations.

And it was amongst the rigid structures of life... that Eddie found the fractal of life.

Bibliography

Australian Dictionary of Biography, www.adb.anu.edu.au, Vol.16. (MUP) 2002

Armstrong, Diane. *The Voyage of their Life; The Story of the SS Derna and Its Passengers.* Flamingo, 2001.

Clarke, Joan. *The Doctor Who Dared. The Story of Henry Price.* Tully Press, 1982.

Price, Dr Eddie. *Health Outcomes. A New Way of Defining and Managing Health.* Tully Press, 1985.

Price, Dr Eddie. *Supramedicine. From Health Outcomes to Outcomes Medicine.* Murray David Publishing Pty Ltd., 1997.

Price, Dr Eddie. *So You Think Medicine is Modern? Revolutionising Health Care for the 21st Century.* AtmInformation, 2008

OUT OF HIS MIND
APPENDIX

written by Dr Eddie Price

Dr Eddie Price's life story has been centred on his ideas derived from applying modern management theory to the healthcare system.

Some readers may be interested in understanding his ideas further. This appendix presents summaries of his conclusions.

APPENDIX CONTENTS
1. Dr Eddie Price's medicine and healthcare system: a summary.
2. Implementation of the new medicine and healthcare system.
3. Hypotheses arising from his theoretical research.
4. Detailed explanations of the evolution of his ideas and theories, see his books:
   - *Is Medicine Really Necessary?* (1985), reprinted as *Health Outcomes: A New Way of Defining and Managing Health* (1994);
   - *Supramedicine* (1997);
   - *So You Think Medicine is Modern?* (2008).

1. **Dr Price's Medicine and Healthcare System.**
   1. Re-definition of health and its measurement.
   2. GP/Primary Care Physicians Practice of Population Health (rather than disease) -
      management and population health improvement.
   3. Vaccine against heart disease, stroke and 40% of cancers.
   4. A hierarchical tree for national health maximisation.
   5. Vertical Total Quality Management (VTQM).
   6. Planting hierarchical trees – the role of health departments/governments.
   7. PROMs as diagnostic tests as authenticated by the WHO 2001 International Classification of Functioning (ICF).
   8. CHI, a person's Comprehensive Health Index.
   9. Disease/Body Part-Specific PROMs – a new medicine.
   10. PROMs treatments.
   11. Survival of the most cooperative and the fittest.
   12. Descartes: The human body is like a well-made clock. Eddie Price: The human body is like a tree.
   13. Evolved Medicine: Dual particle and wave medicine.

2. **Implementation of the New Medicine and Healthcare System.**
   2.1.1   The "What" of Implementation.
   2.1.2   The "Why" of Implementation.
   2.1.3   The "How" of Implementation.

3. **Dr Price's hypotheses arising from his theoretical research.**

4. **Dr Price's books.**

1. DR PRICE'S MEDICINE AND HEALTHCARE SUMMARY

1. Redefinition of health and its measurement.
The first step is to redefine health, to ensure the definition facilitates the change from a disease system to a health and caring system as follows:

Current definition WHO
Health is a state of complete physical, mental and social wellbeing and not merely the absence of disease or infirmity. (World Health Organisation definition)

Dr Eddie Price's definition
Health is a score of Physical Health (PH) of 60+[1], Mental Health (MH) 60+ and Social Health (SH) 60+, where the population norm is 50 (2015 norms) that represents wellbeing for a natural lifespan. Natural lifespan is defined as life expectancy at birth plus 20% life expectancy at birth – currently approximately 100 years.

2. Primary care physicians (PCP/GP) to practice population health management.
Each PCP/GP will encourage every patient aged over 16 years of age for that period, e.g. from 01.01.2020 attending the GP's practice to complete a PROMIS Global 10 Score PROM and Risk Factor (Population Preventive PROM) PROM, with six risk factors: smoking, alcohol, fruit/vegetable consumption, physical

---

[1] See Generic PROMs measurement. PROMs 10-SF, Global SF-12.

activity, weight and height.

After three months, that GP will have a frequency distribution graph in bands of her/his attending population "bands" of physical and mental health scores, and those with associated risk factors.

Individual Patient's PH Score over time

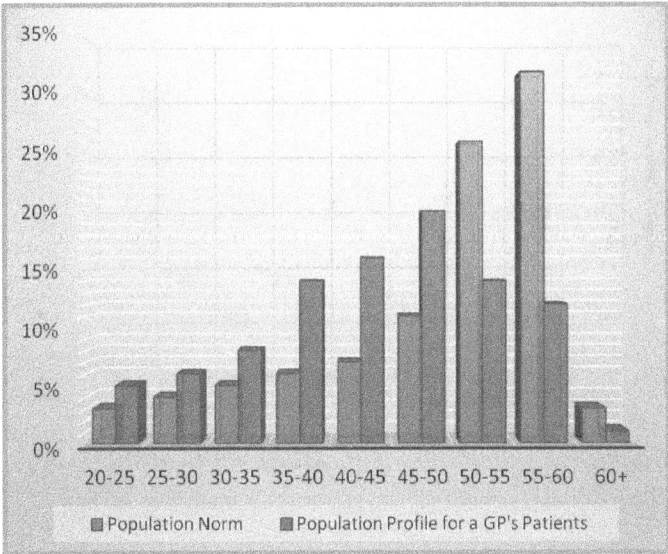

X axis = Physical Health Band Scores. Y axis = Percentage of GP population.
Dr Banks' population graph based on 534 patients attending from 01.01.2020 to 31.03.2020, compared to the population norm.

Risk Factor Incidence

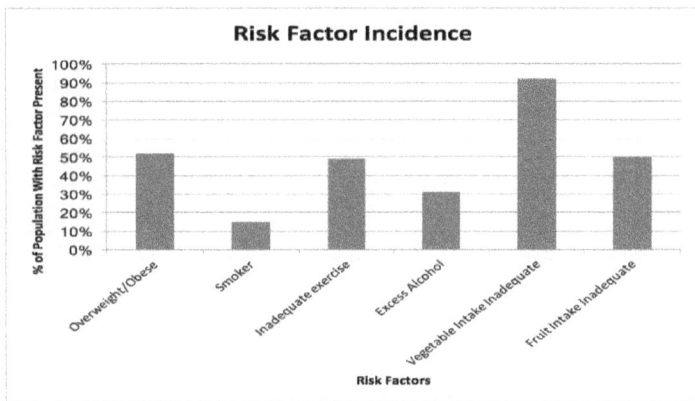

Dr Banks' GP population percentage with various risk factors.

The GP and his individual patient will then reach agreement on an individual's shared care target score to encourage each patient within six months to improve their PH (Physical Health), MH (Mental Health) and SH (Social Health) initial score by 10%, that 10% improvement is the shared care target.

This will be achieved by the GP, utilising motivational interviewing techniques and prescribing lifestyle scripts, PROMs treatments, available as lifestyle apps being a "3-monthly care plan" for the patient.

By the next calendar year, the GP will have moved her/his population's "mean or median score" or the whole population's frequency distribution graph to the right, in a health positive direction, that is, to higher PH, MH and SH scores.

3. Vaccine against heart disease, stroke and 40% of cancers.

The GP can then assert that the number of those of his/her patient population with PH, MH and SH scores above 60 have a vaccine against Heart Disease, Stroke and 40% of Cancers (being a behavioural vaccine) for the next six months.

4. A hierarchical tree for national health maximisation.

The Federal health department representing the health of all Australians can be seen as the top of a hierarchical system that divides into six states and two territories which in turn, divides each state into 1 to 10 PHNS, which are made up of 200 practices and 800 GPs, all with their associated populations, with their PH, MH and SH scores. This hierarchy can be inverted and it becomes a tree with the National Government as the trunk and the states as the major branches.

Now a tree, the hierarchy is a fractal, and it gains more power by not being interrupted at any of the hierarchical levels.

In this way, if we want a Quality Product, i.e. the healthiest nation in the world, all the levels of the hierarchy must first achieve this. We must, as a population, have the healthiest practice populations in the world.

This is vertical total quality management (TQM) and the total quality standards are only achieved if the GP participants and their patients are so motivated.

This can be achieved by utilising social psychology; individual motivational theories that ensure the participants are regularly validated (monthly) for putting in their efforts to achieve the shared goal.

All of these processes are now enabled by the power of

information technology.

In fact, there is no reason why this hierarchical tree cannot be extended from Australia to the OECD and ultimately to all nations. We then would have a health maximisation for all nations united, i.e. the UNO's hierarchical tree for health maximisation.

5. Vertical total quality management (VTQM).

In a manufacturing production line process, total quality management was introduced and developed into lean production and six sigma and lean six sigma.

Essentially, the idea is that if statistics can be implemented along the process line to ensure quality for each part of the manufactured product, the end product, be it a car (such as Toyota) or a TV set, will automatically be, or must be a quality car or television set.

That is to say, one starts with raw materials that need to be converted to widgets, screws, coils, doors etc. to be assembled into the final quality product, this can be assured and is most cost-effectively achieved if each component along the line is a quality component (within statistical limits) and if the production line is smooth etc.

As a nation, if one has a mission such as Australia's from January 2018 Innovation and Science Australia's (ISA's) to be the healthiest nation in the world by 2030, there is a vertical hierarchical tree where the same principal can apply.

That is, for a nation to be the healthiest nation in the world, this will only be achieved if the states that make up this nation are the healthiest states. A state can only be the healthiest state if its regions (Primary Health Networks) are the healthiest. This in turn requires the individual practice population being the healthiest and eventually to each GP and patient being the healthiest.

This hierarchy can be inverted and placed on its end. The nation then becomes the trunk of the tree and the population health as the sum total of the leaves.

Therefore, it is the job of government health departments to "plant these trees". Greater results will be achieved if all the levels or branch sizes are present and there is a smooth continuum.

The statistical process control standards in this vertical hierarchy will only be achieved if the participants (doctors and allied health providers) at each level have their own motivational needs met and furthermore, their motivational needs are continually validated by participating in this process, particularly their sense of achievement.

6. Planting hierarchical trees – the role of health departments/ government.

Once the health departments/government, together with the concurrence of their population, selects a shared health vision, they should then, depending on the vision or goal, carry out a search as to which hierarchy (hierarchical tree) is best placed to assist in achieving the particular health goal or target.

i. Reduction in deaths and injuries from motor vehicle accidents.

The health department, when looking for the correct hierarchy, may look at the GP healthcare system but it is most likely they will end up with the police stations and police departments, together perhaps with local government authorities (LGAs) as the hierarchies to follow. They should then accumulate statistics as to the performance of that particular police station in the previous 12 months and, based on this feedback, then determine a reduction target. The police stations in turn would add up to police regions and it is important in planting or constructing this hierarchical tree that at least one person, preferably the chairperson of the committee, is a member of the committee or organisation above that is charged with achieving its targets. This should establish friendly competition between police stations, police regions and the like. A successful strategy in one police station or region or state could then be utilised in a neighbouring state. There are many benefits of having this whole system of Vertical Total Quality Management as through this peer pressure, friendly competition and other human motivational factors can be utilised at each of the levels to achieve the best outcomes. These would add up to state levels and states would, in turn, compete to reach the national level.

Again, it would be prudent to reward participants on their achievement based on percentage improvements as this would allow the worst areas and regions, those with the greatest need, to have the highest chance of achieving the target of the biggest percentage improvement over the year. In this case, the health department may plant a police station/police region hierarchical tree that they need to nurture to achieve the health target of a prevention of motor vehicle deaths and injuries.

ii. Work Injuries.

Again, the health department needs to, with other departments, assess which hierarchical tree they wish to plant. It is likely in this incident they would plant an employer/workers compensation insurer hierarchical tree charged with setting and achieving targets. This would go up the chain through entities such as licenced insurers, self-insurers, government insurers and the like: each insurer competing on the percentage improvement from prior years. It is noted that the maximum control (even preventing work injuries) is likely to be down at the employer first level supervisor management. These supervisors could set up appropriate preventive procedures in terms of work accidents but also involve his or her workforce in setting and maintaining appropriate targets.

iii.   Health Improvement Hierarchical Tree
This is the major group that has accountability for the health of individuals and this is most likely to be, or ought to be, the patient, together with their primary care physician, and this tree should be planted with all the appropriate hierarchical levels going from practice to cluster of GPs to PHNs (Primary Health Networks) to regions and then to states. Again, the manner in which the tree is planted, cultured and nurtured, and its appropriate use of motivational behavioural peer group pressure and competition theory will help determine how successful it is in achieving its targets year to year.

7.   PROMs are a new suite of diagnostic tests.
This 1994 conclusion of Dr Price, authenticated by WHOs Paradigm Shift from the previous model of disablement known as the International Classification of Impairments, Disabilities and Handicaps (ICIDH, the old biomedical model) to the ICF – the International

Classification of Functioning Disability and Health 2001. In this paradigm shift, the WHO concluded that not only degradation of tissues within body structures could give rise to disease (pathology), under the ICIDH model, but also (1) Degradation in activity, (2) Degradation in participation which in turn could be modified (caused) by a person's (3) Environment, including (3a) physical; (3b) personal and (3c) social environments and also their personal circumstances including (4) Behaviours (e.g. smoking, alcohol consumption, physical activity and (5) Diets or nutrition.

Degradation of all the above activities is measured by PROMs. If degradation is found (that is a lower PROM score) it could be this degradation that, according to the ICF, "caused" the pathology. So, if someone scores low on their alcohol health PROM and their dietary PROM, this below the normal of healthy range test becomes diagnostic of a possible "cause" of the pathology, and so it should be. When Descartes likened the human body to a machine or well-made clock, (a non-living material object), and the biomedical model adopted this metaphor, medicine was disconnected from the person's surroundings.

Descartes might have just as equally likened the human body to a tree – at least a tree is living. We all know what happens to a tree when it is cut from its roots, it dies. It needs a permanent and ongoing connection to its roots. The biomedical model cut the human body from its roots, its connections, the connectors or roots that it needs for nourishment.

PROMs re-present the body to all of these connections and that is activities, participation, and behaviours that

318

are all essential for life and health.

When one highlights a reduction in connections, this may well be diagnostic of the cause of the pathology.

8. A person's CHI (comprehensive health index).

According to Dr Price, medicine and healthcare has always had four aims: restoring function, relieving distress, preventing disease and illness and prolonging life.

With the advance of IT technology and psychometrics in developing validated and reliable PROMs, all of these can be now measured by psychometric measures. According to Dr Price's research, the likely percentage contribution to each person's overall personal health status or CHI (Comprehensive Health Index) is to be 40% from their functional health status or health-related quality of life as measured by a generic measure such as the PROMIS-10.

The medical system's role in relieving distress is reflected in the patient's confidence that care and comfort will be available in times of illness from their social support, as well as their confidence in the healthcare system that appropriate caring and available care will be present at the time of illness is their Cared-For Health Status which is measured by the eHealthier's Cared-For ePROM and would make up 30% of a patient's health status.

The healthcare system's role in preventing disease and illness is reflected in the patient's positive health, which would be made up of the absence of risk factors such as smoking, alcohol, poor diet and excessive weight, together with positive health activity such as physical exercise and stress reduction techniques could make up a generic measure of their preventive health or positive health status.

According to Dr Price's research, this would make up 20%. The residual 10% that is their quantity of life, life expectancy or natural lifespan has been found via large data analytics that it can be calculated through an 11 to 13 question survey and this can accurately predict a person's life expectancy. The best example of this can be found on the website, Ubble.co.uk, as a short questionnaire for 40-70 year olds in the UK.

These individual indices can be scored and all four as a group measure a patient's CHI or Comprehensive Health Index. Anyone scoring one standard deviation above the population norm for each of these indices would be assessed as having achieved the state of complete physical, social and mental health wellbeing and, in all likelihood, for a natural lifespan approximately life expectancy at birth plus two standard deviations.

9. Condition-specific/body part-specific PROMs

To date, we have spoken mainly about generic PROMs which apply to all illnesses and all age groups but there are much more specific PROMs that relate to what would be expected as reduction in functions if a particular body system such as the heart system or the respiratory system or a specific body part such as the hip or knee was the part in question.

ICHOM (International Collaboration on Health Outcome Measurements) have made the development of standard sets to be used across as many nations as possible for each of 50 disease processes or body parts as their goal.

To date, they are beyond the halfway mark in doing so. As these are a new set of diagnostic tests, these can be utilised also in a hierarchy from the more general (generic) to the more specific, depending on their use by the doctor or health provider and their requirements to target a specific treatment regime. This then becomes a new form of medicine that Dr Price previously called "Supramedicine" but now could be readily-called "Complexity Medicine" as its foundations are well-based in Complexity Science.

10. PROMs treatments.

In order to improve his/her patients' PROMs scores, the doctor will achieve this by prescribing lifestyle prescriptions.

These, to be effective, must be well-formulated, just as a drug prescription is set out.

There must be a strength (dosage) of the prescription, e.g. how many repetitions of an exercise, now many serves of vegetables on each occasion.

There must also be a frequency, such as how often a day or a week, as well as a duration, usually a three-month Care Plan.

The GP, aware of his/her patients' likes/dislikes, may prescribe dancing for a patient, rowing or walking for others.

There already are, and will be, lifestyle treatment apps. In this way, the GP will be prescribing, as set out in Dr Price's book, *"Is Medicine Really Necessary?"* the non-pharmaceutical pharmaceutical.

11. Survival of the most cooperative and the fittest.

Following Darwin's Theory of Evolution and the fact that those organisms with the best mutations are likely to survive; it was shortened to survival of the fittest. This really meant the fittest in that environment but others have interpreted this, that if you are not the fittest, i.e. the strongest, you will not survive, and therefore in its interpretation, it has become the 'kill or be killed' in order to survive. However, a small glimpse over human society over the more recent times one should have noticed in fact that most advances have come from humans working together to achieve a better outcome. Therefore, it really is, or should be, survival of the most cooperative or the thriving of the **Most Cooperative.** This does not necessarily mean there cannot be competition for the best outcomes along the way provided that it does not lapse into a 'kill or be killed' mentality. If one truly looks at Darwin, what one is looking at is more the survival of the optimally-adapted, and the optimally-adapted to their environment can be those that cooperate the most.

To work with other human beings for a particular goal requires those with the goal to "harness this human power". In the past, humans harnessed horsepower to carry out tasks of transportation or strength. With human ingenuity, horsepower was replaced by machine power, particularly the steam engines, and this in turn was updated via the information revolution to the power of information and information processing. In order to nowadays "harness human power", one can no longer enslave the human beings but one can understand motivations and emotional needs of the participants towards their goals. The emotional needs of the participants need to be met on a regular basis while all parties work towards the shared vision or goal. There are many "drivers" as to how one can create "the behavioural revolution" that enables people to constructively cooperate to achieve the goal of maximal individual human health and maximum human health for the whole population. Many of these theories have been set out by Dr Price in more detail under chapters 17 and 22 in his 1997 book *Supramedicine*. Accordingly, it becomes part of the participants' role all the way along the hierarchy to ensure that people are validated on a regular basis on their way to helping achieve this goal of improved health outcomes.

12. Each human is like a tree.
    Descartes, who died in 1650, made the observation that he viewed each human as a well-made clock. That the human was machine-like and had mechanisms that allowed the human to work. Unfortunately, a clock is not a living object. Dr Price suggests as well as Descartes' contention that each human is machine-like, Dr Price suggests each human is tree-like. Everybody knows that if you cut down a tree, i.e. separate it from its roots, its nourishment, that that part of the tree that is cut down will die which is not good for its health. Descartes, at his time, represented the latest science and medicine was, and still should be, based on the latest science; so doctors and medicine adopted this model that "the human body is a well-made automated machine". This model, which is still followed today, is called the "biomedical model". When doctors adopted this model, human beings (patients) were separated from their connections and

activities that kept them alive. These connections are what maintain the health of the body structures. Dr Price could have said that the human is like a fish but a fish lives in an ocean of water, whilst the human body lives in an "ocean of air" and within this particular oceanic air environment are certain trees, plants, fruits, flowers and activities that nourish the human. Now PROMs play the role of reconnecting the human to their roots, to their nourishment. The health of the body structures depends upon this human moving like a fish would to eat an appropriate diet in order to have appropriate social connections, avoid toxins and noxious agents.

The interesting thing with the PROMs questionnaire is that in all these questions there is always a subject, the person's illness, injury or health, and an object, i.e. to what extent has this condition interfered with your participation in your work or daily life or opening a jar? PROMs re-establish these connections. Quantum mechanics shows that in the end, all that exists are interconnections and this, together with Complexity Science, gives a scientific basis for this form of medical practice.

13. Evolved medicine.

Dr Price considers that the new medicine would be a dual medicine that would consist of the biomedical model for it is correct at certain points the body is machine-like and requires to keep its machine-like structural and functional integrity, but in other aspects it is more energy-like, it is more interconnected and dependent on its environment. In Quantum Mechanics, one item can be a particle and a wave at the same time. Dr Price asserts that the biomedical model takes into account the material or the particle part, however Complexity Medicine and Supramedicine may be a different model but this takes into account different laws that apply when viewing the human body more "as a wave or an energy structure or a dissipative structure" rather than a machine or material structure. In fact, the competent doctors will be able to, in the future, move from one model to the other and apply those solutions that work best for the particular patient in the particular circumstance. Dr Price attests that he was able to climb off the shoulders of Descartes and Newton, and stand on the much-less stable shoulders of Einstein, Heisenberg, Mandelbrot and the Santa Fe Institute but didn't see further but saw differently. This allowed him to see the invisible and his life's pursuit became to try and convert the invisible to the visible to make it quantifiable and thereby usable by doctors and health professionals. Once both models are applied or this new model added to the old model, Western medicine will have learned from Eastern medicine the yin and the yang. Many procedures that have been based on seeing the human body more as a material will be seen as invasive and unnecessary as the human body is much more plastic and adaptable.

Doctors should be practicing at least 20% of their time in prevention and this does not mean early detection. This prevention involves enabling, encouraging and motivating their patients to become more active in their own health interest to eat better diets, to improve their relationships and their value systems, towards a pro-health orientation. Many commentators say that 30% of medical and surgical procedures are ineffective in improving function and much money is wasted. The evolved medical system, according to Dr Price, if utilised in the OECD nations, with the assistance of IT technology as the essential enabler, will reduce the cost of healthcare by some 8% on an annual basis and at the same time, will improve health outcomes or people's Comprehensive Health Index.

2. IMPLEMENTATION OF DR PRICE'S MEDICINE AND HEALTHCARE SYSTEM: THE WHAT, THE WHY AND THE HOW

This section is mainly about the "how" to implement, for in human affairs the "how" is under-rated. But before we get to the "how", we need some clarification on the "what" and the "why".

2.1   What is Dr Price's healthcare system?
This is set out in Section 1 above. Here, it is important to emphasise that the need was to convert the "what" from Invisible to Visible.

2.1.1   "ePROMs" scoring converts invisible diagnostic tests to be visible.

2.1.2   ePROMs treatments ESTABLISH or RE-ESTABLISH the necessary invisible interconnections of a human body to its nourishments or roots – diets, behaviours, environments - making these invisible treatments visible as a "prescribed whole or three-month individualised care plan".

2.1.3   Motivating the providers (participants) to the shared vision.
This is a set of arrangements, a social psychological systems methodology that will enable the providers to achieve the necessary cultural changes. They will experience self-validation while improving the health of their patients and patient population.

2.2   "Why" is a different system of implementation necessary?
This has to do with evolution and in particular, the evolution of human behaviour.

327

This is best explained by looking at the determinants of "future behaviours" of inanimate objects, early organisms, birds/mammals and lastly, human.

The Evolution of Human Behaviour
1. A small rock.
2. A bacterium.
3. A bird/mammal.
4. A human being.

The question must be asked, *"What governs the future behaviour of a small rock?"* Eddie answers that a **small rock** is subject to external forces and its future behaviour is governed by whatever external forces reign: wind, water, other rocks – all environmental influences that may determine whether the rock stays where it is, stationary, is moved or thrown. The rock itself is totally passive.

Conclusion
The major determinants of the future behaviour of inanimate objects (e.g. a rock) are external forces.

A **bacterium** on the other hand, has evolved and has some very low level information processing. For instance, it can determine that in one direction, let's say to the north, there are multiple nutrients, whilst to the south, there is unsurvivable heat. Accordingly, through the facts of this information processing, the bacterium learns to move to the north where it would survive rather than to the south where it would not survive.

Conclusion
The major determinant of the future behaviour of bacteria is information (facts from its environment) it is able to establish.

A **bird or a mammal**, on the other hand, being somewhat

more evolved than a bacterium, not only has some information processing ability but on top of that, in relation to this information processing, started to develop "emotions" such as fear. Let's say a dog is walking past a bird. Initially the bird does the information processing that this is a dog, but then their emotions have developed such that they experience fear that the dog may attack them, and the fear allows them to react more quickly and to move to safety. On the other hand, a bird may experience the emotion of pleasure from looking at another bird with which they may wish to mate with or from a food offering. This would determine their future behaviour and they may fly or run towards the pleasure and away from the fear. The important thing to note is that, as a later evolutionary development, the emotions act more quickly and in general are the determinant of the bird or mammal's behaviour over and beyond the information processing which nevertheless still plays a minor role. This is called "Primary Consciousness".

Conclusion

The major determinant of the future behaviour of a bird or mammal is its emotions or primary consciousness.

Humans have evolved to develop a second level of consciousness where not only do they assess their emotions of fear, anger, sadness, happiness, joy and so forth, but they put a value or meaning on these emotions. Therefore, they may in fact overcome their fear and take a different stance if it means protecting their country or their family from danger. Again, it is an emotional or sociological reaction that is the pre-determinant cause of their future behaviour. This is "Secondary Consciousness".

Conclusion

The major determinant of future behaviour of people or society is the meaning of emotions.

Meaning <u>not</u> information processing is the major determinant of future human behaviours.

2.3 "How" the new system is implemented.

As meaning, not necessarily facts, "determines" future behaviour, this makes implementation a much more complicated process. Fortunately, there has been a host of knowledge gained since the 1950s. This has informed "how" to implement these changes. Dr Price has grouped all these changes together under the title of "The Behavioural Revolution". Just as the Agricultural Revolution, the Industrial Revolution and the Information Revolution led to major disruptions and advances, so will the Behavioural Revolution when applied appropriately to the healthcare system.

There is not just one theory that has been developed in the last 70 years, i.e. since 1950, and there are at least eight accepted theories, they all come together to form a system of behavioural change or revolution. These theories Dr Price sets out as:

  i.   Management Theory;
  ii. Organisational Theory;
  iii. Social Psychology;
  iv. Psychological Motivational Theories;
  v.   Learning Theories;
  vi. Systems Theory;
  vii. Detailed Management Theory;
  viii. Scientific Theory of Energy.

Dr Price has put these various theories together in an

amalgam of a practical way of achieving behavioural change and orienting them towards the goal of improved health status and healthcare. **Management Theory** can be summarised by the poem, *"Where Am I Going? How will I get there? How will I know that I've arrived?"* So, in the first part of this one has to have a goal at which you need to arrive and essentially the goal should be quantifiable in quantity and in the time when you intend to achieve that goal. "How will I get there?" is the various processes but particularly applying theories of motivation that one uses to get there, and "How will I know that I've arrived?", means that you need to use the quantification and compare the actual result over the current time to determine whether you're going in the right direction and so when you've arrived, these measures will be the same. To achieve a management goal, however, it is not mainly competition between people in order to achieve it, but it is getting something done together with people and therefore there is a need for "cooperation" and therefore a need to motivate people to cooperate. **"Organisational theory"** states that once you have a goal or a target that they state has to be a shared vision, i.e. shared by all members of the organisation for it to work effectively as a motivator, and once you have this goal or shared vision or target, you have created a creative tension "between" the actual current situation and the future target, and there are only two ways of getting rid of this tension or potential energy and that is either by dropping the target, then the energy will dissipate or achieving the target. **Social Psychology** is the psychology of people in society or in groups. People like to be in tune with their society and therefore there are items such as fashion which determine the clothes we wear, the glasses we may buy, the hats we wear, and the arts and music we appreciate. It has been shown in psychology as to be such a powerful force that even if things are incorrect, if enough people agree that that is the way things are, there will be pressure on the individual and most of the individuals will concur with the social norm. The other way of looking at this is in terms of peer pressure and there can be group pressure on individuals to behave in a certain way in order to be consistent and well-viewed by their peers or that one person is not bringing down the whole of the group. Then there are a host of individual **psychological motivational theories** – the best known being that of Hierarchy of Needs by Abraham Maslow who sets out that there are five levels of need of increasing importance or potency and the first order need is the **physiological need or the need for air and food**, and if this is not satisfied, it is the strongest motivator, but if it is satisfied, it is no longer a motivator. The second order need is the **need for safety or security** which is generally being met in Western society and this means safety from lions or crocodiles or the like. However, with the advent of terrorism, this second order need has re-surfaced slightly but generally doesn't interfere in day-to-day life. The third order need is the **need to belong to a group or a family**, and this is a strong need that is generally but not always met in Western society and everybody may be motivated as belonging to a group and this explains partially the peer pressure mentioned previously. The fourth level need is the **need of self-esteem or achievement**, i.e. to see one's goals met and get a feeling of achieving objectives. This is generally not met day-to-day in Western society and therefore this self-esteem and achievement need is a very strong need. This need can be utilised by management and this is why management has goals and one can allow people to meet these needs for achievement when they reach this goal. It also allows for competition between different players to see who more effectively meets these needs and there is a need of self-esteem for doing as well as one can and sometimes better than one's competitor. The firth order need is the **need of self-actualisation**, i.e. achieving one's potential and developing from year to year, and these needs can be used in management organisation or in a whole industry to achieve higher goals that one develops from year to year.

Another psychological motivator theory is **Bandura** with his **Social cognitive theory,** stating that the person, if they do not feel they have enough skills, may not attempt to achieve the goal as set out under "Achievement Needs" and therefore he suggests that they may require some training. First the incentives they should be offered should be positive incentives, based on past successes and the goals should be partially their goals, otherwise the management has to set up the conditions that allow for a successful attempt and this may involve some training of this person to increase their confidence in the area that is required.

Similarly, there are **learning theories** of **Argyris** and particularly learning can be what they call "adaptive learning" where there is one set goal but then there is "generative learning" which allows the person involved to change the goal or objective.

A major contribution theory to this "Behavioural Revolution" is what is known as general **Systems Theory** which states that systems are integrated wholes whose properties cannot be reduced to those of smaller units. The properties of systems come from the inter-relationship and positional structure of one part in relation to the other that make up the overall organisation, i.e. a car could be viewed as a system, as a living cell, as a human organ system, as the educational system or the transport system. Almost all items can be viewed as systems and general systems theory states there are various system levels and each system above another system, can have an effect on the system below and vice versa. This has all been set out on page 37 of his book, *"Supramedicine"* but another major feature of systems is that there must be feedback which would measure what is actually happening and compare it to the goals. So there is a hierarchy of vertical systems, as well as feedback within the individual system horizontally, and there are a whole lot of rules and regulations that go with this feedback. Unfortunately, within the world above the individual human which has inbuilt feedback systems, in the suprasystems, the feedback mechanisms are not always present and they need to be therefore constructed and they need to be constructed in a way that is consistent with Systems Theory, i.e. in a cyclic manner at a regular interval.

These theories then all act together and have great similarities between management reports and we now get down to the "detailed management system" where once one has a goal, one needs to have feedback mechanisms at that particular system level to see where the actual performance matches to the goal. In an air conditioning or cybernetic system, this is readily understood where one may wish to have a temperature of 24° (the goal) and the air-conditioning continuously measures the outside temperature and if it is too low, initiates heating, and if it is too high, initiates cooling. In this way, the goal is reached. In Management Theory, the same is true, only one needs to establish the data that is fed back in what used to be called "Control Statements" that compare the actual results with a standard that was derived from the initial goal, but the data that is presented must be such that it is easily and readily used by human beings. Therefore, the reports need to be of a certain quality and this includes items such as:

i. The speed and the intelligibility of the data;
ii. The data itself;
iii. The presentation of the data;
iv. Its complexity;
v. The frequency;
vi. The way it is integrated with systems above;
vii. The way it is integrated with systems below;
viii. Its consistency; and
ix. Predictability.

This is all set out on page 173 of his book, *Supramedicine*. Once one has a hierarchical system of such reports, as set out on pages 220 to 232 of the book, *Supramedicine*, one creates a system where provided everyone agrees with the goals, there are sequential levels of peer pressure placed on the participants to achieve these desirable goals. The point that needs to be understood from this is it is not only the data itself which plays a secondary importance, according to Dr Price, but the "emotional or behavioural change effect of this data on the individuals involved". It is the power of this data in this format and this frequency to stimulate the desired behaviour in the recipients.

It is also important that the individuals who are receiving this data are the ones who have the biggest influence on the system based on the Pareto Principle (the 20/80 Rule). In general, in healthcare, according to Eddie's theories, this will be the doctors and the large teaching hospitals. To ignore these most important "influencers" causes their effectiveness to achieve results to be radically reduced.

The creation of a hierarchical system of reporting from the individual patient and their GP, to the national level is a system that as a whole is an extremely powerful emotional inducement yet based on legitimate and general theories and has the consent of the participating individuals. As emotions are more important than facts in determining the behaviour of these individuals, all these participants in the system will have emotional reasons of achievement, self-actualisation and belongingness, together with peer pressure from their peers and pressure from those above or below in order to help everybody achieve their interwoven goals. In an ideal management system, these participants would also be incentivised money-wise and paid for the achievement of these goals.

Within the healthcare area, Dr Price contends that this **Behavioural Revolution** will reduce unnecessary or preventable hospitalisations, increase people's functional health status, their cared-for status, and can do so from today, if implemented now.

3. DR PRICE'S HYPOTHESES ARISING FROM HIS THEORETICAL RESEARCH. SUMMARY AND REFERENCES.

1. The big BIF (Bifurcation Theory), a theory that explains the origin of life.
   http://www.ehealthier.net/wp-content/uploads/2018/08/THE-BIG-BIF-THEORY-2.docx

2. A behavioural vaccine against heart attack, stroke and 40% of cancers. (*Supramedicine*, p.263).

3. SOPHTID: State within the human body between solid and fluid, otherwise called Extended Criticality. (*So You Think Medicine is Modern?* p.48, p.95, p.101, pp.135-6).

4. A fractal coding system that competes and cooperates with DNA. (*So You Think Medicine is Modern?* pp.138-41, p.183, p.194).

5. Cellular cognition occurs in each cell of the human body. (*So You Think Medicine is Modern?* p.95, pp.109-10, 119-20, 125-131, p.133, pp.142-3, p.189, p.248).

6. Somaplasticity, not only neuroplasticity.
   http://www.ehealthier.net/wp-content/uploads/2015/11/ALMA-Conference-OHs-161115.pdf

7. Complexity Science Therapies. (*So You Think Medicine is Modern?* pp.189-194).

8. CHI, a person's Comprehensive Health Index or indices. A histogram graph representing each person's health status. (*Supramedicine*, Ch.16, pp.147-157); *Health Outcomes*,

    Appendix 1, pp.144-156).

9. Evolved Medicine: Medicine that combines two models. The Biomedical Model and the Complexity Medicine Model. (*So You Think Medicine is Modern?* pp.39-40, pp.246-247, pp.251-252).

4. DR PRICES BOOKS: DETAILED EXPLANATIONS OF THE EVOLUTION OF HIS IDEAS AND THEORIES:

- **Is Medicine Really Necessary? (1985), reprinted as Health Outcomes: A New Way of Defining and Managing Health (1994)**

  Amazon

  http://www.amazon.com/Health-Outcomes-Defining-Managing-Medicine-ebook/dp/B00WHQCX1O/ref=sr_1_1?s=digital-text&ie=UTF8&qid=1431574251&sr=1-1

  Apple

  https://itunes.apple.com/au/book/health-outcomes/id988295776?mt=11&uo=6&at=&ct=

  Google

  https://play.google.com/store/books/details/Dr_Eddie_Price_Health_Outcomes?id=vit0CAAAQBAJ

  Barnes & Noble (Nook)

  http://www.barnesandnoble.com/w/health-outcomes-dr-eddie price/1121803440?ean=9781925271348

  Kobo

  https://store.kobobooks.com/en-US/ebook/health-outcomes

- **Supramedicine (1997)**

  Amazon
  http://www.amazon.com/SUPRAMEDICINE-Health-Outcomes-Outcome-Medicine-ebook/dp/B00WM19SUS/ref=sr_1_2?s=digital-text&ie=UTF8&qid=1431574251&sr=1-2

  Apple
  https://itunes.apple.com/au/book/supramedicine/id988299471?mt=11&uo=6&at=&ct=

  Google
  https://play.google.com/store/books/details/Dr_Eddie_Price_SUPRAMEDICINE?id=6mt0CAAAQBAJ

  Barnes & Noble (Nook)
  http://www.barnesandnoble.com/w/supramedicine-dr-eddie-price/1121803429?ean=9781925271355

  Kobo
  https://store.kobobooks.com/en-US/ebook/supramedicine

- **So You Think Medicine is Modern? (2008)**
  Amazon
  http://www.amazon.com/You-Think-Medicine-Modern-Revolutionising-ebook/dp/B00WHRL5US/ref=sr_1_3?s=digital-text&ie=UTF8&qid=1431574251&sr=1-3

Apple
https://itunes.apple.com/au/book/so-you-think-medicine-is-modern/id988296882?mt=11&uo=6&at=&ct=

Google
https://play.google.com/store/books/details/Dr_Eddie_Price_So_You_Think_Medicine_is_Modern?id=bIt0CAAAQBAJ

Barnes & Noble (Nook)
http://www.barnesandnoble.com/w/so-you-think-medicine-is-modern-dr-eddie-price/1121803555?ean=9781925271362

Kobo
https://store.kobobooks.com/en-US/ebook/so-you-think-medicine-is-modern

Free Book Offer

I would like to offer you the digital version of one of my 3 earlier books.

Health Outcomes a New Way of Defining and Managing Health, re: the transformation of healthcare.

Supramedicine, re: the transformation of medicine.

So You Think Medicine is Modern, re: the new science as the basis for the new medicine.

This offer is available from my website for a limited time.

http://www.ehealthier.net/book-offer-for-out-of-his-mind-readers/

About PROMs / Complexity Medicine

Dr Eddie Price is the Medical Director of Complexity Science Medical Systems Pty Ltd trading as eHealthier.

He is passionate about bringing medicine out of what he calls the Second Dark Ages in which it currently practices. There is a movement amongst health professionals known as the "Right Care Alliance" who concur that the right care is not being delivered by today's healthcare systems.

Many health and medical organisations state they wish to deliver the right care to the right patient at the right place and at the right time.

Eddie or Dr Price has determined that this only occurs in today's medicine in 25-30% of cases.

In the other 70-75%, he states that the wrong care is being delivered to the wrong patient at the wrong place and the wrong time, based on the wrong maths and based on the wrong science.

Descartes died in 1650 and Newton died in 1727, yet the current biomedical model is based primarily on their theories. This is known as the Biomedical Model and is the underpinning of today's medicine which views the body as a machine, a linear model. Since the deaths of these two great scientists, there have been massive scientific discoveries that current medicine ignores.

343

These include:

1. The Theory of Evolution.
2. The Chemical Revolution, particularly the role of a catalyst in speeding up the rate at which chemical reactions happen. These occur exponentially and power laws become a basis for many things in nature.
3. The Industrial Revolution and in particular the steam engines and the importance of entropy.
4. Systems Theory.
5. Quantum Mechanics.
6. Relativity Theory.
7. The Theory of Dissipative Structures.
8. Chaos Theory.
9. The Santiago Theory of Cognition.
10. Information Theory.
11. Non-linear dynamics.
12. Complexity Theory and Complexity Science.
13. Power Laws and Inverse Power Laws and their role in nature.

None of these breakthrough theories of science and maths have been adopted into the machine model of the body under which medicine practices. Yet it is quite clear that they all play a role, some bigger and some smaller. These theories provide a new basis for health and that good health is adaptability is interconnections. It includes the person's activity and participation in the activities, community and society.

PROMs (Patient Reported Outcome Measures) are the bridge between these two models of medicine. The latter model being best called Complexity Medicine. PROMs are consistent with both models.

PROMs are the catalyst that will enable the modern doctor to move between each model. The models are the yin and the yang that bring balance and homeostasis to healthcare and medicine.

Dr Price has presented training programs and in seminars on these topics.

It is the implementation of these theories that will radically improve the health of nations, whilst at the same time making healthcare sustainable and enable health systems to render "The Right Care".

Dr. Eddie Price

Strategy Session Invitation

Are you in the healthcare field?

Are you a healthcare provider such as a GP, specialist, allied health provider?

Perhaps you are a GP practice manager or a hospital administrator or an administrator in a private health insurer, accident insurer or work for a government health provider.

If you are interested in the ideas in the books and in achieving better outcomes for your patients and wish to brainstorm with Dr Eddie Price, and if you are interested and ready to set up a complementary health service strategy session, all you have to do is tell me how I can help you.

Due to time constraints, the call must be limited to 15 minutes.

Are you ready to get started?

Go to https://calendly.com/ehealthierinterview to set up your complementary strategy session.

About the Author

Kirstine McKay is a freelance journalist, writer, presenter, producer, actor and researcher. She owns a photography business with her husband 'McKay Photography' (www.mckayphotography.com.au) and runs gardening and green living workshops from their property 'Greenlaw' in the Southern Highlands of NSW, Australia - (www.lifeatgreenlaw.com).

Kirstine has studied acting and was part of a theatre company from the age of eight. Her tertiary education included a double degree at Griffith University, Queensland, in Print and Broadcast Journalism, and Film and Media, accompanied with acting and Spanish language studies.

Kirstine has worked in magazine publishing in London and

was a television reporter, producer and researcher for the Nine Network Australia for 12 years where she won a number of awards for her investigative reports.

Kirstine's passion for telling people's stories has aided in international pedophile rings being broken open, stolen children being reunited with desperate families, dangerous drugs being highlighted to communities, and illegal hunting practices exposed. She has profiled hundreds of inspiring people and organisations from all over the world including the stolen children of 'the disappeared' in Argentina following the military coup in the late 1970s, Saddam Hussein's former personal pilot, and Maalika a young Australian nurse turned revered Ethiopian nomad.

Kirstine is an active humanitarian and environmentalist, organising numerous fundraising events, community vigils and demonstrations. She has also been an active executive member of the Bowral Public School Parents and Citizens organisation since 2014, holding the position of Vice President since 2015. Kirstine is an active member of the Southern Highlands Business Women's Network of NSW and has been host and keynote speaker at their International Women's Day events since 2017.